# EARTH FIRE

A Hopi Legend of
The Sunset Crater Eruption

# EARTH FIRE

Ekkehart Malotki with Michael Lomatuway'ma
Photographs by Stephen Trimble

NORTHLAND PRESS · FLAGSTAFF, ARIZONA

*To my son Patrick,*
*Who, at a time of betrayal,*
*Hiked with me*
*The cinder fields of Sunset Crater*
*And beyond...*

FIRST EDITION

ISBN 0-87358-431-7

Library of Congress Catalog Card Number 86-46367

Composed and Printed in the United States of America

Designed by David Jenney
Typography by Prepress Graphics

Library of Congress Cataloging in Publication Data

Earth fire.
English and Hopi.
Bibliography: p.
1. Hopi Indians—Legends. 2. Indians of North
America—Arizona—Legends. 3. Sunset Crater National
Monument (Ariz.)—Folklore. 4. Hopi language—Texts.
I. Lomatuway'ma, Michael. II. Title.
E99.H7M3 1987      398.2'08997      86-46367
ISBN 0-87358-431-7

# TABLE OF CONTENTS

# PREFACE

IN 1980, AT THE HEIGHT of my ongoing effort to salvage Hopi oral literature, I tape-recorded the fragmentary version of a legend entitled "Ka'naskatsina." It was not until three years later, however, when the idea of an oral literature project concerning the Hopi deity of Maasaw took shape, that I realized the full import of the Ka'nas fragment. For once, the legend was linked at some point to Maasaw, the most important Hopi god. More significantly, however, the legend incorporated the eruption of Sunset Crater, an event in Arizona's most recent geologic past. Much to my excitement, the recording represented the first legendary confirmation of this volcanic event, which took place between 900 and 700 years ago. No other evidence has been found to date in any of the mythologies of the various indigenous groups of northern Arizona.

Financial assistance granted by the Organized Research Committee of Northern Arizona University to undertake the Maasaw project enabled me to retrieve additional information on the Ka'nas story. In the course of several field trips, I succeeded in recording a number of details omitted by the storyteller in his original narrative. The phenomenal memory of this storyteller and his unreserved enthusiasm to see the legend committed to print, and thereby salvaged for posterity, deserve the unqualified gratitude of author, coauthor, and reader. Regrettably, I must respect his desire to remain anonymous.

Michael Lomatuway'ma, coauthor of the book, who died shortly after its completion, executed a number of editorial tasks that only a native speaker firmly versed in his language and culture could successfully accomplish. Above all, he aligned the various tape-recorded story segments and ironed out "flaws" typically occurring in natural speech, such as repetitions, unfinished statements, and grammatical inconsistencies. He also helped in the transcription and translation of the Hopi text and contributed most of the cultural information in the glossary. His death was a personal loss. His enthusiasm and respect for Hopi culture will live on in the works in which he participated.

Several other people contributed to this book. Piter Pilles, Coconino National Forest archaeologist, with his long-standing interest in the archaeology of northeastern Arizona, was easily persuaded to write about the Sinagua culture. Richard Holm and Larry Middleton, professors of geology at N.A.U., were equally enthusiastic to share their knowledge, with Richard Holm focusing on the crater itself, and Larry Middleton summing up the geologic information concerning the Little Colorado River Valley, the Painted Desert, Black Mesa, and the Hopi Buttes. While editorially the book, at its core, encompasses the mythology of Sunset Crater, the science discussions give the book a genuine interdisciplinary flavor. For this I am deeply indebted to them.

Stephen Trimble, whose talent in photographing the moods and patterns of the greater Southwest had impressed me for years, readily took on the challenge of capturing aspects of the Hopi story with his lens.

At Northern Arizona University, my colleague Chuck Barnes, and from San Diego, my friend Ken Gary critiqued major portions of the manuscript and contributed many fine points toward improving its readability. Don Vogel, supervisory park ranger at Sunset Crater National Monument, helped out with a number of informative items on the monument. Louella Holter, of the N.A.U. Ralph M. Bilby Research Center, converted the various segments of the manuscript into clean type. Mary Ann Gray, with great zest, took on the chore of proofreading and easily bested both author and coauthor in the number of typos she managed to pinpoint. Elaine Hughes, from the Museum of Northern Arizona, rendered professional assistance in photographing an artifact sampling from the "Magician's Burial." The ease and trust she displayed in permitting me to arrange the delicate items in a configuration appealing to photographer Stephen Trimble was an unforgettable experience. Each of the individuals above I warmly thank for giving generously of their time and showing genuine care for the tasks involved.

I would like to express my special appreciation to N.A.U. administrators Karl Webb, dean of the College of Arts and Science, and Henry Hooper, associate vice-president for Academic Affairs Research and Graduate Studies, for their moral and financial support. Financial assistance in the area of aesthetic production and color photography added significantly to the quality of the work.

Finally, I wish to thank Susan McDonald, editor of Northland Press, for envisioning a basically bilingual book in the press's repertoire, and Associate Editor Betti Arnold for competently taking me through the editorial process. David Jenney, art director at Northland Press, designed the book. I am most grateful to him for enriching the book with an aesthetic dimension, emanating from true sensitivity and creativity. Several sections of the glossary as well as the essay on the Hopi alphabet first appeared in *Hopi Coyote Tales/Istutuwutsi*. I thank the University of Nebraska Press for permission to reprint these passages. I also acknowledge the Museum of Northern Arizona for permitting photographic reproduction of its Ka'naskatsina doll.

E.M.

# INTRODUCTION

THE COLORADO PLATEAU is a storehouse of unique natural and cultural resources. The abundant natural phenomena in this scenic tableland have long
lured geologists and biologists, as well as other natural scientists from a variety of
disciplines. The same holds for scholars interested in the cultural resources of the
area. Archaeologists have dedicated their attention to the material remains of
prehistoric man, whereas anthropologists have focused on the contemporary
Indians. While the majority of their scientifically significant discoveries regarding
the Plateau have been of a tangible nature, the legend described in this book is a
spectacular find in the realm of the intangible.

.To be true, anthropologists, ethnographers, historians of religion, and folklorists
have described the nonmaterial or intangible aspects of Hopi, Zuni, Havasupai,
Paiute, and Navajo Indians, for whom the Colorado Plateau is home. Most of their
work, however, has been done in the English language, a medium that is extraneous
to native American cultures. With the exception of a handful of ethnolinguists,

regrettably little regard has been shown toward the native languages of these tribes.

Having become aware of the rapid demise of all native American tongues under the ever increasing pressure to acculturate to the dominant white society, this writer has undertaken, over many years, to salvage some of the literary heritage of the Hopi Indians in their own vernacular. It was in this context of salvage linguistic fieldwork that the fortuitous recording of the Ka'nas legend was made. The story, which is presented bilingually, features many of the motifs typical of Hopi oral traditions: the mingling of kachina gods and mortals; the testing of protagonists; assistance from Old Spider Woman, the ubiquitous *dea ex machina* in Hopi mythology; marriage and magic; the destructive forces of wicked sorcerers; betrayal and revenge; prosperity and famine; and pity for the survivors of steadfast heart. The ingredient that causes the narrative to stand out, however, from the vast body of Hopi myths, legends, and tales is a climactic scene that portrays an actual event from Arizona's recent geologic past: the eruption of Sunset Crater in A.D. 1064–65. While the narrative does not necessarily reflect the initial explosion—the volcano probably did not cease to be active until about A.D. 1250—the essence of the event has been handed down from one generation of Hopi storytellers to the next for over seven centuries. That seems indeed an impressive achievement of oral transmission.

What is more remarkable, though, is the rather realistic and detailed portrayal of certain aspects of the eruption. In this connection, the effect of massive Anglo information and education on the Hopi must be taken into account. Not only was the narrator of the legend educated in the schools of the dominant society, he also served in the armed forces during World War II in Europe. In addition, he has been exposed over the years to the geologic displays in both the Museum of Northern Arizona and the Sunset Crater National Monument Visitor Center. While certain pictorial and explanatory materials on volcanism in these displays surely must have influenced the narrator's understanding of volcanic phenomena, his linguistic conceptualization of the entire event is nevertheless distinctly Hopi.

The Colorado Plateau, the setting in which the mythological scenario of the eruption unfolds, is a physiographically distinct province, shaped by the Colorado River and its major tributaries, the Green and the San Juan. Centered on the Four Corners, where Arizona, Utah, Colorado, and New Mexico touch, this region covers some 130,000 square miles (337,000 km²).

The periphery of the Plateau landscape is well defined by prominent escarpments and major igneous mountains. Along its southwestern margin is a young volcanic field whose center is dominated by the San Francisco Peaks. Culminating in Mt. Humphreys, an extinct volcano with an elevation of 12,633 feet (3,850 m) (the highest elevation in Arizona), the towering Peaks are surrounded by an area of approximately 3,000 square miles (7,800 km²) in which hundreds of lesser cinder cones occur.

One of the more aesthetically appealing sights in this volcanic "backyard" north of Flagstaff, Arizona, is Sunset Crater. The crater, which nowadays attracts nearly half a million visitors a year from all over the world, was declared a national monument on 26 May 1930 by proclamation of President Herbert Hoover.

This near-symmetrical cinder cone is deservedly included in the network of more than 230 natural areas set aside as national parks and monuments. Now administered by the National Park Service, Sunset Crater National Monument is located some fifteen miles (24 km) northeast of Flagstaff. At an elevation of approximately 7,000 feet (2,100 m), it is easily accessible by a paved road.

Together with the Grand Canyon, Wupatki, Walnut Canyon, Meteor Crater, Oak Creek Canyon, and the San Francisco Peaks, Sunset Crater is one of the seven major tourist attractions within a two-hour driving range of Flagstaff, which in the eyes of city representatives justifies the self-assigned epithet of "City of Seven Wonders."

The crater was originally named "Sunset Mountain" by Major John Wesley Powell, the renowned explorer of the Colorado River, when he paid a visit to the locality in 1879. The name was inspired by the cone's russet red and yellowish crest. While some of the hues result from vapor-deposited minerals, most of the coloration was caused by oxidation of the iron particles embedded in the scoria, or cinders, thus giving the truncated top of the crater, when viewed from a distance in the setting sun, the appearance of being on fire.

The forces that added this most recent member to the geophysically unstable region of the San Francisco volcanic field can still be inferred from a multitude of nearby volcanic remains. The volcano itself, some 1,000 feet (300 m) high and more than a mile (1.6 km) wide at the base, is the dominating feature of the national monument. Its steep slopes, composed mostly of grayish black cinders with barely a trace of vegetation, form the cone. The crater, located at the top of the cone, is approximately 300 feet (90 m) deep and ranges from 1,700 feet (500 m) to 2,500 feet (750 m) in diameter.

The Bonito lava flow, which was extruded at several points along the western to northwestern base of Sunset Crater, is the second most striking feature commanding the attention of an approaching visitor. Virtually untouched by weathering and erosion, the recency of the flow is attested in a wide variety of well-presented structures characteristic of lava flows: fumaroles, or spatter cones; lava bubbles and blisters; tunnels; squeeze-ups; and a legion of fissures, cracks, and crevices. Filling a large basin bordered by older volcanoes, the twisted and gouged magma extrusions of the flow crust make dramatically stark contrasts with the gently mounded cones.

However, that is not all. This forbidding terrain offers still more features associated with volcanism: *aa* lava with its jagged, clinker-like texture, and *pahoehoe* lava with its smoother, more billowy surface; pressure ridges; spatter rampants; ice caves; lava sinkholes; xenoliths; lava bombs; and basaltic rock rubble coated with variegated patterns produced by lichens. Common locally are small dunes of black ash, with intermittent lenses of red cinders among weathered trunks of wind-felled ponderosa pines. Add to this the occasional stands of white-skinned quaking aspen, as well as the splotches of desert-type shrubs such as four-wing saltbush and rabbitbrush, and Joseph Krutch's summary description of Sunset Crater National Monument and environs as a "nightmarishly beautiful scene of unearthly desolation" strikes one as a rather fitting characterization.

Many of the breathtaking sights mentioned above can be experienced by walking the Lava Flow Trail, an easy, half-mile (.8 km) loop that begins near the base of Sunset Crater two miles (3.2 km) east of the Sunset Crater Visitor Center. While hiking up to the crater rim itself is no longer permitted, some excellent views of this bleak, yet inspirational wasteland, may be had from O'Leary Peak, which rises north of the monument.

Sunset Crater, only one of more than five hundred fifty vents in the San Francisco volcanic field, is probably Arizona's youngest volcano. A mere infant in the geologic sense, it is unique in that its prehistoric eruption has been precisely dated. The combined findings of studies in volcanology, archaeology, dendrochronology, and paleomagnetism not only pinpoint the initial eruption as occurring during the winter of A.D. 1064–65, but also provide an exceptionally detailed documentation of the subsequent eruptive span.

Based on tree-ring dates of pit-house timbers from an archaeological site that was found buried under the erupted ash of Sunset Crater, the event of the eruption was first placed between A.D. 875 and 910. Harold S. Colton, founder of the Museum of Northern Arizona, later revised this date. He determined that it took place between A.D. 1046 and 1071. By investigating tree-ring growth anomalies in a chain of dendrochronological samples reflecting the region's climatic conditions of the past two thousand years, Terah L. Smiley, a researcher at the Geochronology Laboratories of the University of Arizona in Tucson, refined Colton's dates once more. On the basis of abnormal tree-ring growth patterns found in trees that survived the initial volcanic activity, Smiley concluded that the eruptive event must have occurred between the fall of A.D. 1064 and the spring of 1065.

On the basis of highly accurate paleomagnetic measurements, coupled with detailed geologic studies of lava flows and volcanic ash associated with Sunset Crater, Eugene M. Shoemaker and Duane Champion, geologists with the U.S. Geological Survey, were able to prove in 1977 that the eruptive chronology of the crater spanned a period of nearly two hundred years. The Kana-a lava flow occurred about A.D. 1150, and the Bonito lava flow ruptured the western base of Sunset

Crater at about A.D. 1220. The final chapter in the history of the crater, the deposition of red cinders, which so strikingly mark the carapace of the volcano, occurred around A.D. 1250. Sunset Crater has been dormant ever since.

Of great interest in connection with this volcanic drama is the question about its impact on the people who were living in the region at the time. Lithic sites along the terraces of the Little Colorado River to the east of the Wupatki–Sunset Crater region are evocative remnants of the early nomadic hunters and gatherers who may have roamed portions of northern Arizona for thousands of years.

As early as A.D. 600, a prehistoric group, Sinagua (Spanish for "without water"), inhabited the area. The Sinagua were sedentary farmers who cultivated crops of corn, squash, and beans in the Wupatki basin and on the alluvial slopes skirting the San Francisco Peaks, including the area now contained in Sunset Crater National Monument.

The havoc created by the initial eruption of the volcano must have had a traumatic effect on them. A number of their semisubterranean living quarters, known as pit houses, have been uncovered—generally burned out and buried beneath successive layers of ash. Yet there seems to be ample archaeological evidence that the increased activity prior to the eruption, such as preliminary earthquakes and cracks opening in the ground, provided fair warning of the impending catastrophe. Only very little wood has been found in the pit houses. The house floor around the postholes is generally disturbed, indicating that the Indians did not simply flee in panic but had time to salvage the beams for subsequent use elsewhere. That they had time to gather their belongings to embark on an orderly retreat before the outburst also seems to be confirmed by the dearth of artifacts in the pit houses. the pit houses.

The posteruptive fate of the Sinagua has been interpreted, for the most part, on the basis of the "land rush" hypothesis advanced by Colton. This theory assumed that the porous ash created an excellent layer of mulch that turned a natural catastrophe into a tremendous agricultural boon. A tremendous population boom occurred as word of the improved soil conditions spread throughout the Southwest.

Based on this hypothesis, an influx into Sinagua territory was postulated for "colonists" who supposedly came from such distant and culturally diverse centers as Kayenta, Chaco, and Hohokam.

That Colton's hypothesis, which still enjoys widespread popularity, is in fact untenable was first pointed out by Peter J. Pilles in 1979. He was able to show that not only had the importance of Sunset cinders as the cause of improved growing conditions been overestimated, but also that the magnitude of the population increase had been exaggerated. Although the local population did expand, this expansion seems to have been induced by the shift of the indigenous inhabitants to a more fecund resource zone. What in all probability took place was an internal redistribution of the population, and not an influx of foreign migrants.

In the course of its two hundred year history, the new volcano spewed forth an estimated one thousand million tons of material. While much of these materials remained localized around the cinder cone and the lava flows, the fallout of black ash probably blanketed an area of approximately 800 square miles (2,070 km²). Substantial quantities of cinders were blown to the southeast and deposits have been identified as far as Meteor Crater, 34 miles (55 km) away. Prevailing southwesterly winds account for most of the ash being found in a broad ellipse extending northeast of the crater. Episodic occurrences of falling ash must therefore also have been experienced by the Indians outside the Sinagua territory. Although the impact of the fiery phenomenon on the individual Sinagua Indian has been lost forever, it is safe to assume that such a "supernatural" event would also have left a profound imprint on the psyche of the neighboring Hopi, whose descendants still live on their ancestral mesas some 65 miles (105 km) to the northeast.

Hopi oral traditions, to the extent that they have hitherto been collected by anthropologists, missionaries, and others interested in their lore, have been closely scrutinized for possible references to volcanic activity.

A dim memory seems to be contained in a story recorded by Henry R. Voth around the turn of this century. The narrative traces the last days of Pivanhonkyapi, a prehistoric Pueblo hamlet 7 miles (11 km) northwest of Oraibi, whose existence, on the basis of certain prevalent pottery types, can be set from about A.D. 1100 to 1300. The community, driven by a gambling rage to the edge of *koyaanisqatsi*, or "crazy life without any regard for human values," must, in the eyes of the village headman and spiritual leader, be razed from the surface of the earth. To this end, he arranges for a fire to be set in the vicinity of the San Francisco Peaks by the Yaayapontsam, supernatural beings with special control over wind and fire. Racing across the desert in four days, the fire storm eventually reaches the wicked village and completely destroys it. The idea of the fiery holocaust might be traceable to one of the many eruptive events that Sunset Crater displayed in those days. There is, however, no mention of any volcanic activity in the narrative. The tradition may allude equally well to a forest or grass fire of large proportions. Colton, who first hinted at a possible link between the story and the eruption, suggested that the tradition not be given too much weight. The Hopi legend that is presented in this book thus constitutes the first folklore account of the prehistoric eruption of Sunset Crater.

There is consensus today among scholars that the Hopi Indians, a Uto-Aztecan speaking group of sedentary agriculturalists in northeastern Arizona, have lived in the semiarid valleys and mesas along the southern fringe of Black Mesa for over a thousand years. The majority of their ancestral pueblos are but abandoned ruins today. This is also true for the residents of Shungopavi, the Second Mesa village in which the legendary Ka'nas materials presented here were obtained. Shungopavi, which today ranks as the largest and culturally most flourishing Hopi community, was originally situated in the foothills of the mesa south of its present-day location. The Pueblo Revolt in 1680 and fear of Spanish reprisals forced the people to move to the mesa top. Archaeological evidence indicates that the original town was well established before A.D. 1250, the approximate year when Sunset Crater finally ceased its volcanic unrest.

Intriguing at this point is the question about the manner in which the eruption found its way into Hopi oral literature in the first place. While it is quite probable that the initial spewings were observed by the Hopi from their mesas some 65 miles

(105 km) away, details such as the flow of the fiery magma could not have been seen from there. However, it is very likely that ashy particles from the first or any of the subsequent eruptions fell on the Hopi villages. This may have induced exploratory parties to investigate the "supernatural" happening.

Another possibility that must be considered as a valid departure point for the legend is the archaeological situation itself. From the early thirteenth century on, a general exodus seems to have been in operation from the populous centers around Flagstaff and along the Little Colorado. The chief reason for this exodus, which in the end led to the total abandonment of the area, was presumably a long-lasting drought. The simultaneous population increase, which can be traced for the Hopi villages during the next hundred years, suggests that several contingents of Sinagua could have been absorbed by the Hopi. Sinagua people would, in this case, have directly related their own eyewitness accounts of the eruption, which were later assimilated into the body of Hopi oral traditions.

One shred of possible corroborating evidence for this origin of the legend is of a linguistic nature. The name of the god responsible for the eruption in the story is Ka'naskatsina. Genuinely native Hopi words only permit velar *q* (formed with the back of the tongue on or near the soft palate) to precede the vowel *a*. Words with the syllable initial sound sequence *ka*, on the other hand, are invariably foreign loans. This phonological rule applies regardless of whether the non-native word is borrowed from such Indo-European languages as Spanish and English or from other American Indian tongues such as Tewa, Keresan, or Navajo. *Ka'nas-*, the Third Mesa form for what is attested as *Ka'na-* on Second Mesa, features palatal *k* (formed with the back of the tongue against the hard palate) before the vowel *a*, hence giving the word a distinct foreign ring. Etymologically obscure *Ka'nas-*, which identifies the kachina god from the Sunset Crater region, might thus represent a word picked up by the Hopi from the otherwise long extinct vernacular spoken by the Sinagua who emigrated to Hopi country after A.D. 1250.

If no Sinagua emigrants joined the Hopi, which is unlikely, we can assume an inverse sequence. Some Hopi may actually have witnessed one of the explosive events while sojourning in the Flagstaff area. They could have gone there either to trade with the Sinagua, to attend Sinagua ceremonies, or to pay homage to certain of their common shrines located on the San Francisco Peaks. That the Hopi had a long and vested interest in the entire region skirting this mountain range is borne out by linguistic evidence attested in the great number of place names relating to that area.

The Peaks themselves, rising more than 5,000 feet (1,500 m) above the plateau on which they rest, are called Nuvatukya'ovi by the Hopi. Possibly a corrupted form of Nuvatukwi'ovi, "Snow mountain high place," the appellation appropriately alludes to the fact that the highest rim of that ancient volcano appears snow-capped for nearly three-fourths of the year.

As one of the traditional boundary markers of Hopiland, the San Francisco Peaks are sacred to the Hopi because they represent one of the mythical homes of the kachina gods. Inasmuch as the latter do manifest themselves as clouds, the summit is regarded as an *oomawki*, or "cloud house." So significant are the Peaks in the ceremonial framework of the Hopi Indians that religious pilgrimages to various shrines located on them were undertaken annually. Most of the villages, at one time or another, seem to have also incorporated a series of distinct features along the mountain range into their horizon calendar, a monumental natural timing device. In fact, so intensely interested were the Hopi of former days in the San Francisco Peaks that they had individual names assigned to their most prominent points. Hu'katsina, "Hu'kachina," and Aaloosakvi, "Aaloosaka place," were named in this way. None of my consultants, however, were capable of identifying specific peaks with these names.

Mount Elden, a volcanic dome along the southern flank of the Peaks, which exhibits thick, pasty rounds of hardened magma, is known to the Hopi under the humorous designation Hovi'itstuyqa, "Buttocks sticking-out point." At its eastern flank lies the important ruin of Elden Pueblo, which has been identified as Pasiwvi by Hopi elders.

The entire panorama extending between the San Francisco Peaks and the Little Colorado River, so markedly studded with dozens of smoothly rounded cinder mounds, is referred to as Löhavutsotsmo, or "Testicle hills." Sunset Crater itself, which forms part of this spectacular cinder cone belt, is named Palatsmo, "Red hill."

Colton, in his summary of principal Hopi trails, lists one that traversed the desert from the Hopi mesas to the San Francisco Peaks. Basically running parallel to Dennebito Wash until it crossed the Little Colorado River south of Black Falls, it led past an ice cave that, due to its close proximity to the crater, is today incorporated in the national monument. The cave, accessible from the Lava Flow Nature Trail, is entered through a sinkhole. Its main passage is a tube—notable for the year-round presence of ice in the form of icicles, stalagmites, and sheets on the wall—winding along for some 225 feet (70 m). Familiar to Hopi under the name Patusungwtanga, "Stored frozen water," it was revered by them along with many other locations associated with any type of moisture. Offerings to the gods in the form of prayer sticks or prayer feathers may have been deposited here by the Hopi since prehistoric times. Whether the Ka'naskatsina was once directly linked with this particular ice cave can no longer be determined. In the version recorded here, an ice cave is identified as the abode of the kachina, but it is placed on top of the San Francisco Peaks. Since no ice cavern is known to exist in the higher regions of the Peaks, this placement may be the result of erroneous recollection on the part of the storyteller.

Grand Falls, nearly 20 miles (30 km) due east, is known as Söynapi, "Swishing/whistling sound place." The name, which is also heard in the variant forms of Söönapi and Söönavi, is an onomatopoeic reference to the mass of Little Colorado River water that occasionally cascades down this fall. The Hopi term for the Little Colorado is Paayu, which translates simply "River."

Wupatki, the Hopi collective designation for the extensive concentration of prehistoric Sinagua sites in the terrain some 20 miles (30 km) north of Sunset Crater, already figures in ancient Hopi migration myths. Famous for its well-preserved ruins, including a large ball court, the place name means "Long cut" or "Long valley" and not "Tall house" as is commonly found in the literature. While the latter designation would be *wupaki* in Hopi, naming a habitation site in this fashion would run completely counter to Hopi practices. *Tuki*,-"cut/valley," which here occurs in its syncopated form of -*tki*, is also attested in Sikyatki, "Yellow cut," the extinct village site east of the First Mesa pueblo of Walpi.

Place names of prominent topographic features to the east of the San Francisco Peaks include Yuvukpu, "Cave-in," or "Sink," a reference to Meteor Crater; Nuvakwewtaqa, "One wearing a snow belt," the term for Anderson Mesa; and Sakwavayu, "Blue river," known today as Chevelon Creek. No indigenous name seems to be remembered for Walnut Canyon.

Familiarity on the part of the Hopi with the Sunset Crater environment is also evident mythologically. Of significance in this connection is their belief that the wind god lived in the vicinity of the crater. In our story, the god, who is characterized as a whirlwind, dwells in a gigantic subterranean hole. According to Colton, this hole is actually supposed to have been a large crevasse in the Bonito lava flow notable for its rather perceptible issuing of cold air. That the Hopi located the wind god, identified as Yaapontsa in other tales, in the Sunset Crater–Wupatki area makes a great deal of sense, considering the rather unusual eolian phenomena that exist here. The limestone formation, which underlies much of the volcanic field in this area, houses an immense interconnected cavern system whose volume and length have been estimated at approximately seven billion cubic feet (200 million m³) and 700 miles (1,120 km), respectively. Most intriguing in this cavern system are so-called blowholes, through which air is either sucked in or rushes out, depending on the barometric pressure. One such blowhole is situated immediately adjacent to the ball court that is associated with the main ruin complex at Wupatki National Monument.

Whatever the circumstances under which the Hopi learned of the explosion of Sunset Crater, whatever the origin of the Ka'nas legend, it is ironic that this awesome account of the eruption, so masterfully woven into a plot of betrayal and revenge, was salvaged at a time when the once-powerful flow of Hopi narrative traditions has already abated to a trickle, if not run dry. With active storytelling nearly extinct, story rememberers can still be found among the older Hopi. What they remember, however, is no longer of great appeal to members of the younger generation. Hopi children are nowadays more in tune with the comic strip adventures of Batman and

Superman than with the mischievous pranks of their Pöqangwhoya and Palöngawhoya; they are more at home with the cosmic topography of Luke Skywalker than with the mythological map on which their own heroes and heroines once roamed.

The command of their language, the all-important vehicle in which native culture is not only anchored but also meaningfully passed on, has deteriorated to a point of crisis proportions. Thus, it was indeed a sad milestone in this development when, during a recent kachina dance rehearsal in one of the Hopi villages, Hopi elders had to resort to English to explain to younger participants such performance aspects as dancing, singing, and costuming.

Whether the Hopi can, before it is too late, make a concerted effort to stem the tide of losing their cultural identity, rooted so deeply in their own vernacular, is uncertain. By committing this legend to print in a bilingual format, one hopes that Hopi interest and motivation to preserve and cultivate their oral heritage may someday be rekindled.

# EARTH FIRE
# A HOPI LEGEND OF THE SUNSET CRATER ERUPTION

ALIKSA'I. They say people were living in Musang-nuvi. The headman of this village had a daughter who was very beautiful. The girl was of marriageable age, but there was no man she loved. Upon reaching this age, a Hopi girl regularly grinds corn. She carries out this task to prepare for the day when she will take a husband. This particular girl, however, had given no thought to getting married. But she ground corn anyway, for she was very industrious. She undertook the chore mainly for her mother who, whenever there was a wedding, cooked the necessary food from the stockpile of corn flour.

ALIKSA'I. Yaw musangnuve yeesiwa. Noq pep yaw pumuy kikmongwi'am hakiy lomamanti'yta. Pu' pam yaw maana naat pas pu' havuukiwkyangw pam yaw qa hakiy naawakna. Noq pay pi hopima-na pan wuuyoqte' pam pay pas sutsep pan ngu-mantangwu. Pam hapi hisat kongtaniqey pangsoq na'saslawngwuniiqe oovi pay pas sonqa pantsak-ngwu. Noq pay yaw i' maana as qa hin kongwu-wantakyangw put pantsakngwu; pay yaw pam qa na'önaniiqe oovi. Pu' pay yaw pam piw yuy engem put pantsakngwu. Pay yaw haqam mö'öngna'ya-niqw, pay yaw put yu'at put angqw hiita noova-tangwu.

As a rule, the girl ground corn in a grinding chamber on the second story of the house, as was customary in those days. A Hopi dwelling generally had one or two rooms built above the main floor. Generally, the grinding chamber contained several metates lined up side by side, although some had only two grinding stones, one for coarse grinding and the other for fine grinding. Exceptionally, there were two fine grinding stones.

Whenever a woman or girl ground corn, she first used the coarser stone to break up the whole kernels. Having crushed the kernels slightly, so that the flour was still lumpy, she dry-roasted the mixture in a cauldron over an open fire. Then the coarsely ground flour was scooped onto the finer metate, where it was ground to the fineness desired. Such was the grinding routine the girls and women adhered to.

Noq pu' yaw pam maana pan ngumante' pay yaw pam sutsep pepeq pumuy tupatsayamuy epeq pantsakngwu. Pay yaw qa hak maana qa pepeq hisat ngumantangwu. Noq pam hopiki pay epha- qam suukw, lööq tupatsa'ytangwu. Pam tupatsa pay sus'atkyaqniiqat kiihut piw atsve suukyawa kii'iwtangwu. Noq pu' pam mata qa suukya ang haqe' leetsiwtangwu. Niikyangw ephaqam pam pay panis lööyömningwu, i' hakomtaniqw pu' i' pingyamtaningwu. Pu' ephaqam i' pingyamta löö- yömningwu.

Noq maana, wuuti ngumantaniqa mooti hakomtavaqe put humitat haakoknangwu. Pu' pam put hihinvingyaqw pam pay naat paasat hakwurkwiningwu. Pu' pam ason put pas tulakne', paasat pu' pam put pangsoq pingyamtamiqwat naalakne', pu' pangqewat pas put hin piingyaniqey pan pangqe piingyangwu. Yan puma mamant, momoyam ngumantotaqam hintsatskya.

The young maiden at Musangnuvi was constantly wooed by the young men, but all was for naught. She never encouraged a man's feelings and she resisted yielding to anyone from her home village. Even though some men appeared wealthy, she felt no desire to marry any of them. From the distant villages of Walpi, Orayvi and Songoopavi the wooers came to win her hand. The girl's parents knew that their daughter had never succumbed to any man. Normally, once a girl had a boyfriend, she would cease grinding corn whenever she wanted to talk to him. But this girl never once interrupted her work.

Thus time passed until one day, surprisingly enough, the girl did stop grinding. Her mother, who immediately noticed it, exclaimed, "Thank heavens!" And her father added, "Yes, indeed. Our daughter must have talked to somebody. Maybe she has found a boy now. For alas, our daughter is grown, and though we have long hoped that she would find a suitable husband, the stubborn girl has discouraged everyone."

"How true!" the mother agreed. "If we're lucky, she may at long last have fallen for someone."

Noq ima tootim yaw as okiw sutsep put aw tutumaywisngwu. Noq pay yaw pam pas qa hisat hakiy aw unangwtavi. Pay yaw pam pas qa hakiy pep naap kitsokiy ep aw uunati. Naamahin pay yaw as himuwa naap a'ni hiita tuwa'ynumqw, pay yaw pam put qa hin amumniqey unangwtingwu. Hikis yaw ima kiyavaqtotim as walngaqwnit pu' piw orayngaqw put aw ökiwta. Pu' yaw yangqw songoopangaqw piw yaw as aw ökiwta. Noq pay yaw pam pas qa hakiywat hisat aw unangwtapqw yaw put maanat yumat puma yan navota. Pay pi yaw as himuwa maana siwatuwte', pay siwatway aw yu'a'aykunik, pay yaw as ngumanqe'tingwu. Noq pay yaw pam pas qa hisat ngumantaqe qe'ti hak aw pituqw.

Noq pu' yaw aapiy pantaqw piw yaw pam suus epehaq ngumanqe'tiqw, yaw put maanat yu'at tuqayvastat pu' yaw pangqawu, "Is askwali," yaw kita. Noq pu' yaw na'atwa pangqawu, "Kwakwhay, owiy," yaw kita. "Pi kya pu' hakiy aw yu'a'aykuy. Sen pi pu' hakiy tuwa. Taq nuwu hapi pay pam wuuyoqtiqw, itam as hakiy put engem naawaknaqw, pas soq pam qa hakiy aw unangwtapngwuy," yaw na'at kita.

"Hep owi, pay pi itam sakinaqw, pi antsa pu' hakiy aw nawis'ewtiqw unangwtavi," yaw yu'at kita.

The parents listened most carefully. A long time passed, still their daughter did not resume her grinding. Eventually she seemed ready to retire, because she came down from the upper story of the house. The parents said nothing to their daughter that night. "We'll wait until tomorrow to ask her," they decided and so held back their questions.

But the girl had been talking to a young man. She had not been at all suspicious of him and, in fact, had taken an immediate liking to him. Actually, the young man was a Ka'nas kachina, but he had not revealed this to the girl. He had no intention of voluntarily giving away his background to her. It would not be until she really wanted him that he would make such a disclosure.

The next night, at about the same time, the girl again quit grinding corn and appeared to be conversing with someone. Once more her parents listened attentively. "Our daughter must finally have found someone. This is the second time that she's quit grinding," they thought, and both were elated.

Then, as on the previous evening, the girl came down from the grinding chamber in the upper story. Her parents asked, "Did anyone talk to you last night and the night before?"

Noq pu' yaw puma oovi pantaqw, pay yaw aapiy pas wuuyavotiqw pay yaw pam pas qa ahoy ngumantiva. Hisatniqw pu' yaw pam pay kur puwtoqe yaw oovi haawi. Noq pay yaw puma naat put qa aw hingqawu. "Ason pi pay kur qa suus pantiqw pu' itam tuuvingtaniy," yaw puma kitaaqe pay yaw puma oovi ep mihikqw pay put qa tuuvingta.

Noq pay yaw pam maana qa hin put hakiy tiyot aw pas hin wuuwanta, pay pi yaw pam kur paasat put hiiyongtiqe oovi. Noq pam tiyo yaw kur i' hak himu ka'naskatsinaniikyangw pay yaw pam put maanat qa aawinta. Pay pi yaw pam son pas put naap put aawintani. Ason pi yaw pay pam pas putniniqw, paasat pu' pay yaw pam son put qa navotnani.

Noq pu' yaw qavongvaqw mihikqw pay yaw pam maana piw aasatniqwhaqam epehaq ngumanqe'tiqe yaw sumataq hakiy aw yu'a'ata. Noq pu' yaw pam piw pan qe'tiqw, pu' yaw put maanat yumat piw tuqayvaasi'yta. "Pu' kya itaati nawis'ewtiqw hakiy tuwaaqe oovi pay pu' hapi löös mihikqw panti," yaw puma yan wuuwaqe yaw puma haalayti.

Pu' yaw pam maana kya pi piw ngumanyukuuqe paasat pu' yaw pam piw haawi. Pu' yaw pam hawqw paasat pu' yaw puma put tiy tuuvingta, "Ya qa hak tookinit pu' hukyaltok uumi yu'a'ata?" yaw puma yan put tuuvingta.

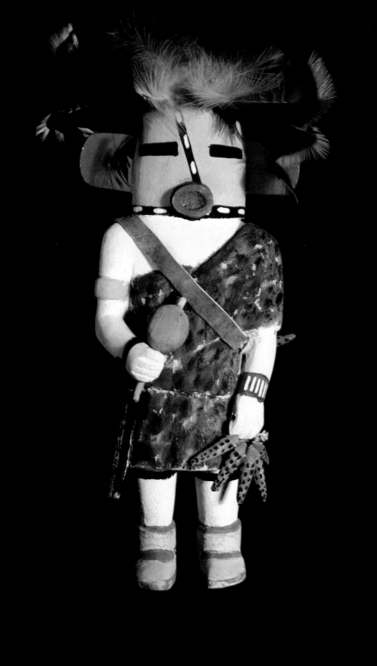

For a while the girl remained silent. Finally, she replied, "Yes, a most handsome young man, but he's not from here. He's from another village."

"Really? How fortunate!" both parents exclaimed. "You're pretty old already, so we've been seeking a husband for you. Still, if we had found one, you might not have cared for him, and therefore we did not trouble. It seems you've found someone yourself though. For that we are grateful. When the time comes that you want to go with him," her mother continued, "you must let us know so we can prepare whatever you need to take along to his home to be married."

The girl replied, "Tomorrow night I'll ask him if he really wants me. If he gives me an answer, I'll let you know which day he intends to take me with him. By the way," she added, "there's something I forgot."

"What is that?"

Noq pay yaw pam qa nuwu pumuy amumi hingqawt pas yaw nawutstiqw pu' yaw pam pangqawu, "As'a," yaw kita, "pas pam hak suhimutiyoniikyangw pay pam qa yangqö. Pay pam haqaqwwat kitsokit angqö," yaw pam maana pumuy yumuy amumi kita.

"Haw owi? Pay tsangawa," yaw puma kita. "Pay um hapi nuwu wuuyoqtiqw oovi itam as yep hakiy ungem heevi'yta. Noq itam hakiy ungem tuwaqw, son pi um put hakiy nakwhaniqw oovi pay itam qa pantsaki. Niikyangw pay tsangaw um kur hakiy tuway," yaw puma put mantiy aw kita. Noq pu' yaw yu'at pangqawu, "Pay pi antsa um hisat amumninik, um itamuy aa'awnaqw, pu' itam hapi ungem hiita na'sastotaqw, pu' um put pankyangw antsa haqami kiiyat aw lööqöktoniy," yaw yu'at aw kita.

Noq pu' yaw pam maana pangqawu, "Pay pi ason nu' qaavo tuuvingtani sen pi pas antsa nuyni- qey naawakna. Pu' ason pi paasat nuy hinwat aa'awnaqw, pu' nu' paasat tuwat umuy hin aa'awnani sen hisat nuy wikniqat," yaw kita. Pu' yaw pam maana piw pangqawu, "Noq mit kur nu' qa u'na," yaw pam maana kita.

"Ya hiita'a?"

"He handed me a gift, all bundled up, which I left upstairs. Let me go back up and bring it." With that the girl climbed to the upper story. Returning with the package, she undid the wrapping and discovered that it contained baked sweet corn. That was what the youth had presented to the girl. The girl tasted it and found that it was fresh out of the pit oven and therefore still tender. As the family feasted on it, the father remarked, "That must be quite an extraordinary man to bring us baked corn out of season. It's just turned summer and there have been no crops in the fields. He must have grown them, for here we had fresh food on account of him."

At about the same time the following night the girl once more stopped grinding corn. Somewhat later, when she had once more come downstairs, she informed her parents, "He asked me to leave with him in two days. But he did not tell me where he intends to take me."

On this occasion, the girl's suitor had brought fresh roasted corn for her. So again the family feasted on it. It was a delicious treat. The next evening the young man came to the girl with fresh roasted corn along with some dried rabbit meat. Thus, when the maiden had finished her grinding, the family again enjoyed a delicious supper.

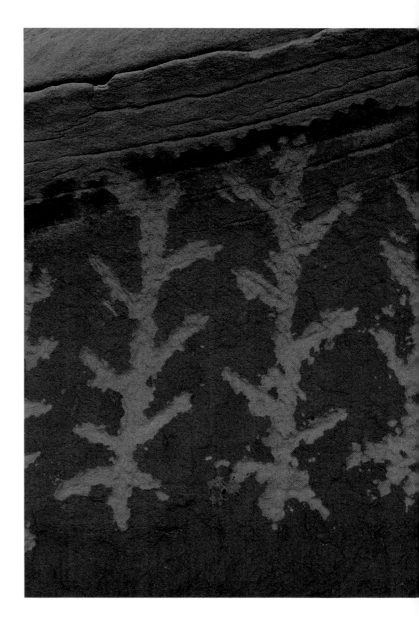

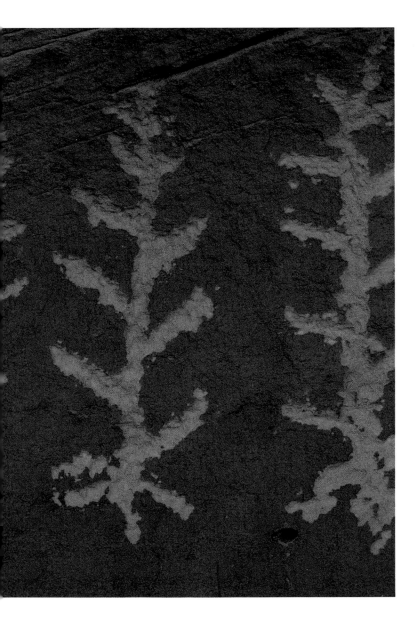

"Pam it hiita mookiwtaqat inumi taviqw, nu' put qa u'naqe oovi aqw oomiq kwistoni," yaw pam kitat pu' yaw pam ahoy oomiqhaqami tupatsmiq, pepeq pam ngumantangwuniiqey, pangsoq yaw pam wuuvi. Niiqe pu' yaw pam pangqaqw hiita mookiwtaqat kwusivaqe pu' yaw puruknaqw, kur yaw pam tuupevu. Put yaw kur pam put maanat maqa. Pu' yaw pam put puruknaqe yaw angqw yukuqw, pas yaw kur pam naat pu' put yaaha. Pas yaw pam naat oovi suphingpu. Paasat pu' yaw puma put oovi noonova. Noq pu' yaw na'at pangqawu, "Pay kur pas pam hak a'niniiqe oovi it piw itamungem oya," yaw pam kita. "Pay pi as naat pu' tal'angwvaqw, naat itam qa hiita uuyi'yyungwa. Noq pay kur pam it aniwnaqw oovi itam atsviy nöönösay," yaw na'at kita.

Noq pu' yaw ep qavongvaqw mihikqw pay yaw piw aasatniqwhaqam yaw pam maana piw ngumanqe'ti. Hisatniqw pu' yaw pam piw haawi. Paasat pu' yaw pam yumuy amumi pangqawu, "Yaw nu' löötok pay amumniqat inumi kita," yaw kita. "Niikyangw haqamiwat pam nuy wikniqey pay pam nuy put qa aa'awna," yaw kita.

Noq ep yaw kur pam put engem pas puhutu'tsit kiva. Pu' yaw puma oovi put piw nöönösa. Is ali yawi'. Qavongvaqw mihikqw pu' yaw kur pam piw pitukyangw ep pu' yaw pam put maanat engem tu'tsitniikyangw pu' sowiskwilakvut enang kiva. Niiqe puma yaw oovi ep mihikqw put maanat qe'tiqw, puma yaw piw putwat kwangwanö- nösa.

Now the girl's parents inquired of their daughter, "How does he talk? Does he speak like a Musangnuvi, a Walpi, or an Orayvi?"

"It's difficult to say where he's from, but his speech seems like that of the people of Songoopavi," she said. "He certainly speaks in a way different from us. Nor is his dialect like that spoken in Orayvi or Walpi. So perhaps he's from Songoopavi."

"Don't you see where he goes when he sets out for home?" they asked their daughter.

"No, the moment he hands me the gifts he goes down from the mesa. Furthermore, it's too dark to tell the direction he takes," the girl asserted.

Pu' yaw puma put maanat tuuvingta, "Noq pam hin tuuqaytay?" yaw puma kita. "Qa pay sen musangnuptuqayta, sen walaptuqayta, sen orayeptuqayta?"

"Pay kur pas haqaqwniikyangw pay piw pas songoopaptuqayta'eway'o," yaw kita. "Pay pas pam alöngöt yu'a'ata. Qa itamun, pu' piw qa orayvituy amunniikyangw pu' piw qa walpituy amun yu'a'ata. Pay sen pi pam oovi pangqw songoopangaqö," yaw kita.

"Noq haqamiwat nimangwuniqw um qa tuwangwu?" yaw puma put maanat aw kita.

"Qa'e, pi pay pam panis inumi it oyat pu' pay angqw hawngwu. Pu' piw qa talngwuniqw, haqamiwat pi pam oovi nakwsungwu," yaw pam maana kita.

The following morning the mother and her daughter began to ready the amount of flour the girl would take along to the home of the man she was going to wed. Thus mother and daughter ground corn all that day. That same evening the youth returned once more and told the girl, "Tomorrow I'll take you away from here. So get ready whatever you care to bring along."

"We've already made our preparations," the girl disclosed.

"Once more I brought some food for you and your parents," said the youth. "Take it downstairs and share it among yourselves. Tomorrow night we'll leave right after you've supped because it's quite a distance to my home." Where he resided, however, he still did not divulge. On this occasion he had brought a watermelon and dried venison in addition to roasted corn, all of which he handed over to the girl. After the young man had departed, the girl carried the food downstairs and the whole family enjoyed a delicious meal.

Sure enough, just after supper the following evening the youth came back again, this time to take the maiden along. In appearance the youth was truly handsome. His skin was light-complexioned, and he had long flowing hair. Inviting him inside their living room, the parents themselves got to look at their daughter's suitor. The youth asserted, "Well, I've come for your

Noq pu' yaw ep qavongvaqw pu' yaw puma naatim put maanat engem na'saslawu, pam maana hiita ngumnit hinkyangw lööqöktoniqat puta'. Niiqe puma yaw oovi ep teevep ngumanta. Ep mihikqw pu' yaw pam tiyo piw pituuqe pu' yaw put maanat aw pangqawu, "Qaavo hapi nu' pay ung yangqw wikkyangwniy," yaw aw kita. "Noq oovi um hiita hinmaniqey put na'sastaniy," yaw pam put aw yan tutapta.

"Pay itam paas put yuki'yta," yaw pam maana put tiyot aw kita.

"Noq nu' yep it piw umungem yanvaqw oovi um ason piw it atkyamiq kimaqw uma piw it nöönösani. Pu' qaavo mihikqw uma hapi pay panis nöönösaqw, pu' itam hapi payniy," yaw pam put aw kita. "Taq ikiy aw pay hihin yaavo'oy," yaw pam tiyo kita. Niikyangw pay yaw pam tiyo haqam ki'ytaqey pay yaw pam piw put qa aa'awna naato. Noq ep pu' yaw pam kur it kawayvatngatnit pu' sowi'ingwsikwilakvutnit pu' tu'tsit enang yaw kur kivaaqe pu' yaw put maanat aw oya. Noq pu' yaw pam tiyo oovi nimaqw, pu' yaw pam maana piw put atkyamiq hannaqw, pu' yaw puma pepeq piw put kwangwanönösa.

Noq pu' ep qavongvaqw tapkiqw pay yaw puma oovi suunönösaqw, pu' yaw antsa pam tiyo put maanat wiktoqe ep pitu. Noq antsa yaw hak suhimutiyo. Pas yaw hak sikyavuhoya, pu' yaw piw wupa'anga'yta. Noq pu' yaw puma put

daughter. I wonder if you're ready and if you've prepared whatever she needs to bring along."

"Yes, everything is ready," came the response.

"In that case, I'll be taking your daughter now. Four days hence I'll bring her back again. She'll return dressed in her wedding costume," he carefully explained to them.

With that the parents handed the girl's ground flour over to the youth. "Carry this on your back for her," they instructed him. The young girl herself shouldered the load of piiki. "Well then, be on your way," the father directed. "You can be certain we'll be waiting for you on the fourth day," he said to the young man. "May you both go with happy hearts," he encouraged the couple.

From the village of Musangnuvi the couple descended from the mesa on the west side, whereupon they proceeded westward taking a route south of Songoopavi. When they were a good distance away from Songoopavi, the youth bade his bride to halt. "Wait a minute," he told her. "If we travel on foot, it'll be ages before we reach my home. So let's use my own special way of journeying. With that he groped around in a pouch dangling from his hip and pulled out some object.

paki'a'awnayaqw, pu' yaw puma maanat yumat put siwatwayat aw pas naap yori. Noq pu' yaw pam tiyo pangqawu, "Ta'ay," yaw kita, "nu' umuumanay wiktoy," yaw pam kita. "Noq sen pi pay uma yuki'yta. Sen pi pay hiita hinmaniqey pay put yuki'yta," yaw kita.

"Owiy," yaw puma kita.

"Ta'ay, nu' hapi it umuumanay wiikye', yaapiy naalös taalat ep pu' hapi nu' angqw ahoy wikniy," yaw pam pumuy amumi kita. "Ason itamuy it pas yuwsinayaqw, pu' nu' it ahoy angqw wikniy," yaw pam pumuy paas yan aa'awna.

Pu' yaw puma oovi it tiyot aw put maanat nguman'iniyat tavi. "It um engem iikwiwmaniy," yaw puma kita. Noq pu' yaw pam maanawa pay yaw naap put piikiy iikwilta. "Ta'ay, yupavey," yaw na'at kita. "Pay ason itam antsa naalös taalat awhaqami umuy nuutaytaniy," yaw put maanat na'at put tiyot aw kita. "Uma oovi haalaykyangw awhaqaminiy," yaw pam pumuy amumi kita.

Paasat pu' yaw puma pangqw musangnuviy taavangqöymiq hawt pu' yaw puma aapiy songoopaviy tatkye' aqw teevengewat hoyta. Noq pu' yaw puma pay pangqw songoopangaqw hihin yaaptiqw, pu' yaw pam tiyo put mantuway huruutapna. "Haakiy," yaw pam put aw kita. "Pay itam hapi naapnen son ikiy aw iits pituniy. Noq oovi itam hapi pay ivokoy akwniy," yaw pam put aw kitat pu' yaw pam put tukput pi'alhaytaqey yaw put aqw hintsaklawt pu' paasat yaw pangqw hiita horokna.

Unmistakably, it was a rainbow. After removing it from the pouch he hurled it westward. The rainbow arched up and alighted at a place far away. "This will be our means of travel now," the young man enlightened the girl. The girl, who had witnessed the spectacle, became frightened. She balked at the idea of riding the rainbow and confessed to her boyfriend, "How scary, I might fall off! I'm afraid of heights."

The youth reassured her, "Nothing will happen to you. I'll watch over you carefully. We just can't afford to travel on foot. It would take us too long, since I live quite far from here."

The girl had no choice but to yield to his wish. After all, she had promised the youth to go along with him, and so she complied. The youth now said to her, "All right, climb up behind me. But keep your eyes shut tight once we fly along, and don't open them until I tell you to do so."

Noq pam yaw kur i' tangaqwunu. Pu' yaw pam put pangqw horoknat pu' yaw pam put teevengewat tuuva. Pu' yaw pam put tuuvaqw, pas hapi yaw pam yaavoqhaqami laholti. Noq putakw yaw pumaniqat yaw pam tiyo put maanat aw pangqawu. Noq pay yaw pam maana yan yorikqe pay yaw pam tsawna. Pay yaw pam as paasat qa suutaq'ewtaqe yaw oovi put siwatway aw pangqawu, "Is uru, piw kya nu' okiw angqw posni. Pu' nu' piw suuya," yaw pam put tiyot aw kita.

Noq pu' yaw pam put aw pangqawu, "Pay um son hintini. Pay nu' ason uumi paas tunatyawmani. Taq pi itam naapnen itam son iits ikiy aw pituni. Nu' hapi pay hihin pas yaap ki'yta," yaw pam put aw kita.

Noq pu' yaw pam maana pay nawus paasat suutaq'ewta. Pay pi yaw pam nuwu pi put tiyot amumniqey aw pangqawqe pu' yaw pam oovi pay paasat nakwha. Noq pu' yaw pam tiyo put maanat aw pangqawu, "Ta'ay, um pew inuukwayngyavo wupniy. Niikyangw um hapi huur uvimaniy. Ason pas nu' uumi pangqawqw pu' um paasat uuposiy puruknaniy," yaw pam tiyo put maanat aw yan tutapta.

Following the youth the girl obediently climbed up on to the rainbow and firmly closed her eyes. No sooner had she done so than she clearly sensed a rising up of the rainbow. It shot along at a great speed. This was apparent from the wind fanning the girl's face, though it was not a very strong wind. Furthermore, the youth's long hair, blowing backwards and brushing against the girl's nose, tickled her so that at one point she sneezed a couple of times.

In no time at all, the rainbow carried its passengers to the place where it touched the ground. Both of them stepped off and when the girl looked back, the village of Songoopavi was no longer in sight. Apparently, they had covered a great distance. Again the youth cast the rainbow skywards and asked the girl to climb up on it behind him. This time she did not hesitate. She got on behind him and again firmly closed her eyes. A second time the rainbow rose and, carrying the couple aloft, proceeded until it touched down. As before, they had covered a vast distance in an instant and came to rest at a place adjacent to Söynapi.

As the rainbow landed, it set the couple down ever so gently. Once more the youth picked up the rainbow and threw it westward. This time it came down near a big hill, whereupon the two climbed aboard and were transported to this location, where they disembarked a third time.

Paasat pu' yaw pam maana oovi put tiyot aakwayngyavo wupt pu' huur uviiti. Noq naat yaw pam oovi pu' pantiqw pay yaw pam tangaqwunu susmataq hölöltiqw, yaw pam maana hihin navota. Pu' yaw pam pan hölöltikyangw pay yaw pam paasat pas suyan a'ni hoyta. Niiqe paasat yaw oovi put maanat taywayat susmataq aw sumawva. Niikyangw pay yaw as piw qa a'ni huuhuktima. Pu' yaw piw put tiyot anga'at susmataq ahoywat huhukhoytimaqe yaw put maanat yaqayat ang tongtimaqw, pam yaw oovi put kuktsuknaqw, pam yaw oovi lööshaqam aasi.

Hiisavoniqw pay yaw pam haqami tsööqökqey yaw pangsoq pumuy pitsina. Pu' yaw puma paasat angqw haawi. Noq pu' yaw pam maana ahoy yorikqw, pay yaw paasat songoopavi pangqw qa maatsiwta. Pay yaw kur puma pas yaapti. Noq pu' yaw pam tiyo piw put pookoy tuuvakyangw pu' yaw piw put maanat aw pangqawu yaw piw angk put pokyat aw wupniqat. Paasat pu' yaw pam pay qa hin naawaknat, pu' yaw pay put angk aw wupt, pu' yaw piw huur uviiti. Paasat pu' yaw pam tangaqwunu piw pumuy tsoki'ykyangw hölöltikyangw pu' paasat haqamiwat yeevaqey pangsoqwat pu' yaw pam piw nakwsu. Noq pay yaw puma antsa piw suuyaaptikyangw pu' paasat yaw puma söynapiy suu'aqlap qatuptu.

Pu' yaw pam tangaqwunu qatuptsiwme' pas hapi yaw pam pumuy paas tavi'ymangwu. Noq pu' yaw pam tiyo piw put ep kwusuuqe pu' yaw pam

That moment, much to her own surprise, the girl felt the urge to defecate. She was puzzled by this, for earlier that morning and the night before she had not eaten a great deal. Also she had emptied her bowels just prior to her departure. Anyway, she told her boyfriend of her need.

He replied, "I understand. I'll wait here for you while you search for a place out of sight. When you are done, come back here. But please hurry, since it gets dark quickly at this time of year."

Thereupon the girl went to defecate. When she had found a spot out of the youth's view, she gathered up her dress, squatted down and began to defecate. She had not finished when a voice spoke to her from somewhere. "Young girl," the voice said, "when you're done with your business, come over here to me."

piw put teevengewat tuuva. Noq paasat pu' yaw pam yuk haqami wukotsomot aqlavo yeevaqw, pu' yaw puma paasat piw put aqw wupt pu' paasat piw pangsowat. Panmakyangw pu' yaw puma put tsomot aqlavo piw qatuptukyangw pu' yaw puma put tiyot pokyat angqw haawi.

Noq suupaasat yaw pam maana piw kwayngyavomoki. Noq hintiqw pi yaw pam piw paasatniqwhaqam kwayngyavomoki. Pi yaw pam as ep talavaynit pu' piw ep tokinen pay qa pas wukonösa. Pu' yaw pam as piw pay paas kwayngyaptaqw, pu' puma pangqw put maanat kiiyat angqw nakwsu. Niiqe pu' yaw pam put siwatway pan aa'awna.

Noq pu' yaw pam put aw pangqawu, "Kur antsa'ay, pay nu' tur haak ung yep nuutaytaqw, um haqami na'uypikya'ytaqat hepte', pu' um ason pep kwayngyaptat pu' piw angqw ahoyniy. Niikyangw pay um hapi hihin pisoqtiniy, taq pi pay suutapkingwuy," yaw pam put aw kita.

Noq pu' yaw pam oovi kwayngyaptato. Noq pu' yaw pam maana haqam na'uypikya'ytaqat tuwaaqe, pu' yaw pam oovi kwasay oomi tsovalat, pu' pephaqam tsukuniltiqe pu' yaw pep siisisi. Noq naat yaw pam qa yukuqw, pay yaw hak haqaqw aw hingqawu, "Maanaa, ason um hintsakqey paas mongvastit pu' um ason pewni," yaw hak put aw kita.

After she was through, the girl stood up and went looking about, but no one seemed to be there. So she called out, "Who spoke to me and where are you?"

"I'm right here next to you. Step a little farther to the east and you're bound to find me." The girl obeyed and moved slightly eastward, whereupon the voice spoke again. "I'm right here below you." Peering in front of her the girl, much to her amazement, spotted what looked like a house.

Since only a tiny opening led into the place, the girl called down, "I don't see how on earth I can get down to you. The entrance in the roof is awfully small."

"If you jam your heel into it and rotate it back and forth, the aperture is bound to get larger," the voice advised her. The girl heeded the instruction and, indeed, the opening grew so wide that she was able to enter. From all evidence it was Old Spider Woman who resided there. "My poor grandchild!" she cried in sympathy for the girl. "I felt sorry for you; that's the reason I waited for you here. You're still young and inexperienced and you've never been so far away from home. What's more, you're walking into an uncertain future. You should be aware that the youth leading you to his home is a Ka'nas kachina. He and his family live west of here in an ice cavern on top of Nuvatukya'ovi. Once he succeeds in getting you there, your courage will be severely tested. Without my lending you a helping

Noq pu' yaw pam oovi yukuuqe pu' yaw pam wunuptut pu' yaw pam as angqe' taynumqw, pay yaw qa hak haqam'eway. Pu' yaw pam paasat pangqawu, "Ya um hak inumi hingqawqa haqamo?" yaw pam kita.

"Pay nu' paysoq yep uqlap'o. Um oovi hihin pew hoopowatnen pay um son nuy qa tuwani." Yaw hak put aw kitaqw, pu' yaw pam oovi aw hooponiiqe pu' yaw pam haqami pituqw, pu' yaw hak piw aw pangqawu, "Pay nu' paysoq yep utpip'o," yaw hak aw kitaqw pu' yaw pam oovi natpipo yorikqw, piw yaw pephaqam hak sumataq ki'yta.

Noq pangsoq pay yaw pas hiisaqhoya hötsiniqw, pu' yaw pam oovi aqw pangqawu, "Pi nu' kur hin uumiq pakini, pi aqw hiisaqhoya hötsi," yaw pam maana kita.

"Pay um uukuktönsiy peqw rooroyaqw, pay son peqw qa wuuyaqtini," yaw hak angqaqw kitaqw pu' yaw pam oovi pantiqw pay yaw antsa aqw wuuyaqtiqw pu' yaw pam aqw paki. Noq yaw kur pam kookyangwso'wuuti pepeq qatuuqe yaw put aw pangqawu, "Okiwa imöyhoya," yaw aw kita. "Nu' ung ookwatuwqe oovi nu' yep ung nuutayta. Um hapi naat tsayniiqe um hapi naat pu' suus uukiy angqw pewhaqami'i. Pu' um piw kur hintaqat aw'i. Noq pu' pam tiyo ung wikqa, pam hapi ka'naskatsina. Noq puma yep taavang nuvatukya'oviy ooveq patusungwtangat epeq yeese. Naat hapi pam ung pangso wikqw, pu' puma hapi

hand, you certainly won't survive the ordeal," the old woman told the girl. "So for this reason I'll go with you. But we shouldn't tarry. The young man may grow suspicious and come to look for you. Let's go right now," she urged the girl. "Place me behind your ear and we'll be off." With that the girl set Old Spider Woman on her ear, whereupon they returned together to where the youth was waiting.

"Have you finished?" he inquired. Since he asked only this much, he was obviously unaware of what had taken place.

"Yes," the girl replied.

"All right then, let's move on. It's still quite a way to my home."

Once again he drew the rainbow out of his sack and flung it upward. As before, it arched, and this time struck the top of the Nuvatukya'ovi range. The young man and his bride mounted the rainbow, whereupon it contracted and headed to the top of the mountain. The place where they came down was right next to the hatch of a kiva. "Well, we've arrived," the youth exclaimed. "Follow me." With that he led her into the kiva and announced their arrival. "Haw! What about some words of welcome! I am not alone," he shouted into the dwelling.

pepeq son uumi hin qa hepyani. Pu' nu' ung qa pa'angwaqw um son ang kuyvani," yaw pam so'-wuuti put maanat aw kita. "Nu' hapi oovi paniqw umumni. Niikyangw itam pay qa sööwuni, taq pay pam tiyo hin wuuwe' sen ung angqaqw heptoni. Oovi itam payni," yaw kita pam so'wuuti put maanat awi'. "Niikyangw pay oovi um yuk uunaq-vuy aakwayngyavo nuy tsokyaqw itam payni. Tu-mu, nuwu pay hisatniqwti," yaw pam kitaqw pu' yaw pam maana put naqvuy aw tsokyaqw, pu' yaw puma naama put tiyot awniqw pay yaw pam naat put ep nuutayta.

Noq pay yaw pam tiyo kur qa navotqe pay yaw oovi panis put aw pangqawu, "Ya um yuku?" yaw kita.

"Owi," yaw pam maana kita.

"Kur antsa'ay," yaw kita. "Ta'ay, pay itam piwniy. Pay naat pas ikiy aw wuuyavo'oy," yaw pam tiyo kita.

Paasat pu' yaw pam oovi piw put pookoy horoknaqe pu' yaw pam piw put tuuva. Noq pu' yaw pam piw laholtikyangw pu' yaw pangsoq oomiq nuvatukya'omiqniqw, paasat pu' yaw puma piw put aqw wuuvi. Paasat pu' yaw pam tangaq-wunu pangqw piw naalangaknakyangw pu' pang-soq oomiq. Noq pu' yaw puma pephaqam qatup-tukyangw piw yaw puma haqam kivaytsiwat aqlap qatuptu. Paasat pu' yaw pam tiyo put aw pangqawu, "Ta'ay, itam pituy," yaw kita. "Um pew inungkniy," yaw pam put aw kitaaqe pu' yaw pam

Sure enough, voices could be heard from down below. "Come on in," they urged. "Please, enter. Maybe you do, indeed, bring someone with you."

When they entered, the girl discovered that the kiva was filled with a great many people. There were women and girls, men and boys. As she carefully ran her eyes over them, she noticed that all the people residing there were unmistakably kachinas. While her boyfriend disappeared into a back room, those gathered cordially welcomed the girl who was to be their new in-law. They relieved her of her bundles of piiki and corn flour and expressed their delight in receiving these foods. One of the women stepped into a room far in the rear and returned with a trayful of items that she presented to the girl. The tray was loaded with everything that could be grown: watermelon, muskmelon, roasted corn. In addition, there were all the dishes that can be made from corn. A meat roast was also on the platter. The girl really savored the food. The kachinas, in turn, helped themselves to the girl's piiki and ate with great relish. At this moment the girl's fiancè emerged from the back room in the guise of a Ka'nas kachina. Now the girl truly believed that he represented this kachina.

put pangqw kivami wikt pu' yaw aqw pangqawu, "Haw, kuwawatotangwuy! Nu' qa naala waynumay," yaw pam aqwhaqami kita.

Noq pu' yaw pam aqw pangqawqw, yaw antsa hakim angqaqw kuwawatota. "Yungya'ay," yaw kitota. "Huvam yungya'ay. Antsa kya um hakiy wiknumay," yaw angqaqw kitota.

Pu' yaw puma oovi aqw pakiqw, antsa yaw hakim epeq qa an'ewakw yeese, momoyam, mamant, tootim, taataqt. Noq pu' yaw pam pas pumuy paas amuupa yorikqw, piw yaw puma kur katsinam pepeq yeese. Noq pu' yaw put siwatwa'at pay paasat aapamiqhaqami pakima. Pu' yaw puma put puhumö'wiy paas taviya. Pu' yaw puma put maanat pikmokiyatnit pu' ngumantangayat kwusunayaqe yaw tuwat haalaytoti. Pu' yaw haqawa yuumoqhaqaminiiqe pu' yaw pangqw hiita ini'ymaqe pu' yaw put maanat aw oya. Pas yaw qa himu natwani pep qa iniwta. Kawayvatnga, melooni, tu'tsi, pu' yaw i' nöösiwqa qaa'öt angqw yuykiwqa piw. Pu' yaw i' sikwitpe pep piw enang iniwta. Pas hapi yaw pam maana put kwangwanösa. Noq pu' yaw puma pep ki'yyungqam put maanat piikiyat tuwat nöönösaqe pay yaw puma piw put maanat an kwangwanönösa. Paasat pu' yaw put siwatwa'at piw ahoy pangqaqw yamakqe pu' yaw paasat ka'naskatsinaniikyangw pangqaqw yama. Pas yaw paasat pu' yaw pam maana tuptsiwa yaw kur pam himu ka'naskatsinaniqw.

When it was time for everyone to retire for the night, great care was taken to make a bed for the girl. Among the people living there was Hahay'iwuuti, who now turned to her and said, "Girl, tomorrow you'll have to grind some corn. When you wake, I'll show you to one of the metates where you'll do your work."

"Of course," the girl acknowledged.

Thereupon everybody retired for the night. The following morning while it was still dark Hahay'iwuuti nudged the girl, saying to her, "Get up, girl!"

The girl had no choice but to get out of bed. Next Hahay'iwuuti told her that they would say their morning prayers together. Thus the two of them went outside and uttered their prayers in the direction of the rising sun. After this brief ritual they came back inside.

Then Hahay'iwuuti selected a place for the girl to sit, and there she squatted with her knees drawn up against her chest, as is customary for any novice during an initiation. Finally, after serving the girl some breakfast, Hahay'iwuuti ushered her to the grinding chamber and positioned her behind one of the bins. She handed the girl a mano and said, "Here! I'm now going to bring what I want you to grind." With that she disappeared into the innermost room at the north end of the kiva. A few moments later she returned bearing some unrecognizable items. When the girl looked

Noq pu' yaw puma tokniniqw pu' yaw puma put engem paas piw aapatota. Noq pu' yaw i' hahay'iwuuti kur piw pep nuutumniiqe pam yaw put maanat aw pangqawu, "Maana, um hapi qaavo sonqa ngumantaniqw oovi pay nu' ason qaavo ung taatayne' pu' ung haqamiwat matamiq panaqw, pu' um paasat ngumantani," yaw pam put maanat aw kita.

"Kur antsa'a," yaw kita.

Noq pu' yaw puma oovi tookya. Qavongvaqw naat pay yaw qa talqw, pay yaw pam hahay'iwuuti put maanat wayayaykinat pu' yaw aw pangqawu, "Qatuptu'u, maana," yaw aw kita.

Noq pu' yaw pam maana oovi nawus pay paasat qatuptu. Put qatuptuqw pu' yaw pam hahay'iwuuti put aa'awna yaw puma kuyvatoniqat. Niiqe pu' yaw puma oovi naama yamakqe pu' yaw talpumiq naama naawakna. Yantit pu' yaw puma paasat piw ahoy paki.

Paasat pu' yaw puma oovi ahoy pakiqw pu' yaw pam put maanat engem haqami qenituwqw, pu' yaw pam maana oovi it kyelewyat an pep tsomo'kyangw qatuwta. Pu' yaw pam hahay'iwuuti put maanat mooti nopnat pu' put pangsoq matamiq pana. Nit pu' yaw pam put aw mataakit tavi. "Yep'e," yaw kita, "um hiita ngumantaniqat nu' put ungem intoni," yaw pam put aw kitaaqe pu' yaw pam kwiniwiqhaqami yuumoq paki. Pu' yaw aqw pakit pu' yaw pam hiisavoniqw pay ahoy angqaqw hiita ini'yma. Yaw pam maana aw yorikqw,

carefully, she realized that they were chunks of ice. Hahay'iwuuti dumped the ice into the grinding bin and commanded her, "This is what you must grind."

The girl just sat there in shock. Never in her life had she heard of anyone grinding ice. No wonder, therefore, that the poor thing balked at the idea. But as she had no choice, she started work. Every so often, after grinding for a short spell, her hands became so chilled that she was forced to tuck them into her armpits for warmth. For a while she merely knelt there shivering. Finally, when her hands warmed up again, she continued. As she resumed her work, she also noticed that there was a chilly breeze coming from the ice. It was extremely cold. Once more she was chilled to the bone. Nevertheless she continued with her task, her entire body shivering. The chunks of ice were terribly rough. Again and again the girl tried to grind them, but with no success. She saw no way that she would ever be able to crush them.

When it had become quite clear that she would not succeed, she became aware that something was stirring on her ear. As she reached up her hand, she realized that Old Spider Woman still clung there. "Ouch, don't scratch me off. It's only me, my granddaughter," the old woman assured her. "You poor, poor thing! I truly sympathize with your misery. That's why I'm here with you," she professed. "The people who inhabit this place are hard-

piw yaw pam patusngwat pangqaqw inta. Pu' yaw pam put matamiq pangala. "Ta'a, it um nguman-tani," yaw pam put aw kita.

Pu' yaw pam pangsoq yanta. Qa hisat pi yaw hak put hiita ngumantaqw pam yan navoti'ytaqe yaw oovi okiw qa suutaq'ewa. Pu' yaw pam oovi nawus ngumantiva. Nit pay yaw pam naat qa wuuyavonit pay yaw pam maasungwmokqe pu' yaw pam may kutsipsömiq pana. Noq pu' yaw pam hiisavo tururutikyangw pep qatuwta. Hisat-niqw pu' yaw pam piw ahoy hihin mukipkiqe pu' yaw piw aapiyta. Pu' yaw pam paasat piw put ngumantaqw, pas hapi yaw put patusngwat angqw huuhukya. Is iyo hapi yawi'. Pay yaw pam paasat piw ahoy sumvakqe pu' yaw pam okiw pangqw tururutikyangw ngumanta. Pu' hapi yaw pam patusngwa anaha'a. Pu' yaw pam as put pangqe haaninkyangw pay yaw pam put qa kyaati. Kur pi yaw hin put piingya.

Pas yaw pam put qa angwutaqw, pu' yaw put naqvuyat ep himu poniniyku. Noq pu' yaw pam naqvuy aqw tongokq, naat yaw kur i' kookyangw-so'wuuti pep tsöpölöwta. "Ana, um qa nuy enang hariknani. Pi pay nuu'u, imöyhoya," yaw pam put aw kita. "Um hapi okiw yephaqam okiwhintsaki. Noq nu' ung ookwatuwa," yaw pam put aw kita. "Ima hapi yep pas qa nun'okwat yeese. Niikyangw pay hapi ima qa paysoq panyungwa. Pay hapi ima son paysoq naap hakiy tuwat mö'wi'yvayaniqey naanawakna. Pas hapi hak pavanniiqa, pasi'na-

hearted. They're not cruel only for the sake of being cruel. It's because they don't want just any girl as a daughter-in-law. She has to be an exceptional person, one of pure heart who can beat them at their own game. I know that you have these qualities and therefore I'll help you for sure. Anyway, you're not just doing this for yourself; once you have beaten them, you will have gained something very special for your people. That's why I brought you this." With that Old Spider Woman laid a soft turkey feather on the mano and added, "This will keep your hands warm without fail. It's bound to melt the ice as well."

ngwa'ytaqa, son imuy qa pö'ani. Noq pay nu' uumi pan navoti'ytaqe son oovi ung qa pa'angwani. Pu' um hapi pay qa neengemsa yep it yantsaki. Um hapi imuy pö'e', um hapi pas hiita soosokmuy uusinmuy amungem aasatani. Nu' oovi yep it ungem angqw enang kima," yaw pam put aw kitaaqe pu' yaw pam put mataakiyat ang it koyongvöhöt pas suphingput tavi. Nit pu' yaw pam put aw pangqawu, "I' pay son uumay qa mukini'ytani. Pu' pam pay son piw patusngwat qapaatani," yaw pam put aw kita.

Once more the girl resumed her grinding. Straight away her hands warmed up again, and the ice began to melt. Apparently, the turkey feather was generating heat and warming the mano causing the ice to turn quickly to water. Eventually, the girl had all the ice crushed, so Old Spider Woman warned her, "I'm sure she'll notice that you've stopped working."

Indeed, it was not long after she had ceased grinding that Hahay'iwuuti came back in. "Thank you! Have you ground it fine?" she exclaimed.

"Yes," answered the girl.

From somewhere Hahay'iwuuti got hold of a gourd dipper and a water vessel. These she brought to the metate, whereupon she scooped the ice water into the container. Evidently this was the purpose of the girl's grinding the ice: she was preparing water for the kachinas.

That night when everybody was about to retire, the girl was put in a room facing north. As soon as she had been taken there, Old Spider Woman came up to her and said, "Now, pay strict attention to me. As you can certainly see, it was Hahay'iwuuti who put you in this room. A mighty wind lives in here. By leaving you here they expect you to freeze to death. They want to test you, of course. And tomorrow you'll have to grind again. However, I foresaw that they would tuck you away in here, and so I have brought you some protection."

Pu' yaw pam oovi piw paasat ngumantaqw pay yaw antsa put maa'at ahoy mukipki. Mukipkiqw pu' yaw pam patusngwa antsa piw pay paasat suupa'iwma. Pam yaw kur i' koyongvöhö put mataakit mukini'ytaqw oovi yaw pam patusngwa pas suupa'iwma. Panmakyangw pu' yaw pam put soosok piingya. Noq pu' yaw kookyangwso'wuuti aw pangqawu, "Pay hapi pam hahay'iwuuti sonqa navotni ung qe'tiqw'ö," yaw aw kita.

Pu' yaw pam qe'tiqw, pay yaw naat qa wuuyavotiqw pay yaw antsa pam hahay'iwuuti navotqe pu' angqawu paki. "Is askwali! Ya pay um piingya?" yaw aw kita.

"Owi," yaw pam maana kita.

Pu' yaw pam haqam tawiykuyapitnit pu' kuysivutniiqe pu' yaw pam put pangso yawmaqe pu' yaw put aqw kuukuya. Noq yaw pam maana pep kur put patusngwat paniqw ngumanta. Pam yaw pumuy amungem kuuyit na'saslawu.

Noq pu' yaw puma ep mihikqw tokniniqw pu' yaw puma put maanat kwiniwiq aapamiq panaya. Noq naat yaw puma pu' put pangsoq panayaqw, pay yaw piw i' kookyangwso'wuuti put maanat aw pitu. Niiqe pu' yaw aw pangqawu, "Ta'a," yaw kita, "um hapi inumi paas tuuqaytani. Antsa i' hahay'iwuuti hapi ung yukiq pana. Yangqw hapi i' wukohukyangw ki'yta. Yukiq hapi pam ung panaqw, um hapi son pu' qa tuusungwtini. Um sonqa mokni. Noq puma hapi uumi hepyaniqe oovi ung peqw panaya," yaw kita. "Pu' qaavo hapi um piw

In revealing this to the girl, Old Spider Woman laid four of the softest turkey feathers on the floor. They were meant for the girl to sleep on. Then Old Spider Woman said, "Now, bed down here." The girl lay down and was covered with four more of the same feathers, which were sewn together. "There," Old Spider Woman muttered, "I'm sure you'll live to see the morning."

Then it was time for the girl to sleep. She had become snug and warm and was dozing off when the wind came up. It blew with such tremendous force that the air turned freezing cold. But because of the turkey feathers, which provided both bedding and covers for the girl, she was comfortably warm.

Early the next morning Old Spider Woman urged her protégée, "Wake up! It's already daylight. They're sure to come and check on you in a minute," she warned her. "They tried your strength, believing you'd probably freeze to death by being in here. Fortunately nothing happened to you. But they're bound to test your courage again."

naat ngumantani. Ung hapi suyan peqw panayaniqw, nu' oovi paniqw it piw yannuma."

Yaw pam put maanat aw kitaaqe pu' yaw pam put koyongvöhöt naalöqmuy pas susuphingput engem tutskwava oya. Put yaw pam put maanat aapatoyna. Pantit pu' yaw aw pangqawu, "Ta'a, um yang wa'ökni," yaw aw kita. Pu' yaw pam ang wa'ökqw, pu' yaw pam piw put naalöqmuy namitskiwyungqat usiitoyna. "Yantani," yaw kita. "Pay um suupan son hin qa talöngnani," yaw pam kookyangwso'wuuti put aw kita.

Pu' yaw pam antsa puwniqe wa'ö. Niiqe pay yaw pam antsa kwangwamukiitiqe yaw puupuwvaqw yaw huukyangw pitu. Pu' hapi yaw a'ni hukvakyangw pu' yaw iyoho'ti. Niikyangw pay yaw pam maana put koyongvöhöt aapa'ykyangw pu' piw ustaqe pay yaw kwangwamukiwta.

Qavongvaqw pay yaw pam so'wuuti iits talavay put aw pangqawu, "Maanaa, qatuptu'uya," yaw aw kita. "Pay taalawva," yaw kita. "Pay son hiisavoniqw angqaqw uumi qa pootawisni," yaw kita. "Yan hapi uumi hepya. Um hapi pay sonqa tusungwmokniqat puma wuuwankyaakyangw peqw ung panaya. Noq pay pi um tsangaw qa hinti," yaw pam kookyangwso'wuuti put aw kita. "Niikyangw pay naat son piw qa heeviwni," yaw kita.

No sooner had the girl risen than Hahay'iwuuti came rushing in. She could scarcely believe her eyes when she discovered that the girl was still alive. She was at a loss what to make of it. She merely managed to blurt out, "Are you up?" and then she disappeared into the west room. She returned with something unrecognizable on a shallow tray and dumped what turned out to be icicles into the grinding bin. "There," she said to the girl, "this is what you'll grind today."

"All right. But these icicles are so cold. How can I possibly grind them?"

"You'll find a way. They aren't very hard," Hahay'iwuuti retorted and left.

No sooner had she disappeared than Old Spider Woman turned to the young girl. "Here, lay one of these turkey feathers on your mano and put one in the palm of each hand. Then you won't get chilled." The girl did as told and once again set to grinding. Sure enough, she did not get cold. Her hands did not freeze so she was able to crush icicles all day.

By the time Hahay'iwuuti returned evening was coming on. She inquired, "Are you done with your grinding?"

Noq pu' yaw pam naat pu' qatuptuqw pay yaw hahay'iwuuti angqaqw suukuyva. Nit pas yaw pam qa yan unangwti pam naat put maanat tayta-qat tuwaaqe. Pas yaw pam hin kur hintini. Pay yaw pam panis put aw pangqawu, "Ya um taata-yi?" yaw aw kitat pu' yaw pam teevengewat paki-maqe, pu' yaw pangqaqw piw hiita inkyangw pu' yaw matamiq put siwukna. Pam yaw paasat kur lepena. "Ta'a," yaw pam put aw kita, "it um pu' ngumantani."

"Kur antsa'a," yaw pam kita. "Is iyo! Noq pi nu' kur hin ngumantani," yaw pam maana kita.

"Pay um sonqa ngumani. Pay as pam qa huru," yaw pam hahay'iwuuti put aw kitat pu' yaw pay yamakma.

Pu' yaw pam yamakmaqw, pu' yaw pam koo-kyangwso'wuuti put maanat aw pangqawu, "Ta'a," yaw kita, "pay um uumataakiy ang it sukw ko-yongvöhöt puhiknani. Nit pu' um sukw nan'ivoq uumapqölmiq panani," yaw kita. "Pante' pu' um pay son tuusungwtini," kita yaw pam kookyangw-so'wuutiniqw, pu' yaw pam maana oovi pantit pu' yaw piw ngumantiva. Niiqe pay yaw pam antsa qa hin tuusungwti. Pay yaw put maa'at qa hin tuu-sungwtiqw pay yaw pam oovi teevep pep put lepenat ngumanlawu.

Noq pu' yaw pam hahay'iwuuti piw hisatniqw angqaqw paki pay yaw piw tapkiwmaqw. Niiqe pu' yaw aw pangqawu, "Ya um pay piingya?" yaw aw kita.

"Yes," the girl answered. "Tell me, what am I to do with the water?"

"Just a moment," Hahay'iwuuti replied. Once more she disappeared somewhere, only to return with yet more vessels. Into these she ladled the water from the metate, which was brimful of the liquid. So slowly did the water level go down that she topped off vessel after vessel. After filling a great many bowls she praised the girl, "Thank you so much. You have labored very hard for us."

This is how things went for the girl that day. In spite of the misery she suffered, the girl managed to pull through. Still, if Old Spider Woman had not come to her rescue, she would have frozen to death on the very first day.

Having survived so far, the girl was elated. Yet her ordeal was not yet over. Once again Old Spider Woman turned to her grandchild and said, "By completing your task the people here will be displeased. They hoped you would freeze to death. That's why they brought you in here, but you beat them at their own game. I will certainly not abandon you yet, for next comes the real test. Here, tuck this under your dress." With that Old Spider Woman slid another soft turkey feather under her dress at the back. Then she added, "Now, let me give you some more advice. I've protected you in this way to prevent you from freezing. But under no circumstances stop grinding. Even if you tire in your work, do not halt, because once you do stop

"Owi," yaw kita. "Noq nu' haqami it hintsanni?" yaw pam maana put aw kita.

"Pay haaki," yaw pam hahay'iwuuti kita. Paasat pu' yaw pam piw haqamiwat pakiiqe pu' yaw pangqaqw kuysivut kima. Kivaaqe pu' yaw pam put ang kuukuylawu. Put matat angqw yaw pam kuuyi opom'iwta. Pu' yaw put aqw kuukuyqw pas yaw pam qa iits sulawti. Qa iits sulaw-tiqw, pam yaw pi'ep put hiitawat kuysivut aqw kuyqw, oopokq, pu' yaw pam piw sukw aqwningwu. Pas yaw pam hiisa'haqam put kuysivut ang opomnat pu' yaw pangqawu, "Is askwali. Yantani," yaw kita. "Pay um itamungem hin'ur tumalta."

Yanhaqam yaw pam yuku. Yanhaqam yaw pam maana tuwat pephaqam as okiwhintsak-kyangw pay yaw pam hin ang ayo' yama. Noq pay pi yaw pam kookyangwso'wuuti as put qa aw unangwtapqw, pay yaw pam son as naat suus talöngnat pay tusungwmokni.

Niiqe pam yaw as oovi put ang ayo' kuyvaqe yaw okiw tsuyakqw, pay yaw naat kur son piw pantani. Paasat pu' yaw pam kookyangwso'wuuti piw put mööyiy aw pangqawu, "Pu' hapi um it ang ayo' kuyvaqw, ima hapi ki'yyungqam son tsuytini. Puma hapi pay ung pas tusungwninayaniqe oovi ung peqw panayaqw um hapi pumuy pö'ani. Noq nu' hapi pay son naat ung tatamtani. Pu' hapi pas uumi hepyani," yaw pam put maanat aw kita. "Noq um oovi it piw yang panani," yaw pam put aw kitaaqe pu' yaw pam put maanat hotpa piw

43

you'll get so chilled that you'll never warm up again. This time while you grind they're going to open up the entrance of the chamber to the north wind. There will be a blizzard and the snow will clog up your eyes, but you must grind on, regardless. I'm sure if we stick together we'll successfully get through this ordeal."

On the last day Hahay'iwuuti went into the room to the east. Again she emerged with something, hailstones of enormous size. These the girl now had to grind. Before long the blanket closing off the north-facing doorway began fluttering, and all of a sudden freezing cold rushed into the chamber accompanied by a gale-force wind. Next the entrance on the west side opened, followed by those on the south and the east sides. The door coverings on all sides were blown away and through each entranceway the ice-cold wind whisked into the room. With it came a blizzard. Everything inside the grinding chamber was tossed about by the wind, whose whistling and howling was deafening. The girl, all the same, forced herself to grind on. Soon the blowing snow covered her eyes, quite blinding her.

sukw koyongvöhöt pana. Nit pu' yaw aw pangqawu, "Ta'a, naat hapi nu' uumi piw tutaptani. Um
hapi qa tuusungwtiniqw oovi nu' ung yan
yuwsina," yaw aw kita. "Niikyangw um hapi qa
qe'tini. Naamahin um maangu'ykyangw um hapi
qa qe'tini; taq um hisatniqw qe'te', um hapi
tuusungwte', um pay hapi son ahoy mukipkini,"
yaw pam put aw yan tutapta. "Niikyangw pu' hapi
ung naat ngumantaqw, puma hapi uumi it kwingyawuy hötayani. Pu' hapi paasat sonqa nuva-
hukvakyangw pu' angk nuvatini. Pam hapi son
uuposiy qa uutani. Pay um oovi nawus uvikyangw
ngumantani. Pay itam suupan naamanen son ang
piw hin ayo' qa yamakni," yaw pam kookyangwso'wuuti put aw kita.

Pu' yaw oovi ep nuutungkniiqat ep pu' yaw
pam hoopaqwwat, antsa piw put hiita kimakyangw yamakqw yaw kur pam lemowa. Lemowat yaw wuuwukoq pöplangput pangqw yaw pam
hoopaqw kima. Pu' yaw antsa pam put ngumanta.
Hiisavoniqw pay yaw pangqw kwiningyaqw yaw i'
tavupu pangsoq uutsiwtaqa pay yaw ayo' puya-
yaykuqw pu' yaw iyoho' angqaqw supki. Paasat
pu' yaw pay pas kyee'ew hukva. Pantsakkyangw
pu' yaw taavangqw piw hötsilti, pu' tatkyaqwnii-
kyangw pu' piw hoopaqw. Pas yaw paasat sooso-
kivaqw pam aqw uutsi'yyungqa ayo' huhukhoyqw
pu' yaw antsa pangqw naanan'i'vaqw i' kwingyaw-
niikyangw pu' piw nuvayoyangw nönga. Panti-
kyangw pu' yaw piw nuvahukva. Pu' hapi yaw

45

So freezing was the temperature that her nose started streaming. Time and again she had to wipe away the mucus with the back of her hand, which, in the end, became quite encrusted with the phlegm. Then the girl recalled her grandmother's warning, "I must be sure not to give up. My grandmother, Old Spider Woman, insisted that I not stop," she said to herself and carried on with the grinding chore in spite of her great fatigue. "If I stop now I will certainly freeze to death."

The poor girl quite failed to break up the hailstones. They were tremendously hard, as though there were pebbles inside. Eventually, she grew so tired that she could no longer crush the hailstones. Tears sprung into her eyes, but the moment a tear emerged, it became stuck to her eyelashes so that her eyes were soon completely shut. Not being able to see anything, her grinding almost came to a halt. At this point Old Spider Woman advised the girl, "Put this in your mouth," whereupon she handed her some medicinal herb and added, "Chew this and then spit it into your grinding bin. That way the hailstones will soften up."

pepeq soosoy himu qöviviyku. Pavan yaw pepeq hin töötöqa. Pu' hapi yaw pay naamahin pantsakqw, pay yaw pam nawus ngumanta. Pu' yaw put posvaqe nuva huurtiqe pam yaw put huur pos'uuta.

Pu' hapi yaw paasat pas iyoho'tiqw, pu' yaw put yaqangaqw yaqaspi mumunqw, pam yaw sööwu put angqw höntikyangw ngumantaqw haqaapiy pay yaw put maqtöyat ang pam paas qaro. Pu' yaw pam put soy tutavoyat u'na. "Ura kur pi nu' qa qe'tini. Ura itaaso yan inumi tutapta," yaw pam naami kitaaqe pu' yaw pam oovi piw aapiy ngumantiva. Pay yaw as pam maangu'i. Pu' yaw pam as pay qe'tiniqey unangwtit, pay yaw pam put soy lavayiyatniiqe pu' yaw pay oovi qa qe'ti. "Taq kur pi nu' pante' sonqa tuusungwmokni." Yaw pam it u'naqe pu' yaw pam oovi pay nawus as mangu'iwkyangw yaw naat ngumanta.

Pu' hapi yaw pam put okiw qa piingi'yma, pas yaw pam anaha'a. Noq suupan yaw put lemowat aasonva o'owawya tangawtaqat pas yaw pam pan a'ni huru. Pu' yaw pam panmakyangw pay yaw pam paapu pas maangu'yqe pu' pay qa piingya. Paasat pu' yaw pam pay paapu pakkyangw. Pu' yaw put posvala'at angqw panis yamakkyangw pay yaw puvuwpiyat aw huurtingwuniqw, hiisavoniqw pay yaw pam paasat pas pos'uutsiwkyangw, qa hiita tuwa'ykyangw, pay paapu hihin ngumanta. Noq pu' yaw so'wuuti aw pangqawu, "It um mömtsani," yaw aw kitaaqe pu' yaw pam

The girl did as instructed. Amazingly, the hailstones began to melt. The girl also grew warm again and started grinding once more. Eventually, she had ground everything into water.

The girl obviously had no notion as to why she was compelled to grind all these odd substances and suffer so miserably. All she knew was that thanks to the help of Old Spider Woman she had successfully passed all her trials. The Ka'nas youth and his people had intended that the girl freeze to death. Thus did they test her courage. She, however, had beaten them at their own game. By grinding such things as icicles and hail the girl had actually prepared water for her own people. Every evening in the course of her four days' labor, the liquid produced by her work filled several large water containers. At the end, uncounted vessels had been filled, and the resulting supply of water was tremendous. The kachinas would carry this water to the Hopiland to produce rain for the people. They would have to take several visits to use it all up. So huge was the supply that even in four years it would probably not be depleted. Thus in this test, the girl had really triumphed over the kachinas on behalf of the Hopi.

put hiita ngahut aw tavit pu' aw yaw pangqawu, "Um it mömtsat pu' um put uumatay aqw pavoyani," yaw pam put aw kita. "Pay as kya um pantiqw pay kya as pam qa huruutini," yaw kita.

Pu' yaw pam oovi put mömtsaqe pu' yaw matamiq pavoyaqw, pu' yaw pam antsa pangqw paa'iwma. Pu' yaw pam paasat piw hihin mukipkiqe pu' piw ngumantiva. Panmakyangw pu' yaw pam put soosok piingya.

Noq pam hapi yaw qa hiita nanvotkyangw pep naanap hiita ngumantaqe yaw okiwhintsaki. Niikyangw pay yaw pam put so'wuutit atsviy ayo' yama. Noq pay yaw pam tiyoniqw pu' put sinomat as put tusungwninayaniqe yaw put aw pan hepyaqw, pay yaw pam pumuy pö'a. Pu' yaw pam pep pan naalös teevep puuvut hiita lepenat, lemowat ngumantaqe, pam hapi yaw pay kur put sinomuy engem na'saslawu. Pam hapi yaw oovi pan naalös pas teveplawqe yaw oovi qa suukw wukokuysivut ang oopoknaqw, pu' tapkingwuniqw yaw pam oovi aw nalöstalay aw hiisa'haqam ang opomna. Is tathihi pi yaw pam oovi niitilti. Put hapi yaw puma katsinam pangsoq hopiikimiq kuuyi'ykyaakyangw pu' yaw pumuy amungem yoknayani. Son pi yaw puma oovi suus pangsoq ökini. Hikis kya yaw naalöq yaasangwuy aqwhaqami pam naat son sulawtini. Yanhaqam yaw pam maana pumuy katsinmuy imuy hopiituy amungem pö'a.

The kachinas, of course, had not tested the girl for nothing. After all, she was to marry a superhuman being, a kachina, and for this reason they had put her through many hardships. This is the way they wanted it for the boy kachina. Not until some extraordinary girl had survived the entire ordeal would they accept her. Thus it was not with evil intent that they tested her. At long last they agreed to have the girl as an in-law. Now they would not test her endurance any longer.

When the girl had completed the crushing of the hailstones, Hahay'iwuuti summoned her and said, "Well, thank you for finishing your work. We'll eat supper now, for evening has come. As soon as we've eaten we'll probably be going to bed."

When everyone had supped and was ready to retire, Hahay'iwuuti did not subject the girl to another cold room. Instead, she made her bed in a warm place and bade her sleep there. And no sooner had the girl bedded down than she fell asleep from exhaustion.

The girl was still sleeping soundly when Old Spider Woman woke her. "Wake up, girl," she commanded, "it's already daylight. The kachinas are bound to come and fetch you. Now that you've beaten them at their own game, they must take you back home," she informed the girl.

Niikyangw pay yaw puma katsinam piw qa paysoq yaw put maanat aw hepya. Pam hapi yaw kur pas put hiita katsinat amumtiniqw, paniqw yaw puma oovi put pep okiwhintsatsna. Pan yaw puma put tiyot engem naanawakna. Pas ason yaw hak pavanniiqa put soosok hiita ang ayo' yamakqw, paasat pu' yaw pay puma put hakiy naanakwhani. Pay yaw as puma qa nukpanvewat put aw pan hepya. Niiqe puma yaw oovi nawis'ewtiqw pu' put pay mö'wi'yvayaniqey naanakwha. Paasat pay yaw puma oovi pay paapu put qa piw aw hepyani.

Noq pu' yaw pam maana soosok put lemowat piingyaqw, pu' yaw i' hahay'iwuuti put aw pangqawu, "Ta'a, askwali um yuku. Itam noonovani, taq pay hapi tapki. Ason itam pay panis nöönösat pu' pay sonqa tokni."

Paasat pu' yaw puma oovi nöönösaqe pu' yaw puma pay paasat tokniniqw, pu' yaw pam hahay'iwuuti pay paasat qa haqamiwat iyoho'pumiq put panat, pay yaw pam haqamwat yongive put engem aapatat, pu' yaw put aa'awna yaw pam pu' pay pang puwniqat. Nit pay yaw pam naat pu' wa'ökt pay yaw kur pam mangu'yvuwva.

Noq pu' yaw pam naat oovi pas kwangwavuwqw, pay yaw piw kookyangwso'wuuti put maanat taatayna. "Taatayi'i, maana," yaw aw kita. "Pay taalawva. Pay son ung angqw qa wikwisni. Pay hapi um pu' pumuy pö'aqw, pay puma son pu' ung nawus qa taviwisni," yaw aw kita.

So it was that, on this morning, the maiden was already awake when Hahay'iwuuti made her entrance. When she had risen she turned to Hahay'iwuuti and without a trace of enmity said, "Since you know where my flour is, tell me so that I can cook for you this once before I leave for home. For certainly the time has come."

Hahay'iwuuti told her where her flour was kept and led her to the storage place. Then she left. The room had a fireplace and a piiki stone. After lighting fires both in the fireplace and under the piiki griddle she set to mixing a batch of batter. It was her intention to ready a good amount of batter, but Old Spider Woman, who was still with her, stopped her. "Wait, girl! Even if you make a large amount of batter and cook a lot of food, the many people here will not be able to eat their fill. So for every dish you're planning to fix, just prepare enough batter for four portions, and I'll help you with the rest."

The girl did exactly as instructed. Upon completing the batter she began cooking. Thus she fixed just four portions each of tsukuviki, somiviki, and pövölpiki; of the piiki, too, she baked only four pieces that were folded and four that were rolled. When all the food was done, she again followed the old woman's advice and placed

Noq ep pay yaw pam maana taytaqw yaw pam hahay'iwuuti pep paki. Noq pay yaw pam maana oovi paasat qatuptut pu' yaw put hahay'iwuutit aw pangqawu, pay yaw piw qa hin put aw unangwa'y-kyangw, "Ta'a, haqam kya um ingumniy tuwa'yta. Put um nuy aa'awnaqw, nu' suus yep umungem noovatat pu' antsa ahoyni. Pay pi itam pu' aqw pitsinaya."

Yaw pam put aw kitaqw pu' yaw pam oovi put aa'awna haqam pam ngumni tangawtaqw. Pu' yaw pam hahay'iwuuti oovi pangso put maanat panat pu' yaw pay piw ahoy yamakma. Noq pep pay yaw kur piw paas qöpqö'ykyanqw pu' piw tuma'ytaqw, pu' yaw pam oovi mooti pangsoq qöönat pu' paasat yaw novavavaqwrini. Niiqe pay yaw pam pas aapiyniikyangw as pas wukova-vaqwriniqw, pu' yaw pam kookyangwso'wuuti naat pay put amumniiqe yaw put aw pangqawu, "Haaki, maana! Pay as um naamahin pan wuuyaq paavaqwrikyangw pan wuuhaq noovataqw, ima hapi yep kyaastaqe son put öö'öyani. Noq pay um hiita yukuniqey pay panis um put naalöq aw ap-tsiwtaqat engem paavaqwriqw, pu' pay nu' ason ung pa'angwani."

Yan yaw pam put aw tutaptaqw pu' yaw pam oovi put tutavoyat anti. Noq pu' yaw pam oovi paavaqwriqe yukuuqe pu' yaw noovativa. Niiqe pay yaw pam oovi panis naalöq tsukuvikitnit pu' naalöq somivikitnit pu' naalöq pövölpikit yuku. Pu' yaw it piikit pam piw pay panis naalöq

everything into one pile. Thereupon Old Spider Woman covered it with something and sprayed some sort of medicine on the pile, as a result of which it grew into a huge feast. Every dish was available in abundance now.

Next the girl uncovered the pile, carried all the food into the front room, and spread it over the entire floor. She set the dishes out in long lines, yet the supply of food did not give out. The kachinas residing there marveled at the maiden when they saw what quantities of food she had prepared in such a short time. Then the girl invited them to eat, so everybody sat down and ate. What a delicious meal it was! In this fashion Old Spider Woman helped the girl again. She enabled the girl to feed all the kachinas with her own cooking.

Hahay'iwuuti now beckoned her grandson, whereupon he approached her and the girl. Prior to this she had soaked some yucca roots on the north side of the fire pit, and it was there that she escorted the boy and girl. She bade them kneel down side by side, which they did. Then she washed their hair with the yucca suds and twisted their tresses together. This symbolized that the two had become one. They were truly husband and wife now. Hahay'iwuuti spoke these words to the couple: "All right, as of this moment you really belong

muupiwtaqatnit pu' naalöq nömömvut yaw yuku. Yantiqw pu' yaw pam put kookyangwso'wuutit tutavoyat piwniiqe pu' yaw pam put suuvo haqami tsovala. Pantiqw pu' yaw pam pep put aw hiita akw naakwapnat pu' ngahuy aw pavoyaqw, pay hapi yaw pam pep nuwu wukomo'olti. Pas pi yaw pam pep niitilti.

Paasat pu' yaw pam maana put ayo' höloknat pu' pangqw put oo'oylawkyangw pu' pep iipovewat put tunösvongyalawu. Noq pas pi yaw pam as wupatunösvongyaataqw, pas yaw put noova'at qa hin sulawti. Pu' yaw puma pep ki'yyungqam put aw kyaataayungwa pam hiisavonit pay pan pumuy amungem wukonovataqw. Paasat pu' yaw pam pumuy tunös'a'awnaqw pu' yaw puma oovi pep noonova. Is ali, pas pi yaw puma kwangwanönösa. Yanhaqam yaw pam kookyangwso'wuuti piw put pa'angwa. Yanhaqam yaw pam pumuy pas naap noovay nopna.

Paasat pu' yaw pam hahay'iwuuti put mööyiy wangwayqw pu' yaw pam pumuy amumi. Noq yaw pep qöpqöt kwiningqöyve pam hahay'iwuuti pay yaw kur paas moovit qeeni'ytaqe pu' yaw pam oovi pangso pumuy wiiki. Nit pu' yaw pam pumuy amumi pangqawu yaw puma naqlap pangsoq möyiqtuptuniqatniqw pu' yaw puma oovi panti. Paasat pu' yaw pam pumuy naama asna. Pu' yaw pam pumuy asnat pu' yaw pam pumuy höömiyamuy murukna. Pantiqw pu' yaw puma suukyatiniqat oovi pam panti. Paasat pu' yaw puma pas

to each other. So step outside and pray toward the direction where the sun rises. Pray for a good life. Beseech the sun that both of you may live without sickness and that you may grow old together." Obediently the couple made their exit and uttered the prayers.

Next, Hahay'iwuuti turned to making up the girl as a bride. She asked the girl to sit down and fixed her hair in the style proper for a married woman. Then she went into a back room and emerged carrying a beautifully spun, brand new woman's dress. She dressed the girl in it and, surprisingly enough, it fit exactly. Then she girded a belt about the girl's waist and helped her into her wedding boots. They were huge and quite heavy, being fashioned from a large buckskin. The leather, a beautiful white, had been tanned so carefully that it was very soft to the touch. The boots, too, were exactly her size and extremely comfortable.

Following this, Hahay'iwuuti daubed the girl's face with white cornmeal. Next, she draped the large wedding cape over her shoulders. Someone had also spun a cape smaller in size than the one she had on, together with a large wedding sash.

naamati. Paasat pu' yaw pam pumuy amumi pangqawu, "Ta'a, pu' hapi uma pas naahimu'yva. Uma oovi tuwat yuk iipo yamakye' pu' uma ep aqw talpumiq naawaknani, nukwangwqatsit oovi. Qa hiita akw uma naami hinte', uma naama wuyootiniqey put uma oovi naawaknani," yan yaw pam pumuy amumi tutaptaqw, paasat pu' yaw puma oovi yamakmaqe pu' yaw antsa yanhaqam pep pangsoq naawakna.

Paasat pu' yaw pam put mö'öngyuwsinaniqe pu' yaw oovi haqam put qatuptsina. Noq pu' yaw pam pep qatuwtaqw paasat pu' yaw pam put aw torikuyna. Pu' yaw pam put mö'wi'ytaqa put yuwsinaniqe pu' yaw haqamiwat aapamiq pakiiqe pu' pangqw yaw pas nukngwat kanelkwasat horokna, pas yaw naat suupuhut. Pu' yaw pam put ang panana. Noq piw yaw pam put su'aasay'o. Pantit pu' yaw pam put kweewat piw kwewtoynat paasat pu' yaw totsvakna. Pas yaw pam put wukomö'öngtotsit ang pananaqw, pas yaw pam oovi pay hihin a'ni putu. Pas pi yaw pam wuyaqsowi'yngwat angqw yukiwta. Niikyangw pas pi yaw piw qöötsaniikyangw pu' piw yaw kur pas paas pöhiwniwtaqe yaw oovi pavan pas suphingpu. Pu' yaw pam tootsi piw put su'aasay; pas yaw kwangwahinta.

Pantit pu' yaw pam put ngumanqömatoyna. Paasat pu' yaw pam put it wuuyaqatwat oovat usiitoyna. Pu' yaw haqawa kur tsaaqatwat oovatnit pu' it wukokwewat engem yukuqw, put yaw

Hahay'iwuuti folded both these garments neatly and rolled them up inside a reed mat. In this way the girl received a complete bridal outfit. Now that she was fully garbed, all the kachinas became aware of how beautiful an in-law they had gained.

Hahay'iwuuti next stepped outside and made a proclamation: "My people living here, gather here so that we may all go and return our in-law to her home." This was the announcement she made.

It did not take long for the kachinas to begin making their entrance. With them they brought an assortment of items: watermelons, muskmelons, peaches, fresh corn, squash, as well as a variety of other foods the Hopi use for sustenance. The new in-law thanked the kachinas for everything they had brought her and in turn invited them to eat. So they too ate and took great delight in the meal. The Hehey'a, who were feasting among them, again and again exclaimed, "It tastes terrible! How tough everything is!" The girl could not help but smile inwardly, for she knew of course that it was the habit of these kachinas to express everything by its opposite. The two Sikyaqöqlö did not eat at all, so busily were they engaged in conversation. The Suyang'ephoya typically munched from their left hand and kept jostling their neighbors just as they were about to put food into their mouths. Thus, in-

pu' pam oovi put paas mupipiykinat pu' piw it songooqekit akw paas mokyaata. Yan pay yaw pam oovi soosok hiita mö'öngyuwsit makiwa. Noq yan yaw pam put yuwsinaqw, pas pi yaw puma kur put hakiy lomamö'wi'yvaya.

Pantit pu' yaw pam hahay'i paasat iipoqhaqami yamakqe pu' yaw pam pepeq tsa'lawu. "Pangqe' kya uma inatkom yeese. Uma pew tsovaltiqw, itam soosoyamyakyangw it itaamö'wiy ahoy taviwisni." Yan yaw pam epeq tsa'lawu.

Hiisavoniqw pay yaw angqaqw hakim sinom yungta. Niikyangw pu' yaw puma piw hiihiita oo'oyaya, kawayvatngat, meloonit, sipalat, samit, patngat. Pas yaw puma soosok hiita hopit nöösiwqayat kivaya. Noq pu' yaw pam puhumö'wi'am pep pumuy amumi haalaylawu puma put hiihiita engem kivantaqw. Pu' yaw pam pumuywatuy piw tunös'awinta. Noq pu' yaw puma oovi tuwat nöönösaqe yaw tuwat kwangwanönösa. Noq naat yaw pumuy noonovaqw yaw ima hehey'am nuutum noonovaqe yaw pangqawkyaakyangwya, "Pas qa kwangwa! A'ni huru!" yaw kitikyaakyangwyaqw yaw pam maana amumi na'uytaya'iwta. Pay pi yaw pam suyan navoti'yta puma ahoytuqayyungqw. Pu' yaw ima sikyaqöqlöt tuwat qa tuumoytat tuwat yaw puma naami lavasoq'iwta. Noq pu' yaw ima suyang'ephooyam tuwat suyngaqw noonovaqe, yaw hiitawat aqlangaqw qatuuqat okiw naat pu' mo'ami nöösiwqat yanmaqat tongoknaqw, pay yaw pamwa okiw qa

stead of placing food into their mouths they smeared their chins, cheeks, or other part of their faces with it. The many Kooyemsi in turn only helped themselves to pövölpiki. This dish was round in shape, exactly like the openings of their mouths. They would hold one of the corn balls up to their mouths to suck on it, whereupon it would quickly disappear into their mouths. The girl thought all of this very amusing.

As the guests became satiated, they got up and moved away from the food placed before them. The girl repeatedly urged them not to be modest and to put aside whatever they cared to save for later. So everyone helped himself to two or three dishes and then took his leave. The Kooyemsi really outdid everyone else in this regard. They had arrived with bags full of gifts slung over their shoulders. Since they had bestowed all their gifts on their new in-law, their sacks were now empty. So when they could eat no more, they began stuffing their bags with all sorts of food. They were the only guests to get a large share of the girl's cooking. This is what took place at the wedding feast.

When the feast was over, Hahay'iwuuti announced, "Now, my people, we'll return our in-law to Musangnuvi. Let no one hesitate. I want all of you to accompany me, even down to the last child."

mo'amiq nöösiwqat panat, tuwat soq öyiy sen taywami sen yaqay naap haqami akw tsöö-qöknangwu. Noq pu' yaw ima kookoyemsim tuwat pay pas pövölpikitsa noonova. Pam yaw pumuy mo'ahötsiyamuy su'an pongokpuniqw himuwa yaw oovi put sukw mo'ay aw iite', pu' yaw put kwangwasölökqw pay yaw pam mo'amiq supkingwu. Niiqe pas pi yaw puma put pep no'i'yyungwa.

Pu' yaw puma ööyiwwiskyangw tunösvongyat angqw ayo' watkitaqw, pu' yaw pam pumuy amumi pangawlawqe qa pevewma, yaw angqw paatsonlalwaniqat. Noq pu' yaw himuwa oovi angqw paatsontanik, pay lööqhaqam, paykomuy-haqam hiita angqw yawkyangw ayo' waayangwu. Noq pu' yaw ima kookoyemsim tuwat pas yuu-kye'lalwa. Puma pi tukpuy angqw na'mangwuy mooki'ykyaakyangw put torikiwkyaakyangw öki-kyangw pu' put mö'wiy aw soosok o'yaqe pay yaw qa hiita pangqw tanga'yyungwa. Niiqe pu' yaw puma ööyiwwiskyangw pu' yaw hiihiita put noovayat tukpuy ang opomintota. Nanalt yaw puma oovi put noovayat kyaahaktoti. Yanhaqam yaw puma pep hintoti.

Pantotiqw pu' yaw pam hahay'iwuuti pumuy amumi pangqawu, "Ta'a, isinomu," yaw kita, "itam hapi itaamö'wiy kiiyat aw ahoy taviwisniniqw oovi uma soosoyam inumumyani," yaw kita. "Qa hak nanahinkinani. Tsaatsakwmuy aqwhaqami itam it itaamö'wiy ahoy taviwisni," yaw kita hahay'iwuuti.

Everyone consented, "Let it be so. What a beautiful in-law we have!" they all cried.

"So true. Let's get going straight away. We'll be leaving from the plaza," Hahay'iwuuti informed them.

At this moment the girl's husband entered and inquired, "Is everyone ready?"

"Yes, we're ready," came the answer.

"Very well. The sun is about to rise. Let's all meet in the dance court in the meantime."

When all the Ka'nas kachinas were gathered there, the young man came out with his new wife and said to her, "All right, let's climb aboard. Then I want you to close your eyes again tightly. And you're not to open them until I tell you to."

This time on their way home, the two were going to travel by flying shield. Together they climbed onto the shield and the girl firmly shut her eyes. As the shield lifted off, the kachinas all gave out a boisterous yell. The spectacle was incredible; every sort of kachina conceivable was present. All of a sudden as the couple flew along, flashes of lightning were visible in the air and the rumble of thunder could be heard. When the shield rose higher, drizzle began to fall. The kachinas were now accompanying them. They actually followed the pair in the form of clouds.

Noq pu' yaw puma pangqaqwa, "Kur antsa'ay. Pas kur itam hakiy lomamö'wi'yvayay," yaw kitota.

"Pas hapi antsa'a," yaw kita. "Noq itam payyani. Itam yangqw pay sonqa kiisonngaqw nankwusani," yaw pam pumuy amumi kita.

Noq paasat yaw kur pam tiyo put maanat wikqa ep paki. "Ya uma pay yuki'yyungway?" yaw pam kita.

"Owi, itam pay yukuyay," yaw hak kita.

"Kur antsa'ay," yaw kita. "Taawa hapi pas pay angqw kuyvaniy. Oovi itam pay yuk kiisonmi angwu tsovaltiniy," yaw pam tiyo kita.

Pu' yaw puma pangso tsovaltiqw pu' yaw pam tiyo put nöömay wikkyangw yamakqe pu' yaw aw pangqawu, "Ta'ay, itam yuk wupni," yaw kita. "Itam it aqw wupqw, um hapi pay haak piw uviitiniy," yaw aw kita. "Ason nu' uumi pangqawqw pu' um piw uuvosiy puruknaniy," yaw kita.

Noq paasat kur yaw puma it paatuwvotat akw ahoyni. Paasat pu' yaw puma oovi naama put aw wuuvi. Yaw aw wupqw pu' yaw pam maana piw uviiti. Pu' yaw pam tuwat oomi höröltiqw yaw ima katsinam sa'a'ayku. Uti, pas pi yaw soosoy hinyungqam katsinamya. Pantiqw yaw puma naat oovi panmaqw, pay yaw susmataq talwiptakyangw pu' yaw piw a'ni umta. Pu' yaw puma oovetiqw pay yaw paasat suvuvuyku. Pangqw pu' yaw puma katsinam pumuy amumumyakyangw paasat yaw kur puma imuy oo'omawtuy akw pumuy amungkya.

Thus the entire entourage traveled along until it neared Musangnuvi. Everyone landed on the west side of the village. The youth and his new wife, who had not yet opened her eyes, were the first to make their descent, followed by the kachinas. At this point the husband turned to his young wife and said, "Come on, open your eyes." Doing so, she discovered that they had landed at Kyeletip-kya, a place west of Toriva. A host of kachinas had accompanied them, bearing a variety of gifts. The youth prompted his wife, "All right, climb down. We've arrived."

Pangqw pu' yaw puma panwiskyaakyangw pu' yaw puma yuk musangnumi hayingwnaya. Niiqe pay yaw puma oovi pep taavangqöyvehaqam yesva. Noq yaw i' tiyo put puhunömay amum mooti pephaqam qatuptuqw, pu' yaw ima katsi-nam pumuy amungk pep yesva, pay naat yaw pam maana poosiy qa puruknaqw. Noq pu' yaw pam koongya'at put wutiwyat aw pangqawu, "Ta'ay, uuposiy purukna'ay," yaw kita. Noq pu' yaw pam poosiy puruknaqw pay yaw kur puma yep torivat aatavang kyeletipkyave yesva. Noq pay yaw paasat ima katsinam piw pep pumuy amumumya, puuvut hiita na'mangwuy enang yankyaakyangw. Noq pu' yaw pam tiyo nöömay aw pangqawu, "Ta'ay, haawi'i. Pay itam ökiy," yaw kita.

His wife did as bidden, whereupon her husband proclaimed, "From here we'll all go on foot."

Hahay'iwuuti, who was at the head of the procession, laid out the cornmeal path for all of them. "All right, daughter, let's go." With this cue the entourage started out for the village.

As the young girl looked over her shoulder, she saw a host of kachinas following in a nearly endless line, among them the many Kooyemsi who hauled large quantities of watermelon, fresh corn, and roasted corn on their backs. The instant the procession set in motion, something happened to the girl's foot so that she could not step on it. Immediately, she remembered her medicine, which she chewed. After spraying it on her foot, it became well again and the procession continued on in the direction of Musangnuvi.

Since the Ka'nas youth had told the girl's parents of their daughter's arrival on this day, they were, of course, waiting for her. Customarily, a bride is returned to her residence in the morning. Therefore the parents had headed to the edge of the mesa at this time to look out. Looking down from the rim of the mesa, they saw an incredible number of people coming across the plain. To their great amazement all were kachinas, singing and crying out their calls in a pandemonium.

Pu' yaw pam pangqw hawqw pu' yaw pam koongya'at pangqawu, "Ta'ay, itam yaapiy pay naapyaniy," yaw kita.

Noq pu' yaw pam hahay'iwuuti mooti'ymaqe yaw oovi pep pumuy pöötapna. "Ta'a, mö'wi, itamyani," yaw kitaqw pu' yaw puma oovi kiimiwat nankwusa.

Noq yaw pam maana ahoy yorikqw, pas pi yaw is tathihi katsinam. Qa an'ewakw yaw pumuy amungk katsinam leetsiwta. Pu' yaw ima kookoyemsim kawayvatngat, samit, tuupevut wuko-'ikwiwyungwa. Noq pu' yaw pumuy nankwusaniqw pay yaw put maanat kuk'at hintiqw pam yaw kur hin akw wuukukni. Pam yaw kur hin kwangwawaymani. Pu' yaw pam ngahuy u'naqe pu' yaw pam oovi put angqw kyatkut, pu' put mömtsat, pu' kukuy aw pavoyaqw, pay yaw pam piw antsa kwangwahintiqw, paapiy pu' yaw puma musangnumiya.

Noq pay pi yaw pam maana pu'haqam pituniqat yaw pam tiyo pumuy amumi tutaptaqw, pu' yaw oovi put maanat na'atniqw yu'at yaw put nuutayta. Pay pi yaw maanat lööqökqat taviwisqam paasatniqw talavay wikvayangwuniqw pay yaw puma oovi paasat tumpoq kuyvato. Pu' yaw puma pangsoq pituuqe yaw aqw yorikqw, pay yaw pangqw atkyangaqw hiitu qa an'ewakw hinwisa. Niikyangw piw yaw katsinamya. Puma yaw pangqw taatawtiwiskyangw pu' töötöqtiwisa. Pavan yaw hin töötöqa.

The girl's father walked down to the foot of the mesa to greet the kachinas. Encountering them, he laid down a path of cornmeal toward the village for them and then led them into the plaza. The girl's mother approached her child and took her home. At this point the young Ka'nas man directed his relatives, "Now, my people, I want you to spread out the gifts of food you brought along."

Apparently, some of the guests had come with stewed meat, which was actually stewed venison. In addition to the meat, a variety of other foodstuffs, such as watermelons, fresh corn, and peaches, decked the plaza ground. The young Ka'nas man next turned to his father-in-law. "Would you make a public announcement?" he said. "Tell your people to come forth and join us in the feast we have provided."

So the father cried out the following announcement: "People, I take it you are fully awake by now. We have our daughter back. Her in-laws have come with a great many dishes. Come down here, therefore, and eat."

When all the food was set out, the villagers began pouring into the plaza. There they ate to their hearts' content and truly had a great feast. As it turned out, the kachinas had brought along such

Noq pu' yaw put maanat na'at aqw tupoq pumuy amuupewtoqe, pepeq pu' yaw pam pumuy amumi pituuqe pu' yaw pam tuwat pumuy amungem kiimi pöötapna. Pangqw pu' yaw pam pumuy tsamqe pu' yaw pam pumuy kiisonmi tangata. Pu' yaw pam mö'wi'iwtaqat yu'at angqw tiy awniiqe pu' yaw paasat put kiy aw wiiki. Noq paasat pu' yaw pam tiyo pangqawu, "Ta'ay, isinomuy, uma yep umuuna'mangwuy soosok hiita tunösvongyaatotaniy."

Noq piw yaw kur puma peetu amumumyaqam nöqkwivit enang oyi'yvaya. Put sowi'ingwnöq- kwivitnit pu' aapiy pay hiihiita kawayvatngat, samit, sipalat yaw puma pep tunösvongyaatota. Paasat pu' yaw pam tiyo put maanat nayat aw pangqawu, "Ta'a, um tsa'lawniy," yaw kita. "Um tsa'lawqw, ima yep sinom angqw pew haane', pu' yep tuwat itamutsviy nöönösaniy," yaw pam tiyo put maanat nayat yan ayata.

Noq pu' yaw pam oovi tsa'lawqe yaw yan tsa'lawu: "Pangqe' kya uma sinom talahoyyay," yaw kita. "Itam yep itaamanay ahoy pitsinayaqw, yep put mö'wi'yyungqam hiihiita kivayay. Noq oovi uma pew haane' yep nöönösaniy," yanhaqam yaw pam tsa'lawu.

Pu' yaw puma oovi pep tunösvongyaatotaqw pu' yaw antsa sinom aw naakwusta. Pu' yaw puma oovi pep paas öö'öyakyangw antsa yaw naanasna. Noq pas hapi yaw puma kur hiita wukokivayaqw, pas yaw puma sinom qa hin soosok hiita soswa.

enormous quantities of food that the people could not consume it all. So the Ka'nas youth urged them, "Don't be bashful, but take whatever pleases you. There's a great deal left yet. Help yourselves to whatever you want and take it home with you. There's still more for my new wife and her relatives." Thus encouraged, the inhabitants of the village lost their inhibitions and, indeed, began to stock up with various dishes for later.

Thereupon the youth announced to the people, "Well then, before they go home, they'd like to entertain you." And turning to his relatives, he said, "Come on, I want you to provide some dance entertainment for these people and then you can return home. I, of course, will remain here," he asserted.

Next, he directed the girl's father, "Now then, sprinkle the dancers with cornmeal. The Kooyemsi right in the middle is their leader and starts the songs for them."

Upon receiving these instructions the girl's father strode along the line of kachinas, blessing each of them with the sacred cornmeal. As he approached the Kooyemsi at the center of the line, he spoke these words to him: "Now, let it start! Dance joyfully and vigorously! I'm glad so many of you could come." With that the Kooyemsi shook his rattle and the dance commenced.

Noq pu' yaw pam tiyo pumuy amumi pangqawu, "Uma qa nanahinkinayat tatam angqw paatsonlalwaniy. Naat himu ep niitiwtay. Hak hiita aw kwangwa'ytuswe' put angqw paatsontamantaniy. Pay naat itam piw it ipuhunömaynit pu' put sinomuyatuy amungem peehut hiita kivayay," yaw pam pumuy amumi kitaqw, paasat pu' yaw puma sinom antsa pay qa nanahinkinayat yaw hiihiita paatsonlalwa.

Noq pu' yaw pam tiyo sinmuy amumi pangqawu, "Ta'ay," yaw kita, "ason ima umuy mooti tayawnayat pu' yangqw ahoy ninmaniy." Pu' yaw pam pumuy katsinmuy amumi pangqawu, "Ta'ay, uma yep imuy hiisavo tiitaptotat pu' ason ahoy ninmaniy," yaw kita. "Nu' pi pay sonqa yep huruutiniy," yaw pam kita.

Pu' yaw pam put maanat nayat aw pangqawu, "Ta'ay, um ang homnaniy. Noq pam pepeq sunasaveqniiqa kooyemsi pam hapi pumuy mongwi-'amuy. Pam pumuy amungem kukuynay," yaw pam put aw kita.

Yan yaw pam put aw tutaptaqw, pu' yaw pam pumuy oovi ang homni'ymakyangw pu' yaw pam pangsoq sunasamiq put kooyemsit aqw pituuqe pu' yaw aw pangqawu, "Ta'ay, pay namuy. Pay uma haalaykyaakyangw tiivaniy, qa tsako'nangwa'y-kyaakyangoy. Tsangaw kur uma angqaqw kyaysiway," yaw pam pumuy amumi kitaqw pu' yaw pam kooyemsi antsa ayaknaqw pu' yaw puma paasat tiivantiva.

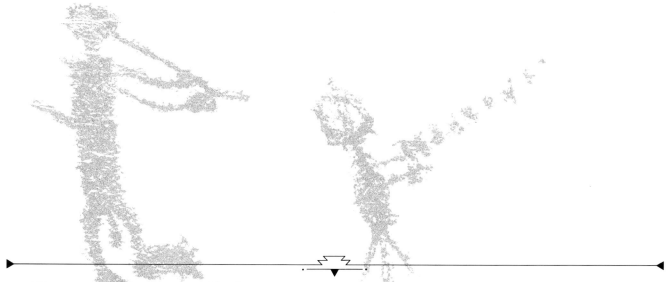

The man continued to sprinkle the remaining dancers and then stood among them to call out his directions. The rest of the people, too, approached the kachinas to bless them with cornmeal, for they were delighted to have them and felt indebted to them for the food.

The whole mixed group of kachinas was dancing now, and people took great pleasure in witnessing the performance. How enjoyable the songs were! Later, when the kachinas were ready to leave, the man in charge of them presented each with a prayer feather. Then, just as before, he drew out a path of cornmeal on the ground, which they followed as they descended from the mesa. Already during the dance it had started to drizzle. It rained a good deal that day. Not once did the rains cease, and it was still pouring when the kachinas made their way down to the plain to depart for home.

Noq pu' yaw pam taaqa aapiy pumuy soosokmuy homnat pu' yaw pam pumuy pep amumi tsaatsa'lawu. Noq pu' yaw mimawat sinom piw haalaytoti pumuy ökinayakyangw pu' piw amutsviy a'ni nöönösaqe. Pu' yaw puma tuwat pumuy amumi naakwustakyangw pu' yaw pumuy piw hoohomnaya.

Pu' yaw puma katsinam pep tiiva; yaw soyohimkatsinamya. Pu' yaw puma sinom pep kwangwatitimayya. Is ali, yaw kwangwatatatawi'yyungwa. Hisatniqw pu' yaw puma angqw ninmaniqw, pu' yaw pam taaqa paas pumuy piw nakwakwusit huyta. Nit pu' yaw pam pumuy pangqw amungem piw pöötapqw pu' yaw puma put anawit haani. Noq naat yaw puma pep tiivaqw pay yaw paasat suvuvuyku. Pas pi yaw ep a'ni yokva. Noq pay yaw pas ep qa suusa yoyngyalqw, pay yaw puma oovi pantaqat ang hant pu' yaw ninma.

The girl's parents and the villagers now built a house for the newlyweds at a promontory on the west side of Musangnuvi. The people, grateful to the Ka'nas youth for having provided so much to eat, helped in the building. As a result, the project was completed in no time. Here the newlyweds were to make their home.

Year after year the Ka'nas youth, while living at Musangnuvi, grew an abundance of plants and consequently raised large amounts of crops. And every year without fail he freely shared his plentiful crops with the people, especially the husbandless women who had children. Thus, each and every one thrived because of him.

This generosity, however, was not looked upon favorably by all the villagers. There were some troublemakers who did not like the youth's success. These people were vulgarly referred to as "the turds." As a group they were evilminded and shared the same kiva. They detested the young man and plotted among themselves to steal his wife. To implement their plan the turds formally announced their intention of putting on a kachina dance. The young Ka'nas man, who still had nothing against them, decided to join them. While he was rehearsing for the dance with the others, the sorcerers devised a scheme. One of them, of the same stature as the Ka'nas kachina, would dress to resemble the latter and, so disguised, approach his wife. The turds were convinced that the young

Noq pu' yaw put maanat yumatniqw pu' ima sinom pumuy puhunawuutimuy musangnuviy taavangqöyveq tuyqamiq amungem kiitota. Pay yaw ima sinom put tiyot atsviy a'ni nöönösaqe pay yaw haalaytotiqe oovi. Niiqe pay yaw puma it tuwa'ykyaakyangw yaw pumuy amumi a'ni unangwtatve puma kiilawqw. Niiqe pas pi yaw puma oovi pumuy amungem it kiihut sungwnuptsinaya. Pepeq yaw oovi puma puhunawuutim qatuptu.

Noq pu' yaw pam tiyo pep qatukyangw pas yaw pam sutsep a'ni uuyi'ytangwu. A'ni yaw pam hiita aniwnangwu. Pu' yaw pam aasakis pan a'ni hiita aniwne' pu' yaw pam pay nanap'unangway pep sinmuy angqw put natwaniy maqangwu, pu' yaw tis oovi imuy nalqatmomoymuy timu'yyungqamuy. Niiqe pay yaw puma oovi soosoyam put atsviy a'ni yeese.

Noq pay yaw kur peetu piw put ep qa naaniya. Noq puma yaw kur ima hiitu kwitavitya. Puma yaw piw pay pas nuunukpant. Pu' yaw puma piw pay haqam suup kiva'yyungwa. Pu' yaw puma put tiyot aw qa kwangwataayungqe yaw pangqaqwa yaw puma as hin put tiyot nömanawkiyani. Noq pu' yaw puma kwitavit oovi imuy hiituy katsinmuy tiingapyaqw, pu' pay pi yaw pam tiyo naat pumuy amumi qa hin navoti'ytaqe yaw oovi nuutumni. Noq pu' yaw pam nuutum tuwanlawqw, pu' yaw ima popwaqt kya pi pan naawinya. Yaw haqawa tiyo pumuy amungaqw put ka'naskatsinat su'aasava, su'aasay yaw put an yuwse', pu' yaw

woman would willingly succumb to him. This was the scheme they hatched. Thus, they proceeded to fashion a mask, and then chose an impersonator who looked like the Ka'nas kachina.

The real Ka'nas youth now informed his wife, "I'll be going to my folks for a little while. I intend to stay just one night and should be back by tomorrow." With that he departed for his home at Nuvatukya'ovi.

Somehow the turds got wind of his absence. "He has just left for his parents' home and won't be at his wife's house tonight. So go to her," they said to the appointed man. "When you get to her, she'll of course ask you why you returned. Then you must say to her, 'I came back because I longed for you so. I'd just like to spend some more time with you before I leave and return again tomorrow.' When you tell her that she'll believe you."

The man did as instructed. That very night he slept with the wife of the Ka'nas kachina and left her again early the next morning. The Ka'nas kachina, of course, was endowed with great powers and was already aware of what the sorcerers had in store for him. Upon his return he knew right away that he had been deceived. His

pam put maanat awniqw, pay yaw pam son put aw qa unangwtapni. Yan yaw puma naanami yuku-yaqe, pu' yaw puma kwaatsit yukuyat, pu' put hakiy ka'naskatsinat su'aasakw namortota.

Noq pu' yaw pam tiyo pas ka'naskatsina yaw put nöömay aw pangqawu, "Nu' hapi hiisavo ikiy awniy. Niikyangw pay nu' hapi suus ep mihiknat pu' pay nu' son ason qaavo qa piw angqw ahoyniy," yaw pam nöömay aw kita. Kitat pu' yaw pam oovi yuk nuvatukya'omi kiy awi'.

Noq pu' yaw puma kwitavit piw pay kur put hin nanaptaqe yaw pangqaqwa, "Ta'ay, pay pi pam kiy awniiqe son pu' mihikqw nömakiy epniy. Noq um hapi oovi awni," yaw kitota. "Noq um awniqw ung hapi sonqa tuuvingtani hintiqw um ahoy pituuqat'ay. Noq pu' um ason aw pangqawni, 'Pay nu' ung sölmokqe oovi ahoy pitu. Niikyangw pay nu' hiisavo yep umumnit pu' nu' piw ahoynen pu' nu' ason pay qaavo piw angqw ahoyni.' Pay um put aw kitaqw pay pam sonqa tuptsiwni." Yan yaw puma put hakiy aw tutaptota.

Noq pu' yaw pam oovi pantiqe, pay yaw pam oovi put ka'naskatsinat nöömayat ep mihikqw amum puwt, pu' yaw qavongvaqw pay su'its put maatavi. Noq pu' pam katsina pi pay a'ni himunii-qe pay yaw pam piw sunvoti'yta puma put hin-tsatsnaniqw. Pay yaw puma oovi put tsöntotaqw, pay yaw pam oovi sunvoti'ykyangw ahoy pitu. Pu' yaw pam ka'naskatsina pay pas ahoy pituqw, pu' yaw pam nööma'at pan aqle' qahoptiqey yaw na-

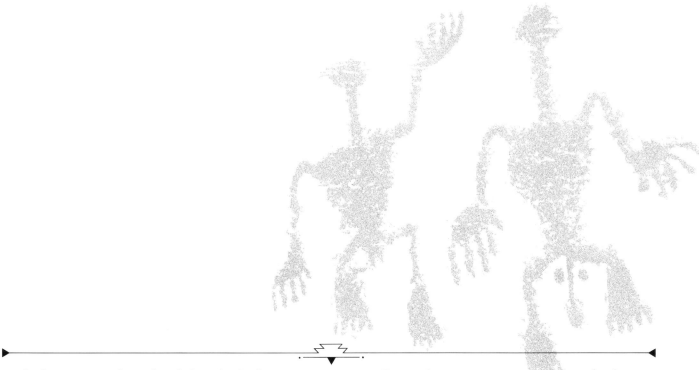

wife, however, only realized that she had committed adultery when her husband was back. Consequently, she felt depressed, and noticing this her husband said, "There must be something causing you sorrow."

"Yes, I'm not at all at ease," she confessed.

"And what is the reason for this?" he asked.

So she revealed to her husband what had happened. And even though he already knew, it grieved him much hearing it from his own wife. But he did not grow angry with her. After all, she had not done it intentionally. He merely replied, "Is that so? How terrible!"

vota. Sunvoti'ytaqe yaw pam putakw qa haalayqw, pu' yaw put koongya'at tuuvingta, "Um sumataq hiita ep qa haalayiy," yaw pam put nöömay aw kita.

"Owi, pas nu' antsa qa kwangwahinta," yaw pam aw kita.

"Ya hintiqw'öy?" yaw kita.

Paasat pu' yaw pam put koongyay aw naatuutu'ala. Noq pay yaw as pam it navoti'ykyangw, pas yaw pam qa haalayti put nöömay angqw it naap yan navotqe. Niikyangw pay yaw pam put qa aw itsivuti. Pay pi yaw pam qa nanap'unangway panti. Paasat pu' yaw pam pan lavayti, "Haw owi? Is ohi, antsa'ay."

His wife continued, "Those turds have ruined me. One of their group approached me, and since he looked exactly like you I believed what he told me."

"Of course, I'm aware of that. The turds became jealous of me. I suppose I have no choice but to return home," he said. "I can't very well stay here. They did this because they disliked me. I assure you, they will no longer benefit from the powers I possess. Had they not committed this crime against me, they would have prospered from my powers. My relatives would certainly have brought rain for them. That was the reason you filled so many ollas with water for the Hopi. It was our intention to bring it all here in the form of rain, but I guess this is the way things must be." Then he bade his wife, "Tell your father to come to me."

His wife did as bidden and got her father out of bed. "My husband would like to speak with you," she told him.

His son-in-law then related to him, "Really, it never occurred to me that something like this would happen when I married your daughter. But my people had tried to warn me. They told me that some of you, particularly those turds, would become envious. Now you will have to bear the

"Hep owi, pay ima kwitavit yep nuy nukushintsatsna. Pay pumuy angqw haqawa yep pitukyangw, pas pam piw su'un soniwqw oovi nu' tuptsiwa pam inumi hin lavaytiqw'ö."

"Hep owi, pay nu' navoti'yta. Puma pay qa tsuytiqe oovi'oy. Noq pay pi nu' oovi nawus nimaniy," yaw kita. "Pay pi nu' son pas yep nakwhani'ytani. Pay pi nuy qa himuyaqe oovi pantoti. Pay pi oovi puma nawus yaapiy qa inutsviy mongvasyaniy," yaw kita. "Pay pi suupan as puma nuy qa pantsatsne' puma yep inutsviy mongvasyani. Pu' isinom as sonqa pumuy amungem angqw yoknawismantani. Paniqw oovi um paasa' put kuysivut ang peqw imuy hopiituy amungem as na'sastaqw, put hapi itam angqw peqw as oo'oyayaniy. Put hapi as itam akw peqw yoknawismantaniqw, kur pay antsa yanhaqam hintaniqw pay pi antsa oovi yantaniy," yaw pam kita. Nit pu' yaw pam piw pangqawu, "Niikyangw um unay aw pangqawqw angqw pewniy," yaw pam nöömay yan ayata.

Pu' yaw pam oovi nay taataynaqe pu' yaw aw pangqawu, "Yaw ikongya uumi hingqawni," yaw pam nay aw kita.

Pu' yaw pam mö'önangw'at put aw pangqawu, "Ta'ay," yaw kita, "pay nu' qa hin yan wuuwankyangw it uumanay amumti. Noq pay yaw ima sonqa yantotiniqat antsa puma pep isinom inumi kitota," yaw pam aw kita. "Yaw ima son tsutsuyni. Noq pay pi oovi puma tur nawus qa inutsviy

consequences. You will no longer prosper on account of me. It was to prepare rain for you that your daughter went through her marriage rites at Nuvatukya'ovi. The rain was to have been carried here by the kachinas. But since I have been wronged in this way, no one will derive any benefits from me any more. If you do not care to forsake me, go and find a place for me where I can live. There you can pray to me."

Thereupon his wife's father took his son-in-law to a mesa spur north of Musangnuvi. At that place he erected a shrine for him. "Now, here you will reside," he told him.

"Very well," the Ka'nas kachina replied. "Here I want you to come and pray to me for rain and for all your crops. If you sincerely plead for these things, I'll grant them. But there is one thing I desire more than anything else: a paaho that has the male and female sticks side by side. At the time of the Soyal ceremony I expect you to make such a neveqvaho as the first thing you do and then bring it here. Use it to pray here to me and I will be merciful toward you." Next the Ka'nas youth handed his father-in-law a short object, which turned out to be the butt of a baked corn cob. "Take this and stick it into the lowest tier of your corn stack. It will be your assurance always to have crops."

mongvasyaniy," yaw kita. "Noq i' umuumana hapi paniqw oovi pep lööqökiwta. Pam hapi umungem yooyangwuy as peqw na'sastaqw, nuy hapi yantsatsnaqw oovi pu' hapi pay nawus qa hak inutsviy mongvasni. Niikyangw kur um nuy qa tatami'ymanik um haqami inungem kiituwqw, nu' antsa pay pep qatumantanti. Pangso um inumi naawakinmaniy," yaw pam kita.

Noq pu' yaw oovi put nöömayat na'at put mö'önangwuy yukiq musangnuviy kwiniwiq tuyqamiq wiiki. Niiqe pepeq pu' yaw pam put engem pahokit wunuptsina. "Ta'ay, yep hapi um qatuni," yaw pam put aw kita.

"Kur antsa'ay," yaw kita, "yuk hapi um inumi tur naawaknamantani. Yokvaniqat pu' hiita um aniwnaniqey put um oovi yuk inumi naawakinmani. Pu' um inumi antsa it hiita tuuvingtimaqw, pay nu' son ung put qa maqamantani. Niikyangw suukw nu' pas naawakna, it neveqvahot. Put um hapi soyalangwuy ep inungem pas susmooti yukut pu' um angqw put pew yawmamantani. Yep um put akw inumi naawaknaqw, pay nu' son ung hiita akw qa ookwatuwmantaniy," yaw pam put aw kita. Niiqe pu' yaw pam put hiita maqa, yaasavat. Noq yaw kur pam it tuupevut öövi'at. "It um yawme' it um uutuu'oyiy mumuyiyat ang panani. Pante' pay um sonqa uyi'ytamantaniy," yan yaw pam put aw tutapta.

Then he turned to his wife and said, "Well, I'm leaving. This is the way it'll have to be. I've left some instructions with your father. Since you yielded to those sorcerers, though, you are theirs now. I have nowhere to go except back to my people," he said.

With that the Ka'nas kachina left for home. Upon his arrival his anger welled up over the turds getting to his wife. As he mulled his situation over, he professed, "All right, they caused me a lot of grief. I must take my revenge. Granted, not all the villagers harmed me, but they knew of the scheme. Not a single person warned my wife, however. The outcome was that she succumbed to one of them. I don't believe I can live with this adultery. Therefore I'll kill the lot of them." This anger the Ka'nas kachina shared with his people.

His people advised him, "Don't do anything that drastic. Rather you should shake them up a little. Once they get frightened, they may ponder their conduct," the elders suggested.

"Very well then, how should I go about scaring them?" he queried.

Pantiqw pu' yaw pam angqw nöömay awnit pu' yaw aw pangqawu, "Ta'ay, nu' hapini. Noq pay oovi nawus yantani. Niikyangw pay nu' unay aw tutaptay," yaw pam put aw kita. "Pay pi um nuwu pumuy amumi uunatiqe um pumuy himu'amniwti. Noq pay nu' kur haqaminen nawus qa ahoy isinomuy amumi ahoy nimaniy," yaw pam kita.

Pu' yaw pam oovi pangqw nima. Nit pu' yaw pam kiy ep pituuqe pu' yaw itsivuti puma kwitavit put tsöntotaqw. Niiqe pu' yaw pam put ang wuuwaqe pu' yaw pangqawu, "Ta'ay, pay pi pas nuy tuuhototaqw pay nu' son tuwat qa amumi naa'oyni. Pay pi as naamahin puma qa soosoyam nuy pantsatnakyangw, pay as puma pep ki'yyungqam navoti'yyungwa, puma it yan pasiwna-yaqw'ö. Niikyangw pay pas qa haqawa ngas'ew put iwuutiyniqat yan it navotnaqw, pam oovi antsa put hakiywat aw pay nakwha. Pay hapi nu' kur son it tsönawuy ang kuytani. Niiqe pay nu' oovi pumuy soosokmuy qöyani." Yanhaqam yaw pam itsivutiqe pu' yaw pam yan sinomuy aa'awna.

Noq pu' yaw put sinomat pangqaqwa, "Pay tis um qa pas panhaqam hintsakniy," yaw kitota. "Niikyangw pay pi um ngas'ew pumuy tsaawinani. Tsaawinaqw pay sen puma antsa put ang hin wuuwayaniy," yaw puma wuuwuyom kitota.

"Ta'ay, noq nu' hin pumuy tsaawinaniy?" yaw pam kita.

"We've given the matter some thought," the elders said. "To accomplish your goal you'll need to gather certain items. Collect some snakeweed. From the pine get some bark; also gather the dry, soft needles, and the sap that runs from the wood. Then dig a hole on top of this mound to the east of us and place everything you collected into it. Lastly, take your flint and strike it until sparks fly. At some point, if you're lucky, you'll get a fire started and the material will burn. But mind our next instruction carefully. Don't drive the hole too deep into the ground. Just dig a little way, then let it be. North of that hill, by the way, resides a mighty wind, the whirlwind. Plead with him to come to you and fan your fire so that it turns into a great blaze."

Receiving these instructions from his elders, the Ka'nas youth collected the various items. Then he climbed the mound pointed out to him and, after creating the hole at the top, filled it with the accumulated materials. The elders, who had accompanied the youth, remained at the foot of the hill. The youth now started striking the flint. He struck

"Owiy," yaw kitota, "pay itam ungem aw wuuwayaqw, um it hiitakw put mongvastiniqey put um tsovalani. Um it maa'övitnit pu' it löqöt tsiipuyat, pu' put naapiyat lakput suphingputnit pu' piw put saanayat, paasa' um tsovalaniy," yaw kitota. "Pantit pu' um yep hoop tsomot ooveq aqw hangwat, pu' um it hiita tsovalaqey put um aqw oyani. Paasat pu' um it uuyoysivay akw put aqw pilakintaqw, pu' put angqw tövutslamtimantani. Pu' um pantsakkyangw hisatniqw um sakinaqw pay pam son put qa taqtsoknaqw, pu' pam uwikniy," yaw puma put aw kitota. "Niikyangw it suukw itaatutavoy hapi um pas su'antini. Um hapi pay qa pas a'ni aqw hangwani. Pay um aqw hiisa-vooyat hangwaqw pay pantani. Noq pu' put tsomot aakwiningqöyve piw i' wukohukyangw, tuviphayangw, ki'yta. Put um ason aw naawak-naqw pam uuminen pu' pam put ungem aw huu-kyantaqw, pu' pam pavan uwikniy," yaw aw kitota.

Pu' yaw puma wuuwuyoqam put tiyot aw pan tutaptotaqw, pu' yaw pam oovi put hiihiita tsovala. Noq pu' yaw pam pangsoq tsomomiq wupqe pu' yaw pepeq ooveq aqw hangwat pu' put aqw oya. Noq pu' yaw ima wuuwuyom pay as put tiyot amumyakyangw pay yaw puma put tsomot atkyaq huruutoti. Noq pu' yaw pam put yoysivay akw put aw pilakinta. Noq i' saana yaw su'uwik-ngwuniqw pam yaw oovi put aw pantsaki. Hisat-niqw pu' yaw pam su'an pilaknaqw, pu' yaw put

it toward the pine sap, which usually burns readily. One moment when he hit the flint just right, a spark flew forth and set the pitch alight. As it flamed up, he added more fuel so that the fire began to burn a little more steadily. The youth, however, wanted a roaring blaze. He bellowed it and bellowed it, but before the flames grew any larger, he became dizzy from blowing. At this point he recalled one of the elders' directives. "There's a wind supposed to live just north of here. I guess I'll summon him." With this idea occurring to him he headed over to the north side where he came to a large cavern. Into this cavern he now directed his plea. He knelt down at the opening and shouted inside, "You, who live here. I'd like to ask your help. My elders told me to come here, and so I've come to you."

Barely had a few moments passed when a breeze emerged from the cave followed by a wind of such force that it hurled him aside. The wind rocked back and forth, stirring everything up that was in his path. "What is it that you want of me?" the wind howled.

The youth related how he had fared at Musangnuvi and why he intended to take revenge on the villagers. In addition, he mentioned how the elders had suggested the idea of frightening the people there and that he had built a big fire on top

angqw tövutslamtikyangw pu' yaw pay saanat uwikna. Paasat pu' yaw pam uwiwiykuqw, pu' yaw pam wuuhaq kohot aw oyaqw pu' yaw pam paasat pas hihin kyee'ew uwi. Pu' yaw pam pavan uwikna. Paasat pu' yaw pam uwiwiykuqw, pu' yaw pam wuuhaq kohot aw oyaqw pu' yaw pam paasat pas hihin kyee'ew uwi. Pu' yaw pam pavan uwikniqat pam naawaknaqe, pu' yaw pam oovi aw pooyantakyangw pay naat qa pavan uwikqw, pay yaw pam poyansuwi. Poyansuwqe pu' yaw pan wuuwa hin put ura aw tutaptotaqw. "Ura yep kwiningqöyve piw i' huukyangw ki'yta. Kur nu' put wangwayniy," yaw pam yan wuuwaqe pu' yaw pam oovi pangso kwiningqöyminiqw pephaqam yaw aqw atkyamiq wukohötsiniqw, pangsoq yaw pam naawakna. Niiqe pu' yaw pam pangsoq tamötswunuptut pu' yaw pam aqw pangqawu, "Ta-'ay, ki'ytaqay. Nu' as okiw uumi taqa'nangwtiy. Pay nuy pew aa'awnayaqw oovi nu' antsa angqw pew uumi'iy," yaw pam aqw kita.
put aw pam sumaw a'ni öqalat yamakkyangw yaw put ayo'haqami tuuva. Pantit pu' yaw pam pep naanahoy yannumkyangw pu' hiihiita suqvivitoyni'ynuma. "Ta'ay, ya um hintiqw nuy naawakna?" yaw pam kita.

"Owiy," yaw pam aw kitat pu' yaw put aw pam naatu'awi'yta hintiqw pam imuy musangnuvituy amumi naa'oyniqey. Pu' yaw pam pep wukoqöhe' kya yaw pan pumuy pay hihin tsaawinaniqat yaw puma wuuwuyom put tiyot aw tutaptotaqw, yan

of the hill. "In case my fire should fail to grow into a great blaze, I was told to come and get you. Now I'm here to seek your assistance," the youth explained. The wind readily agreed to accompany him.

The Ka'nas youth escorted the wind back to the mound. "Well then, here it is," he said to the wind when they reached their destination. By this time the fire was about to die. The wind blew on it. Immediately it came back to life and turned into a huge blaze. Before long the fire raged so intensely that flames licked the clouds.

The elders, who had suggested the idea of the fire in the first place and who were there with the youth, now exclaimed, "How terrible! It looks as though you dug the hole too deep, and now the fire is moving in the wrong direction. It's burning downward. Let's all step back a little, for the heat is unbearable!" With that they retreated somewhat from the hill. A few moments later one of the elders exclaimed, "Oh no, it is burning its way down into the hole. Look at the force with which it rages!"

yaw pam put aw tu'awi'yta. "Noq yaw iqöhi qa pavan uwikqw, nu' yaw ung angqw pew wiktoniqat yan piw ima wuuwuyom inumi tutaptotaqw oovi nu' antsa uumi pew taqa'nangwti." Yaw pam put aw yan lalvayqw pay yaw pam huukyangw sunakwha put amumniqe.

Pu' yaw pam paapiy put huukyangwuy wiiki. "Ta'ay, yep hapiy," yaw pam put aw kita puma pep tsomove ahoy pituqw. Noq pay yaw put tiyot qööhi'at ahoy tsootso'iwmaqw, yaw puma pantaqat aw pitu. Pu' yaw i' huukyangw put aw hikwsuqw, pay yaw pam piw ahoy suu'öqawtaqe yaw oovi a'ni pepeq uwiwita. Panmakyangw pu' hapi pay yaw pam a'nitaqe pu' yaw pay angqw wupa'leleyku.

Noq yaw pu' ima wuuwuyom put tiyot aw tutaplalwaqam put amum epyaqe yaw put aw pangqaqwa, "Is ohiy," yaw kitota, "pay hapi um sumataq pas qa atsat a'ni atkyamiq hangwaqw oovi pam soq tuwat atkyamiqwat a'ni'ymay," yaw puma wuuwuyom kitota. "Itam oovi pay hihin ahoy hooyokyaniy, taq hapi is utuy," yaw puma kitotaqe pu' yaw oovi ahoy hihin hooyokya. Hiisavoniqw pu' yaw pam suukya wuutaqa pangqawu, "Is ohiy, pay hapi pas i' soq atkyamiq a'ni hoytakyangw pas hapi piw a'nitay," yaw pam kita.

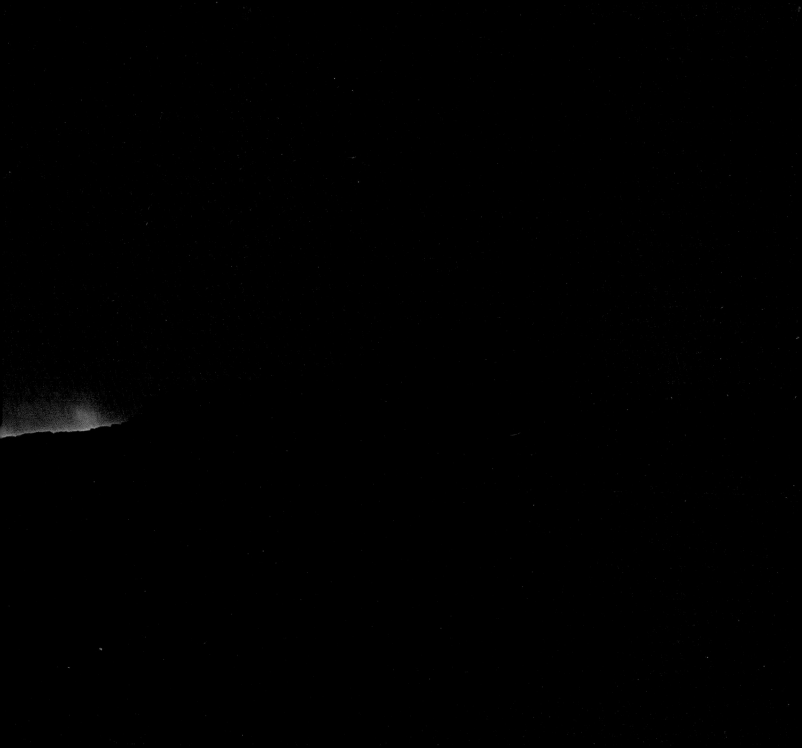

Sure enough, by then the fire had eaten its way into the ground. Once again the elder cried out, "Dear me, I believe the blaze has reached the people who tend the fire underground. They are relatives of Maasaw. They keep the fire there for him and know no pity. I believe the two fires have joined together," the old man exclaimed.

Inside the flames something rose up now. What the elders beheld was a flow of boiling embers. "Didn't we know it!" they cried. "We had a feeling this might happen. That's why we warned you not to dig down too far, but evidently you ignored us," they lamented. "Well, we'll just have to wait and see what happens. Besides, you wanted to scare the Musangnuvi people. Perhaps they'll reflect upon their misdeeds if they see this. They may realize what misery they inflicted on you by forcing you to leave. They'll also be remorseful for losing you. They lived in prosperity because of you and yet they cheated you out of your wife. Now their survival is also in our hands. So let it be this way," one of the elders exclaimed. He had to resign himself to the situation.

Meanwhile at Musangnuvi someone spotted the fire. West of Nuvatukya'ovi a blaze was rearing upwards. This he reported to the village leader,

Noq antsa yaw pam qööhi nuwu pangsoq atkyamiq pitu. Pu' yaw pam wuutaqa piw pangqawu, "Is ohiy, pay hapi pas amumiq pituy," yaw pam kita, "pep qööhi'yyungqamuy aqwaa'. Puma hapi pepeq atkyaqwat qööhi'yyungqam it maasawuy sinomatniiqe puma hapi pepeq put engem it qööhit aw tunatyawyungwa. Puma hapi pas qa nun'okwatuy. Noq pay hapi pam qööhi sumataq pas naami pitu."

Noq pangqw yaw uwiwitaqat angqw yaw himu wungwnuptu. Pu' yaw puma aqw yoyrikyaqw angqw yaw töövu a'ni kwalalata. "Puye'emoy," yaw kitota, "puye'em pi yantaniqe oovi itam ung meewaya um qa pas a'ni aqw hangwaniqat'ay. Noq pas um kur a'ni aqw hangway," yaw kitota. "Noq pay pi'iy," yaw kitota. "Pay pi itam hin nanaptani. Pay pi um pumuy tsaawinaniqey kita. Noq sen pay antsa it tutwe' sen ang hin wuuwayani. Sen ang hin wuuwaye', nanaptani ung okiwsasnat pu' ung pew hoonayaqe'ey. Pu'sa pi sonqa ung kyaakyawnani. Pay pi as puma suyan utsviy a'ni yeskyaakyangw ung okiw tsöntota. Pu' son pi as qa itamumi enang yankyaakyangw pi hin yesni. Pay oovi nam yantaniy," yaw pam suukyawa wuy kitaaqe pay yaw nawusta.

Noq pu' yaw yep musangnuve yaw hak put uuwingwuy tuwa. Yaw yep taavang nuvatukya-'oviy tup yaw qööhu wungwnuptuqw, pu' yaw pam it kikmongwit yan aa'awnaqw pu' yaw pam pangqawu, "Is ohiy," yaw kita. "Pay pi puye'em

who cried out, "Oh my, I knew this was going to happen. But you evil ones always have to find fault with something. I'm certain it's your vile deed that caused this fire to turn against us," he said unhappily.

When the people learned of the fire, they looked across to Nuvatukya'ovi. Right inside one of the hills there was a mass of what looked like boiling coals pushing upward. As this was going on, the fire rose sky-high. Some time later, as it reached its peak, it spewed out molten embers that were extremely hot. Bursts of sparks kept shooting into the air just as from a torch someone is running along with. Finally the embers reached up so high that they poured over the rim of the fire pit, thereby enlarging the hill. Eventually the hill sprung leaks at several places around its base. Spewing forth in every direction, the molten embers started running everywhere. Nothing seemed able to block the flow. From all appearances, the flow was heading straight toward the village of Musangnuvi. By now, the embers were only oozing out from underground and flowing outward. The top of the hill had apparently cooled off and was quiet. But the hill had increased in size considerably. Also due to the cooling action there now stood an enormous red mountain. In its vicinity several other mounds

sonqa yanhaqam hintiniqw, pas uma nuunukpant hiita ep qa naaniyangwuy. Pay pam son it qa umuuqa'antipuy akw pu' itamumiwatniwtiy," yaw pam kitaaqe qa haalayti.

Pu' yaw sinom it nanaptaqe pu' yaw puma aqw yoyrikyaqw pay yaw as pep put suukw tsomot aasonngaqw i' töövu a'ni kwalalatakyangw pay hapi yaw pam pas angqw oomiq sus'ö'qala. Pantsakkyangw pu' yaw pay piw paasat i' uuwingw pangqw pavan pas oomiq wungwnuptu. Pu' hapi yaw pam hisatniqw pas kur a'nitaqe paasat pu' yaw pas tis it töövut a'ni mukit paa'iwtaqat yaw pangqw pavoyanta. Pay hak it kopitsokit yawkyangw a'ni warikiwnumqw, pan yaw pangqw a'ni tövutslalata. Pantsakkyangw pu' yaw pam angqw pas naamolqe pu' yaw pay pam angqw naanan'i'voq wehehetaqw, pavan yaw pam pep tsomo nuwu aw hoyta. Panmakyangw pu' yaw pam pay qa suup atkyahaqam pokwaymakqe pu' yaw pam oovi naanan'i'voq wehekkyangw pu' naanan'i'voq mumuntiva. Pu' hapi yaw pay put pas sumataq qa himu qe'tapnani. Pas pi yaw pam suyan yuumosa musangnumiqwat hoyta. Noq pu' pam haqe' pokwamtiqey pay yaw paasat pas pangqwsa nööngankyangw pu' pang mumuna. Noq put tsomot ooveq pay yaw pam kur paasat hukyaaqe pay yaw oovi paapu qa hinwat hinti. Niikyangw pas pi yaw pam kur aw wuuyoqti. Pu' yaw pam piw hukyaaqe pavan yaw pam pep wukopalatsmo wunu. Pu' put ang aqle' piw yaw kur pam peehu tsomo yukiltoti-

had formed, but they were not as large. Today they are known to the Hopi as Löhavutsotsmo, or "Testicle Hills." Since both the fire underneath these hills and the one raging on top had joined forces, the upper sections of the hills had all caved in. Cooling off, they took on a red hue, and for this reason the terrain is red there today.

When the fire really began to blaze, the elders took shelter on a hill to the north and from this vantage point they looked on. Meanwhile the fire storm had taken on such proportions that one elder shouted, "How dreadful! We simply wanted to strike terror into their hearts, but it appears that everything has gotten out of control. Come on here, young man!"

When the Ka'nas youth approached him, the elder advised him, "Go fetch the wind again and run with him along the edges of the burning ground. Take him around there so he can blow the fire back in this direction. That way he may be able to subdue it."

Already the flowing lava had advanced a great distance, and the elders begged the youth to hurry. The fire was running right through the grassland and the forest. Anything in its path that could burn flared up as soon as the fire came upon it.

kyangw pay yaw qa angsay. Noq pang pu' put i' hopi löhavutsotsmo yan tuwi'yta. Pu' yaw pam pang tsotsmot ang i' qööhi naamiq pas pituqw oovi yaw pam angqw oongaqw aqw yuvum'iwta. Pu' yaw pam hisat hukyaaqe pu' yaw pas pan paalangpu hukyaaqe paniqw yaw oovi pu' pan pas palatutskwa.

Noq pas hapi yaw put angqw a'ni uwiwiykuqw, pu' yaw ima wuuwuyom pangqw ayo' kwiniwiwat tsomomi watqaqe pangqw pu' yaw puma put aw taayungwa. Pu' hapi pay yaw nuwu pas wuuyoqtiniqw pu' yaw pam wuutaqa pangqawu, "Is ohiy," yaw kita, "pay hapi as itam panis pumuy tsaawinayaniqw, pas i' sumataq qa tuuqayniy. Ta'ay, um pewniy, tiyoy," yaw pam put aw kita.

Pu' yaw pam tiyo oovi awniqw pu' yaw pam wuutaqa put aw pangqawu, "Ta'ay," yaw kita, "um yuk it huukyangwuy piw awnen pu' um put wikkyangw, haqe' paasaq qööhi qalawtaqw, pangqe uma warikniy. Pu' um put pangqe wikkyangwniqw, pu' pam paasat put uuwingwuy peqwwat ahoy huhukhoynaniy. Pay sen as pam pante' put angwutaniy," yaw pam put tiyot aw kita.

Noq paasat pay yaw pam töövu pang munqa nuwu pay yaw yaaptiqw, pu' yaw puma wukw'aymat put aw pan pisoqtoti. Noq antsa pay yaw paasat pam uuwingw it tusaqqölöt, löqöqlöt pas qa hiita'yma. Pas pi yaw naap himu uwikngwuqa atpip yantaqw pay yaw pam panis put aw pitut pay yaw pam antsa put uwiknangwu.

The Ka'nas youth went to summon the wind once more and together the two dashed to the fire. Running along the edge of the burn the wind drove the flames back, and by blowing into the area already aflame he eventually succeeded in quelling the blaze.

As a result the flames did not reach the village of Musangnuvi. When the villagers noticed this they were greatly relieved. For surely the fire had been coming nearer with the intention of destroying them. The village elders berated the sorcerers now. "You see, how it is. That young man was no ordinary person. He was a kachina, and his people must not have appreciated how you mistreated him. Also, they held dear their in-law, so they probably won't show us any pity now. That must have been your objective when you hatched your evil plan to hurt that young man. We knew, of course, that you disgraced the man's wife by tricking her to commit adultery. But I suppose we were not smart enough to intercede. So your plan came off. For this reason we're just as much at fault as you. Even so, it was you who caused him all this suffering. No man or woman can stand going through the shame of being cheated on. Therefore

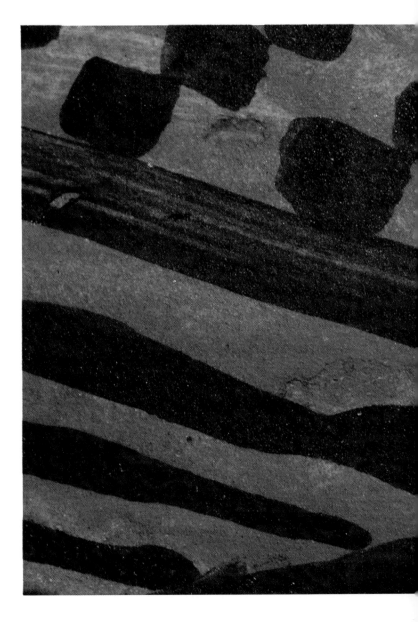

Pu' yaw pam tiyo oovi put huukyangwuy piw wiktamaqe pu' yaw pam paasat put wikkyangw pu' pangqaqw wari. Pu' yaw pang haqe' qööhi qalawtaqw, pang yaw pam tiyo put huukyangwuy wikkyangw warikiwtaqw, pu' yaw pam put ahoywat laalayi. Haqe' pay uwikiwtaqw pangsowat yaw pam put aw pooyanmakyangw pu' yaw pam put angwuta. Yanti yaw pamniiqe pu' yaw pam put tookya.

Pan yaw pam musangnumiq qa pituqw, pu' yaw yepeq musangnuveq yaw puma sinom yan yoyrikyaqe paasat pu' yaw puma hihin yan unangwtoti. Suyan pi as yaw pam qööhi pumuy haqami hintsanniqe pumuy amumiq hoyta. Noq paasat pu' yaw puma wuuwuyom tuwat pumuy popwaqtuy amumi pangqaqwa, "Ta'ay," yaw kitota, "yanta hapi. Pam hapi son pay himu'uy. Pam hapi katsinaniqw put sinomat hapi son put engem haalaytoti uma put hintatsnaqw'öy. Pu' puma it mö'wiy son as qa kyaakyawnayaqe oovi puma son itamuy ookwatutwani. Noq yanhaqam kya pi uma itamungem tunatyawyungqe oovi put yephaqam okiwsasna. Noq pay pi as itam piw navoti'yyungwa uma put taaqat tsöntotaqw'ö. Noq pay pi itam piw kya pi ngasta wuwni'yyungqe oovi umuy qa meewayaqw oovi uma antsa pi put pantsatsnay. Noq pay pi itam oovi songyawnen piw qa antotiy. Niikyangw uma pas put okiwsasnay. Son hak taaqa, wuuti tsönawuy ang kuytangwuy. Noq oovi uma hapi pas wukoqa'antotiy. Noq

you've committed a grave sin. But all that can't be helped now, the crime's been committed." Thus spoke the elders to the turds as they rebuked them harshly. In trepidation, they watched the fire in the west moving closer and closer at a tremendous pace. Then suddenly, and much to everyone's surprise, the entire blaze petered out.

When the Musangnuvi people saw the blaze die down on its own, they exclaimed, "Surely, this fire was our doing. If the flames had reached us, it would have spelled disaster. For some reason, though, the kachinas had compassion on us and the blaze went out by itself. Otherwise it would certainly have consumed us with its flames. It is unlikely, however, that our trials are over." These were the words of the wise leaders.

Days went by, and the planting season came. The people planted their various crops, but when the shoots broke through the ground it only rained once. Midsummer was still some time off, but already the weather was getting hotter and hotter, and all their crops withered.

Time passed and in the second year the people planted anew. Once again everything sprouted and

pay pi'iy," yaw kitota. "Pay pi nuwupi itam qa antotiy," kitota yaw puma pumuy amuminiiqe pas yaw puma pumuy a'ni qööqöyya. Niiqe puma yaw oovi tsawiniwkyaakyangw pangqw pangsoq teevenge taayungwa. Noq angqw yaw pam qööhi a'ni hoytakyangw, piw yaw hiisavoniqw pay yaw pam soosoy tooki.

Piw yaw pam qööhi naap tsootso'q, pu' yaw ima yangqw musangnungaqw sinom yan yoyrikyaqe yaw pangqaqwa, "Ta'ay, pay pi i' as naap itaahimuniqw, itam as suyan hintaqat aqw ökiniqw oovi pam qööhi angqw as peqwniqw, pay puma hintaqat akw itamuy ookwatutwaqw oovi pam qööhi pay naap tsootso'a. Pay as pam qa pante', pam peqw pite', pam hapi as son itamuy qa uwiknani. Noq pay itamuy aw wuuwantotaqw pay naat son yantaniy," yaw puma kitota, ima wuwni'yyungqam, momngwit.

Noq pu' antsa yaw aapiy pantaqw, pu' yaw puma uyismiq öki. Noq pu' yaw puma as oovi hiita uu'uyayaqw pay yaw as uuyi'am kuyvaqw, pay yaw ep panis suus yokvakyangw pay yaw naat as pay qa tal'angwnasami pituqw, pay yaw pangqaqw pas u'tuhu'lawqw pay yaw okiw pam uuyi'am soosoy laaki.

Panmakyangw pu' yaw lööq yaasangwuy aw pu' yaw puma piw uu'uyayaqw, paasat pu' yaw pay as soosoy himu kuyvaqe yaw oovi as ang siitalawvaqw, pavan yaw puma sinom as okiw tsutsyakya. Pu' yaw kur puma put natwaniy

grew, and when the plants blossomed the poor people were overjoyed. Hoping to feed themselves from their crops they were full of anticipation. But it was not to be. That year the rains came in the form of hail. For eight consecutive days and nights the hail pelted down without letting up. The noise outside was awful. Even houses were destroyed by the hailstones. It was such a terrible experience that no one dared go outdoors.

Eventually the storm subsided. Men walked out to their fields, brokenhearted. The hail had ruined all their plants. When they realized the extent of the disaster, they returned home weeping. This was the second year that they had failed to raise crops. It simply would not rain. The leaders congregated to fashion prayer feathers. Pronouncing the name of the kachina in the west, they uttered their prayers. But it was all to no avail. The Ka'nas kachina was apparently still smarting from the adultery and showed no pity toward them. The Musangnuvi people still possessed certain reserves of food but, though they grew unhappy, they had to resign themselves to the adverse weather.

The following winter it snowed, but even before the warm season was upon them the days were searing hot, and the heat parched their crops. This time none of their plants even sprouted. It was obvious that a serious situation was at hand.

angqw hiita nöönösaniqey yan wuuwayaqe yaw kwangwtotoya. Noq pay yaw kur qa pantani. Ep pu' yaw i' yooyangw pitukyangw yaw soq i' lemoyoyangw. Pu' hapi yaw pam pituuqe pas yaw qa suusta. Pas yaw ep nanalsikis teevepniikyangw pu' tookyep pan lemoyoyoki. Pas pi yaw iikye' hin töötöqa. Pu' yaw pam it kiihut pas enang pang sakwitima. Is ana, yaw himuwa yamakninik qa suutaq'ewningwu.

Panmakyangw pu' yaw pam yaala. Paasat pu' yaw ima taataqt uuyiy angyaqe yaw qa haalaytoti. Pas pi yaw pam put pang uuyit soosok nukushintsana. Yan yaw puma nanaptaqe pas pi yaw puma okiw tsaykikyangw pangqw ahoy nimanta. Paasat pay yaw löös puma pas qa hiita aniwnaya. Pas yaw qa yokvangwu. Pu' yaw ima momngwit as tsovaltiqe pu' yaw paaholalwa. Pu' yaw puma pangso it katsinat tungwniyat tungwankyaakyangw yaw aw naanawakna. Noq pay yaw kur puma haktonsa put aw yoynanawakna. Naat yaw pam ka'naskatsina kur put tsöntiwqey ep naatuho'ytaqe pay yaw pam oovi pumuy pas qa ookwatuwa. Noq pu' yaw puma musangnuvit pay naat hiisa' hiita nitkyamaskya'yyungkyangw pay yaw oovi as qa haalaytotikyangw pay yaw nawustota.

Paapiy pu' yaw ep tömö' pay as nuvayokvakyangw pay yaw naat qa pas tal'angwmiq pituqw pay piw yaw aapiy u'tuhu'lawqe pay yaw piw pumuy uuyiyamuy lakna. Ep pu' yaw pay tis qa

When wintertime came again, snow did fall but so powder dry that the ground never absorbed any moisture. In addition, a blizzard came that blew away all the snow. Again the weather turned warm, and the people planted what seeds they had saved. But the seeds were evidently not destined to sprout. All through the summer the wind never ceased blowing and completely desiccated the soil. The wind blew day in, day out, and even the erecting of windbreaks to shelter the plants was useless. There was no recourse against the wind. In the end all the plants became covered by drifts of sand. By this time the people had used up their entire supply of seeds and no longer had anything to eat. In desperation, some went from field to field like thieves, digging up seeds and devouring them. Though it was not yet midsummer, all their provisions were gone. Their reserve food, too, was quite depleted. Further and further the Hopis fell into a state of famine.

himu uuyi ngas'ew kuyva. Pay yaw puma pas susmataq hintaqat aqw ökiwisa.

Pu' yaw piw tömöngvakyangw paasat pay yaw as nuvayokvangwuniikyangw pay yaw pas sulakpuniiqe yaw oovi tutskwat qa mowanangwu. Pu' yaw ep piw i' wukonuvahukyangw pituuqe paasat pu' yaw pam pas soosok nuvat huhukhoyna. Pay yaw puma oovi as piw tal'angwvaqw yaw piw hiisa' poshumiy warani'yyungqe yaw put tangatotaqw, pay yaw pam kur pas son kuyvani. Pu' yaw ang tal'angwnawit piw yaw pas sutsep huuhukqe yaw oovi it tutskwat pas paas lakna. Pas pi yaw angqe' naaqavo huuhukqw, haktonsa yaw puma uuyiy angqe wayonglalwa. Pas pi yaw qa himu put huukyangwuy angwu'yta. Pas pi yaw i' nöönga pumuy uuyiyamuy soosok aama. Noq ep pay yaw puma pas soosok hiita poshumiy soosokyaqe pu' yaw kur paapu hiita nöönösaniqw, pu' yaw pay peetu pang pasnawit put poovoshumit u'uyingwvewat ipwanvayaqe pu' put paasat noonova. Noq pay yaw naat qa hin tal'angwnasamiq pituqw, pay yaw pumuy nöösiwqa'am, tunösmaskya'am pas sulawti. Noq paasat pay yaw ima hopiit pas suytsepngwat it tsöngösiwuy aqw ökiwisa.

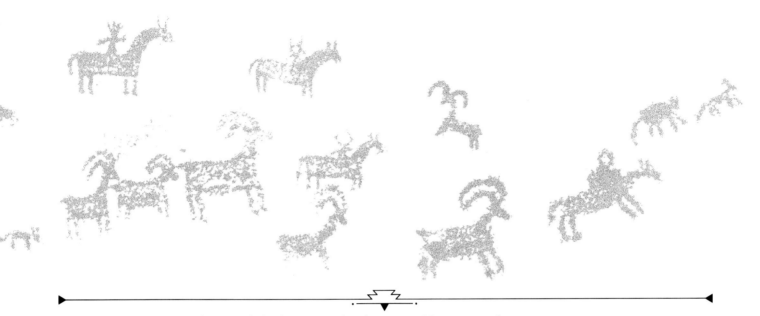

By the fourth year the people had no more food in storage. All anyone could think of now was begging, but even though the person entreated might have had a little food on hand, he would not share it. Famine was truly overtaking them now.

Those who could no longer carry on were forced to leave Hopiland. To seek better living conditions somewhere else, they trekked off in all directions. Some went to the eastern pueblos along the Rio Grande, others migrated among the neighboring tribes. A few even headed into the land of the Paiutes.

Noq aw naalöq yaasangwuy aw pay yaw puma pas qa hiita tunösmaskya'yyungwa. Pu' yaw himuwa as hakiy aw pan wuuwe' pu' yaw pam as put aw tunöstungla'ytangwuniqw, pay yaw as himuwa naamahin hiisa' oyi'ykyangw pay yaw put qa angqw maqangwu. Noq yan pay yaw puma pas suyan tsöngösiwuy aw öki.

Noq pu' yaw ima peetu pay pas paapu kur hin kya pi ayo' nöngakniqe, pu' yaw puma yangqw hopiikingaqw haqamiwat nawus qatsihepwisniqe, pu' puma yaw yangqw naanan'i'voq nankwusa. Peetu yaw hopoqkimiqyaqw, pu' peetu kya pi pay yangqe haqe' himusinmuy amuupa nankwusa. Hikis pi yaw peetu pas payotskivahaqe' e'nangya.

The game animals, no longer having plants to browse on, also disappeared. When game was no longer available, the Hopis began to eat every other creature. They had no choice now but to consume dogs, cats, and even mice. However, these animals did not last long before they, too, were wiped out. There even came a time when the older people descended to the plain below the mesa to hunt such creatures as grasshoppers, cicadas, and prairie dogs. Others traveled about looking for water and disappeared. Before long the people could no longer find even these little animals.

There were some who sustained themselves by consuming cactus, the only plant the soil still bore in abundance. The cactus tasted quite bitter though, and since it was gummy, it was very hard to swallow. Moreover, it was quite tough to chew. Yucca was also eaten, but its flavor was even more unpleasant. At least its fruit tasted a little better, though. There was nothing the people did not try. In this fashion they gained much knowledge of what was edible. At times a person ate something poisonous and fell ill as a result. Others even died.

The Hopis were at a loss to know what to do. They took to ferreting around in their garbage heaps. It was as if they had turned into chickens. They scavenged through the ash piles and turned

Pu' yaw ima tuutuvosipt piw kur hiita noonovaniqe pay yaw puma piw sulawti. Noq pu' yaw pay pumawat piw sulawtiqw, pu' yaw puma pay paasat soosokmuy hiituy noonova. Paasat pu' yaw puma pay nawus imuy popkotuy, moomostuy, pu' hikis pöövöstuy enang noonovaqw, pay yaw puma piw qa wuuyavoyat pay yaw sulawti. Pu' yaw haqaapiy ima wuuwuyoqam pay yaw paasat atkyami hanqe pu' yaw puma pangqe' imuy hiituy töötöltuy, maatuy, tukyaatuy, puuvumuy hiituy oovi maqnumyangwuniqw, pay yaw pumawat piw tuwat angqe' paahepnumyaqe pay yaw kur haqamiya. Niiqe pay yaw naat qa wuuyavotiqw pay yaw puma pumuy piw qa tuwa'ynumya.

Pu' yaw peetu it öösöt noonova, pamsa yaw naat pay ang tutskwava a'niniqw oovi. Noq pay yaw as pam qa kwangwa. Yaw pam himu wiwsaavisaniqw yaw hak peep put qa kwu'ukngwu, peep hak yaw qa piingyangwu. Pu' yaw as puma it moohot piwyaqw pam yaw pas tis qa kwangwa. Pay yaw i' piite'atsa yaw pay ngas'ew kwangwa. Pas pi yaw puma qa hiita qa tuwantota. Niiqe pan yaw puma hiita kwangwngwuniqw put nanapta. Pu' yaw himuwa kur qa suuput hiita nööse' pay yaw himuwa okiw putakw tuutuytingwu; pu' yaw peetu pas tis so'a.

Pu' hopiit yaw kur hintotiniqe pu' yaw puma qöötsaptsomova hiita hepnumyangwu. Pu' yaw puma songyawnen kowaakomniwti. Puma yaw pan qöötsaptsomovaniikyangw pu' piw soosovik

over every clod of earth in search of edibles such as corn kernels. The children also hunted various things in trash piles along the edge of the village. And when one of them unearthed so much as an old piece of deerhide, he took it home and roasted it in the firepit. As soon as it became brittle, the whole family gnawed on it. Some people even, who knew where drums were kept in the kivas, took them out, removed their skin coverings, then baked them and devoured them. This was how poorly they fared. Miserably they carried on their lives from day to day.

It was at this time that a great many men died. Those who perished had all been the evil ones. With great amazement the people realized that neither women nor children were among those that died. Even though all of them had been exposed to the same ordeal, only the evil men died.

The wife of the Ka'nas kachina and her parents did not have to endure the same hardship as the rest. Since it had been her husband's intention to bring famine upon the Hopi, he had foreseen these events and made sure that his family was well provided for. There was always corn in their corn stacks from which they cooked their meals. They always had plenty to eat. And because, during

tutskwava hiihiita humita'ewakw oovi kwetsti-numyangwu. Pu' yaw ima tsaatsayomwat pay pep kiive pang kwayngyava piw tuwat hiihiita hep-numyangwu. Yaw haqam himu hisatsowi'ingwvukya'ewayniqw, put yaw himuwa kiy aw yawme' pu' yaw qöpqömiq tuupe'ytangwu. Pu' yaw pam hihin kolakqw pu' yaw puma pep naanatim put ang kyaaritotangwu. Hikis pi yaw peetu it pusu-kinpit kivaapa tuwa'yyungqam put pangqw ip-wankyaakyangw pu' yaw put ang puukyayat ayo' qapuminkyaakyangw pu' piw put tutpeyakyangw noonova. Pas pi yaw puma yan okiwhinyungwa. Pantsatskya yaw puma, okiwhintsatskya; okiw-yese yaw puma'.

Noq paasat pay yaw ima taataqt pas wuukosu-lawti. Noq puma yaw pay kur ima nuunukpantya. Noq oovi yaw puma naanami kyaataayungwa im-uy momoymuy, tsaatsakwmuy qa haqawa amun-gaqw sulawtiqw. Naamahin pi yaw as puma soo-soyam okiwhintotiqw, angwu yaw ima taataqtsa so'a.

Pu' yaw it ka'naskatsinat nööma'atniqw pu' yumat pay qa hin mimuywatuy amun kyaananvotya. Put wuutit koongya'at pi pay yaw pumuy tsöngösiwuy aqw ökinaniqe it paas yan navoti'yta-qe pam yaw oovi pumuy amungem paas tunös-maskyata. Niiqe pumuy yaw tuu'oyiyamuy pay sutsep ang qaa'ö oyingwuniqw, put yaw puma naatim angqw noovalawqw, pay yaw puma oovi a'ni noonova. Noq pay pi yaw puma qa sutsep

these days, people visited one another less and less, being too occupied in their search for food, others were not aware that this family was not starving. The kachina, of course, had provided only enough for the three of them, and they did not tell anyone that they still had food.

An old woman living next door, however, was puzzled that they never went out in search of something to eat as did everybody else. Thus one night, after parents and daughter had gone to sleep, this same woman began piercing the wall to make a passage into her neighbors' house. She did not accomplish this task that first night, however. She continued for about three more nights before she broke through the wall. Lo and behold, as she entered she found herself in a room with large quantities of stored food still remaining. There was plenty of corn arranged in stacks. When she discovered this she nearly swooned. She headed back into her house only to return with a sifter basket. Into it she heaped some of the corn and then hid it in her own house. This discovery, though, she kept to herself. For surely, if people found out about this, they would be flocking there for the same purpose. She alone would continue this practice secretly and thereby somehow survive. The old woman's husband had been involved in carrying out the evil plan against the Ka'nas kachina. The young wife of the latter was aware of this.

paapu naanaapa kiikinumtinumya pisoq tunöshep-numyangwuniiqe yaw oovi qa nanvotya pumawat qa hin tsöngso'iwtaqw. Noq pay yaw pam piw pas pumuy amumisa aptsiwtaqat amungem na'sastat-niqw pay yaw puma qa hakiy aawintota puma naat nöösiwqa'yyungqey.

Noq pu' yaw kur i' hak so'wuuti pumuy amuqle' nalki'ytaqa yaw pumuy amumi pan wuuwa pas yaw puma qa hisat mimuywatuy amun angqe' tunöshepnumyangwuniqw. Niiqe pu' yaw puma oovi hisat mihikqw tokvaqw, pu' yaw pam hak wuuti pangso pumuy kiiyamuy tuupelva ang aw porokinta. Nit pay yaw pam qa ep pay pangsowat porokna. Pay yaw aapiy pas paayishaqam pam pantsakt pu' yaw aw porokna. Noq antsa yaw pam aw pakiqw, pay yaw naat pumuy nöösiwqa'am pep wuuhaq pee'iwta. Naat yaw pumuy tuu'oyi-yamuy ang qaa'ö'am niitiwta. Pas pi yaw pam yan yorikqe yaw qa yan unangwti. Noq pu' yaw pam paasat ahoyniiqe pu' yaw pam pangqw it tutsayat yawkyangw pu' yaw piw ahoy awi'. Paasat pu' yaw pam pangqw put peehut qaa'öt intat pu' yaw put kiy ep haqami tupkya. Nit pay yaw pam qa hakiy piw it aa'awna. Son pi yaw sinom put nanapte' qa pay pangso put oovi sasqayamantani. Pay yaw pam naala nana'uyve pangso pantsakye' pay yaw son hin qa qatuni. Noq put yaw koongya-'at nuutum put ka'naskatsinat engem pan put qa lo-mahintaqat pasiwna. Noq pay yaw put katsinat nööma'at it yantaqat navoti'yta.

The old woman had pilfered corn about seven times when the family found out. Since they did not enter the storage room too frequently, they were at first quite unaware of what was going on. Once, however, when the wife of the Ka'nas kachina was about to cook a meal and entered the place to fetch some corn, she noticed that their corn stack had dwindled considerably. Rummaging about she discovered the hole in the wall and immediately informed her parents.

So that night they lay in wait for the thief. Sure enough, it was not very long before they heard the old woman removing their corn. She was still busy doing this when the bride's father rushed upon her and seized her by the wrist. "Hey, what's the big idea of stealing here?" the father demanded. "You know very well that this corn doesn't belong to you and yet you're pilfering it. You really shouldn't be doing this. After all, your husband was one of those who brought this famine on everyone; he helped hatch the evil plot against my son-in-law. So put the corn back and leave!" he scolded the woman at length, who now had no alternative but to depart empty-handed. For some reason she never revealed to anyone that her neighbors still had corn.

Noq pay yaw aapiy pam so'wuuti tsange'sikishaqam pantiqw pu' yaw puma naanatim nanapta. Noq pay pi yaw puma naanatim qa pas sutsep pangso yungtaqe, pay yaw oovi as mootiniqw qa nanapta. Noq pu' yaw pam ka'naskatsinat nööma'at piw noovataniqe pangsoq put qaa'öt ooviniikyangw, paasat pu' yaw pam navota yaw kur pumuy tuu'oyi'am angqw a'ni söopukqw. Niiqe pu' yaw pam angqe pooti'ynumkyangw pu' yaw put pangso porokput tuwa. Niiqe pu' yaw pam oovi pumuy yumuy yan aa'awna.

Noq pu' yaw ep mihikqw puma oovi pep put mokmani'yyungwa. Noq antsa pay yaw puma naat qa wuuyavo pep panyungqw pay yaw pam so'wuuti piw pangqaqw pumuy qaa'öyamuy langamintaqw yaw puma nanapta. Naat yaw pam oovi pep pantsakqw, pu' yaw pam taaqa put aw nakwsuqe pu' yaw put matpikyaqe sung'a. "Soo, ya um hintiqw piw put u'uyingway?" yaw put wuutit na'at put aw kita. "Suyan pi i' qa uumuniqw piw um it u'uyingwaa. Son pi um as pantsaknikyangw. Pi uukongya umuy tsöngso'iwtaniqat naawaknaqe oovi nuutum it imö'önangwuy engem panhaqam qa lomavasiwna. Pay um oovi put ahoy pew oyat pay nawus qa hiita hinkyangwniy," pam yaw pay put pas wuuhaq hiita aw lavaytiqw, pu' yaw pam nawus pay pangqw qa hiita hinkyangw ahoy. Nit pay yaw pam piw hintiqw qa hakiy aa'awna puma naat pep qaa'ö'yyungqw.

Before long there came a time when there was no longer anything edible to be found. Occasionally, when someone did come upon a morsel of food and another would catch him in the act, he would walk up to him and grab it from him. And if he failed to snatch the food from him, they would fight over it like dogs. In this way people made enemies of each other.

Meanwhile, several years had gone by since the outbreak of this catastrophic famine in the land of the Hopi. Thus had the Ka'nas kachina wreaked his revenge on the Hopis and made them suffer. Once, however, when he mulled the matter over again, he commiserated with the Hopi. Evidently his anger had abated, and so he related his feelings to his relatives. "Well, maybe it's about time we ended their suffering. Of course, they brought destruction on themselves. But then not really everyone had a hand in this crime against me. Yet I affected each and every one of them when I carried out my plans. In any case, all of those who did me wrong have now perished. Moreover," he continued, "only the Hopis know how to make prayer feathers. To those prayer feathers we owe what we accomplish here. So maybe we should put an end to their misery, for only by using their prayer feathers can we attain our spiritual goals. I think we should help them again. If, however, they go back to their bad ways, we will abandon them completely.

Noq hiisavoniqw pay yaw paasat pas qa himu haqam. Pu' yaw ephaqam himuwa hiita tuwaqw pu' mi'wa yaw ayangqw put tuwaaqa yaw awnen pu' put nawkingwu. Pu' ephaqam pay yaw qa nawkiqw pu' yaw puma pep put hiita pookotuy an oovi naayawvangwu. Yan pay yaw puma piw naatuwqalalwa.

Noq pu' yaw antsa yepeq hopiikiveq i' yaniwtikyangw pu' yaw pay paasat aapiy pas hiisakishaqam yaasangwva. Yan pu' yaw i' ka'naskatsina pumuy hopiituy amumi naa'oyqe yaw pumuy panhaqam okiwsana. Nit pu' pay yaw pam piw ahoy ang wuuwaqe pay yaw piw pumuy ookwatuwa. Pay yaw kur pam ka'naskatsina ahoy pöhikqe pu' yaw pam yan sinomuy aa'awna, "Ta'ay, pay kya itam yaasavo yep pumuy okiwsaasanyaniy," yaw pam kita. "Pay pi as puma naap qa'antipuy ep it aqw naa'ökinayay. Pu' pay as pi piw qa pas soosoyam inumi nukpantotiqw, pay nu' pas soosokmuy amungem antsa pan qa lolmat pasiwnakyangw aw antsanay. Noq pay ima pas inumi nukpantotiqam pu' soosoyam so'ay," yaw pam kitat pu' yaw pam piw aapiyta, "Pu' pay piw puma hopiitsa it hiita paahot tuwi'yyungwa. Pu' itam pumuy paahoyamuy akw piw tuwat yep mongvasya. Noq oovi pay kya itam son pas peqwhaqami pumuy okiwsaasanyani. Taq pi itam pumuy paahoyamuysa akw yep enang itaatuwiy hintsakwisqe pay oovi itam ahoy amumi unangwtatveni. Pu' kur ason hisat piwyaniqw, paasat hapi pay itam paapu

These are the things that went through my mind and for this reason I'm asking your permission to bring the drought to an end," he pleaded with the leading elders.

The elders considered the plea. Finally the oldest leader who sided with the Ka'nas youth answered, "Indeed, they've suffered a long time. Maybe they've realized the full extent of the crime they committed against you. Perhaps they will never do anything like it again. At least, let's give them another chance. Let's show some pity and go to them to wipe away their tears. They may then reflect on what they have done and never again cause any of us such grief."

All the elders agreed. "Yes, it's really been a long, long time. They must know what they did. Maybe they've mended their ways. So let's go and end their suffering."

Since none of the elders raised any objections, they proceeded to prepare for their journey to Musangnuvi. Above all, they gathered the various crops they intended to take along as gifts. Since they were kachinas, they always had crops on hand. Next those willing to accompany the Ka'nas kachina began to come forward. When they were

qa ahoy amumi unangwtatveni. Yanhaqam nu' wuuwantaqe oovi nu' yep umumi maqaptsilawuy," yaw pam katsina pumuy wuuwukmuy, mong'iw-yungqamuy amumi kita.

Pu' yaw puma ang wuuwayaqw pu' yaw ha-qawa pangqawu, "Is ohiy," yaw kita, "pay hapi antsa pas qa atsat wuuyavoti. Wuuyavo puma okiwhinyungway. Noq sen pi antsa nanapta ung yanhaqam okiwsasnaqe'ey. Pay kya antsa paapu qa piw hisatyaniniqw oovi pay itam kur ngas'ew piw tuwantotani. Antsa itam pumuy ookwatutwe', amumiqye', pumuy oknayani. Noq pu' sen puma it ang ahoy wuuwaye' pay paapu qa hisat yephaqam itamuy haqawat yan okiwsasnaniy," yaw pam suswuyoqa mongwi'am kitaaqe pay yaw put tiyot angvati.

Paasat pu' yaw pay puma soosoyam put aw suntiqe yaw oovi pangqaqwa, "Owiy," yaw kitota, "pay pi antsa wuuyavoti. Pay pi sen antsa pu' nanaptaqw, pay pi itam oovi antsa aqw oknawisniy," yaw puma kitota.

Yan yaw puma it aw suntiqe pu' yaw puma oovi paasat pangsoq musangnumiqyaniqe yaw oovi yuuyahiwta. Pu' yaw puma oovi it hiihiita natwanit na'mangwu'ywisniqey put yaw puma oovi tsovalanvaya. Puma hapi yaw pay katsinam-niiqe oovi pay yaw sutsep puuvut hiita aniwni'y-yungwa, maskya'yyungwa. Pu' yaw puma put ka'naskatsinat amumyaniqam yaw naa'o'ya. Hisat-niqw pu' yaw puma soosoyam yuuyaaqe pu' yaw

all prepared and dressed, they congregated at a certain site. It was evident that a host of kachinas was ready to leave for Musangnuvi. So many presents were amassed that they could not carry them all by themselves. Therefore the Hehey'a would go along to haul some of the extra loads. When they had placed everything on their backs, the kachinas set off toward Musangnuvi. The procession stretched out in a long line. As they all kept uttering their individual cries, a tremendous noise filled the air.

The very moment the kachinas were approaching from the plain below, a young child happened to be rummaging about along the rim of the mesa. All of a sudden he heard noises. But because it had been such a long time since any kachina had visited the village, the youngster was not familiar with them. Every so often a shout rang out, yet he did not know what to make of the sound. He surmised that they might belong to some birds. There were other children present who likewise heard the calls, but they were also unfamiliar with kachinas. As they looked from the mesa's edge, they spotted some beings making their way toward them from the west, shrieking out their peculiar calls. Now it dawned on them what those beings were, even though no kachinas had ever performed during their lives. Their grandparents and parents had frequently told them about the kachina gods, so they had learned about them from listening to stories.

puma oovi haqam suvotsovaltiqw pas yaw kur puma pangso musangnumi kyaysiwni. Pu' hapi yaw kur puma it na'mangwuy a'ni hintotiqe yaw oovi puma put kur hin soosok naap hinwisniniqw, pu' yaw oovi ima hehey'am yaw pumuy amungem peehut iikiwwisni. Paasat pu' yaw puma oovi put soosok iikwiltotaqw, pu' yaw puma paasat pangqw nankwusaqe pavan yaw puma aqwhaqami wupawisiwta. Pu' yaw puma piw töötökiy qa pewewwisqw pavan yaw hin töötöqa.

Noq pu' yaw i' hak tsayhoya suupaasatniqwhaqam puma katsinam pangqw atkyangaqw ökiwisqw, yaw pam tumkyaqe hintsaknumkyangw piw yaw pam hiita navota. Noq pay pi yaw wuuyavo qa himu katsina pep hintsakqw, pam yaw oovi pumuy qa tuwi'ytaqe yaw oovi haqam himu töqtingwuniqw, pam yaw kur hin put aw wuuwa. Pay sen pi yaw tsiro'ewayniiqat yan yaw pam wuuwa. Noq pay yaw piw peetu tsaatsayom put amumyaqe puma yaw tuwat nanaptakyangw pay yaw pumawat piw pumuy qa tuwi'yyungwa. Pu' yaw puma pangsoq taayungqw piw yaw pangqw taavangqw hiituya, niikyangw yaw panhaqam töötöqtiwisa. Noq pay yaw puma pumuy maamatsya, naamahin as puma katsinmuy qa tuwi'ykyaakyangw. Pay yaw naamahin pumuy tsaatsakwmuy qatsiyamuy ep qa hisat himu katsina hintsakqw, pay yaw puma pumuy maamatsya. Pay yaw pumuy somat, kwamat, yumat, namat pumuy amumi imuy katsinmuy yu'a'atotangwuniqw, pan yaw puma pumuy tuwi'yyungwa.

When these children realized what they were seeing they notified all the villagers in Musangnuvi. The village leader at once set out to meet them. Reaching the procession, he directed it toward the village, and when he had brought the long line up to the mesa top, he accompanied it into the plaza.

The Hehey'a, who had come along with the kachinas, merely unloaded the gifts and immediately journeyed back home. But prior to their departure the village leader presented each of them with half a handful of sacred cornmeal. The Ka'nas kachinas were most handsome. How beautiful they were to behold. Their masked faces were divided into two fields with a black line running down from the right side of the temple to the left just above the snout. This line was stippled with broken white stripes. The right half of the face was yellow, the left side red. The eyes were of the rectangular shape typical of many kachinas, while the

Noq pu' yaw ima tsaatsayom pumuy pan yoyrikyaqe pu' yaw puma soosokmuy musangnuvituy aa'awnayaqw, pu' yaw i' kikmongwi pumuy amuupewto. Niiqe pu' yaw pam pumuy amumi pituuqe pu' yaw pam pangqw pumuy musangnumi tsamkyangw, pu' yaw pam pumuy pangso kiimi yayvanat pu' yaw pumuy kiisonmi tangata.

Noq pu' yaw ima hehey'am pumuy katsinmuy amumumyaqam pay yaw panis pep pumuy na'mangwuyamuy o'yat pu' yaw pay paasat ahoy ninma. Niikyangw yaw pam kikmongwi pumuy hoomat amumi mooti oyaqw puu'. Pavan yaw puma katsinam sushiitu; pas yaw puma lomahinyungwa. Noq yaw puma natukvukuwyungwa. Niiqe yaw oovi pumuy yangqw putngaqwwat atkyamiq motsovuyamuy atsva qömvit akw tuuwuhiwkyangw yaw ang qöötsat akw longna'yta. Noq pu' yaw pumuy taywa'am putkyaqewat si-

Since the people had not tasted food such as this for a long, long time and were ravenously hungry, they fell to gobbling it down heartily. So great was the excitement that the plaza resounded with a cacophony of munching and lip-smacking. The noise resembled the clacking sounds of the deer hoofs striking the tortoise shells that the kachinas wore just below their knees. The very instant someone received any foodstuff he started to devour it.

Now the Ka'nas kachina responsible for leading the other kachinas there bade the people of Musangnuvi not to consume all the food. "Wait!" he directed them, "do not eat everything up we brought you. Save a few ears of baked corn, and deposit at least one into every place where you usually stack your corn."

Heeding his instructions the people broke off their eating and no longer gulped down the entire handout. Some actually began putting ears aside. For with such enormous quantities were they blessed that it would have been impossible to devour them all anyway. Everyone spoke to his neighbor of his joy at the visit of the kachinas and of how all the Hopi people owed this feast to them.

When the kachinas showed signs of returning home, the leader as well as all the villagers pleaded with them to remain. "Don't leave," they urged them. "Stay here with us forever. We so much appreciate the knowledge and skill you use to grow

Noq yaw puma hisat puuvut hiita angqw qa yukuyaqe yaw oovi tsöngmokiwyungqe yaw pisoq naanaqle' put sowawatota. Pas pi yaw puma hin unangwa'ykyaakyangwyaqe yaw oovi naanaqle' mo'ay taptoynayaqw, pavan yaw pep kiisonve hin töötöqa. Pas pay yaw imuy katsinmuy yöngösona-'am pep töötöqa. Pas pi yaw himuwa panis hiita makiwt pay yaw paasat put sowangwu.

Noq pu' yaw pam katsina mimuywatuy pangso tsamqa yaw pumuy musangnuvituy meewaqe yaw amumi pangqawu, "Haakiy," yaw kita, "pay itam it hiita umungem kivayaqw, pay uma put qa pas soosok soswani. Pay uma suskomuyhaqam tuupevut angqw peetote', uma put haqe' umuutuu'oyiy ang ngas'ew suskomuy o'yani," yaw yanhaqam pam katsina pumuy amumi tutapta.

Pu' yaw oovi puma hopiit put tutavoyatyaqe yaw oovi paasat pay hihin peveltotiqe pay yaw oovi qa soosok soswa. Pay yaw antsa himuwa hiita angqw warantangwu. Pay pi yaw puma piw put hiihiita niitiyaqe yaw son put as soosok ep pay soswani. Pu' yaw puma pumuy amutsviy piw a'ni nöönösaqe yaw yanhaqam naa'a'awnayaqe yaw oovi halaytoti puma ökiqw.

Noq pu' yaw puma angqw ninmaniniqw, pu' yaw ima momngwitniqw pu' soosoyam hopiit pep ki'yyungqam yaw pangqaqwa, "Pay uma qa ninmaniy," yaw amumi kitota. "Pay uma sutsep yep itamum yesni. Tsangaw uma it hiita kur a'ni tuwi'yyungqe itamuy yep nopnayaqw, oovi itam

all the crops you have fed us with. We feel quite revived now," said the village leader as spokesman for the entire group.

But the kachinas declined. "No," they said, "we can't live here among you, for we are not mortals like you. We are kachinas who must live in our own way. So to remain here is out of the question. We must return to the place we have always inhabited," they replied. The people felt so unhappy and disappointed that some of them wept.

During their progression homeward the kachinas stopped at the mesa promontory west of Musangnuvi where the father of the Ka'nas youth's wife had erected the shrine. They opened it up and informed the village leader, "Here is our home. We will therefore enter this shrine and return underground. And since this home belongs to us, it shall henceforth be known as "Ka'naskatsinki." This is the reason that, west of Musangnuvi at a little promontory, a shrine where paaho are deposited is present today.

kur pu'haqam itakw angqw ahoytotiniy," yaw kita pumuy kikmongwi'am. Pam pi yaw pumuy amungem yu'a'ata.

Noq pu' yaw katsinam pay qa naanakwhaqe yaw, "Qa'ey," kitota. "Pay itam kya so'on yep umumum yesni. Itam qa umun hopiituy. Itam katsinamniiqe pay naap tuwat yesqe itam son oovi yephaqam umumum yanyungwni. Pay itam pi tuwat haqam ki'yyungqe pay itam sonqa pangso ahoy ninmaniy," yanhaqam yaw puma pumuy amumi lavaytoti. Noq pay yaw oovi ima sinom as qa haalaytotiqw oovi yaw antsa ima peetu ang tsaykita.

Noq pu' yaw oovi puma angqwyanikyangw pu' yaw puma pangsoq musangnuviy teevenge tuyqamiqyaqe pu' yaw puma pepeq it ka'naskatsinat nöömayat na'at put katsinat engem tuskyataqw, pangso yaw puma ökiiqe pu' yaw pangsoq hötaya. Hötayaqe pu' yaw pangqaqwa put kikmongwit awi', "Yep hapi itam ki'yyungway," yaw kitota. "Itam hapi oovi peqw yungye' itam hapi pay yangqe aatöqe ninmani. Noq i' hapi itaakiniqw oovi yaapiy hapi i' pu' ka'naskatsinki yan maatsiwniy," yanhaqam yaw puma put mongwit aa'awnaya. Noq oovi pangsoq musangnuviy taavangqöymiq tuyqahoyaniqw pepeq pam pahoki naat panta.

These were the events that took place in Musangnuvi, and then the kachinas returned home. From that day on the Hopis once again began to fashion the various prayer feathers and prayer sticks that they deposited at the Ka'nas shrine when they prayed. Thenceforth the life of the Hopi eased somewhat. The rains came again, enabling them to grow crops and to eat well. It was much later, however, that life returned to its former prosperity, and the people were able to carry on their existence as they had in the old days. And here the story ends.

Yanhaqam kya pi puma hiniwtapnayat pu' pangqaqw ninma. Paapiy pu' yaw ima hopiit piw yaw ahoy it hiihiita paahot hintsaktivakyangw, pu' piw pangso ka'naskatsinkimi naawakinwiskyangw, pu' pangso put pahotmalay oo'oyaya. Paapiy pu' yaw imuy hopiituy qatsi'am piw ahoy angqwti. Niiqe pu' yaw puma paapiy piw yoknayangwu. Paapiw pu' yaw puma piw hiita a'aniwnayaqe pu' piw ahoy noonoptivaya. Haqaapiy pu' yaw i' qatsi piw pavan naatuwa. Noq paapiy pu' yaw puma piw antsa yeese. Pay yuk pölö.

103

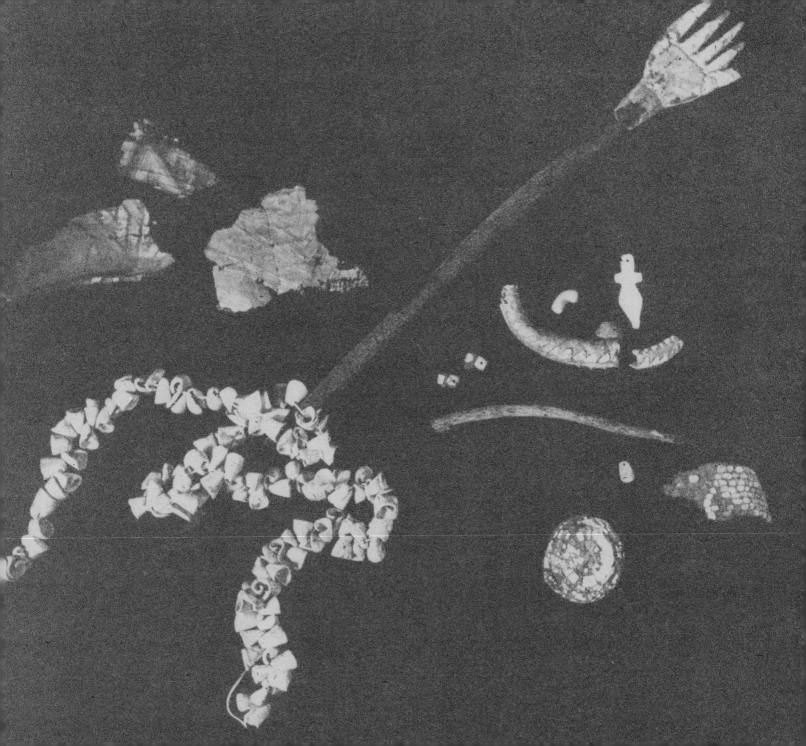

# HISATSINOM
## The Ancient People of Sunset Crater

Peter J. Pilles, Jr.

T HROUGH YEARS OF RESEARCH, archaeologists have identified a number of different prehistoric groups that once inhabited Arizona. In southern Arizona, the Hohokam, a Pima word for "all used up," were the masters of the desert. Over the centuries, they developed an elaborate irrigation system that allowed them to successfully cultivate the hot deserts of the Gila and Salt River valleys. In the high deserts of northern Arizona lived the prehistoric Pueblo people. Early day archaeologists were directed to their cliff dwellings, hidden in the recesses of the deep canyons of the San Juan River, by the Navajo, who called the former inhabitants Anasazi, "enemy forefathers." The Anasazi developed techniques for growing their crops in sand dunes to make use of the moisture-retaining qualities of the sand. Between these northern and southern groups, occupying the forested belt along the Mogollon Rim, were the Mogollon. These people developed into a number of regionally distinct groups. One of these was centered around the San Francisco

Peaks and is called the Sinagua, after the name given to the Peaks by early Spanish explorers, the Sierra Sinagua, "Mountains Without Water." It is this particular Mogollon group that we will examine in greater detail in this chapter.

## THE SINAGUA

The Hopi do not recognize the different names archaeologists have given to prehistoric groups, but call them all *hisatsinom,* "ancient people." According to their traditions, after their emergence from the underworld, individual clans moved slowly across the Southwest and beyond, settling for a period of time in various places and then moving on. Eventually, the clans came together, one at a time, at the Hopi Mesas, where they were destined to meet. Hopi traditions relate the Bear, Bear Strap, Water, Snow, Bluebird, and Sun clans to the Flagstaff area and the numerous ruins around the base of the San Francisco Peaks. Early archaeological work tried, with limited success, to relate Hopi clans to specific prehistoric groups. While this continues to be a topic of current archaeological research, most archaeologists agree that the Sinagua were one of the groups that eventually came together to form the Hopi culture.

This history of the Sinagua stretches from about A.D. 600 to 1400 and focuses on the area to the north and east of the San Francisco Peaks, an area of about 3,100 square miles (8,000 km²). There is much debate in the archaeological literature concerning the relation of the Sinagua to other prehistoric groups and the extent to which they were influenced by them. Central to all such discussions has been the impact of the Sunset Crater eruption. This importance is reflected in our classification of the Sinagua. Their history is broadly separated into two major periods, marked by the occurrence of this notable event in about A.D. 1064.

In the past, most literature has treated the Flagstaff area as a cultural backwater, and the Sinagua as an impoverished group "living in miserable pit houses." Traditionally, they have been viewed as incapable of developing new industries or progressing culturally on their own. Migrations of different people to the Flagstaff area are usually viewed as the mechanism by which change occurred in Sinagua society.

Recently, however, archaeologists have begun to reexamine traditional theories and are realizing the Sinagua were as viable and creative a culture as any in the Southwest. Local cultural developments stimulated by trade and contact with other groups, rather than migrations of people, is now seen as the important factor in Sinagua cultural change.

## THE PREERUPTIVE SINAGUA

The earliest appearance of the Sinagua cultural tradition is about A.D. 600, when people expressing a general Mogollon cultural background moved into the Flagstaff area. At this time, occupation was concentrated in transitional areas between ponderosa pine and juniper woodland zones. Large open areas containing deep deposits of alluvium were near these settlements. While soils over most of the Flagstaff area were unsuited for productive crop raising, these alluvial expanses, locally known as parks, were quite fertile and were the best farmlands to be found in the entire region. By settling in such locations, the Sinagua were able to take advantage not only of the best farmlands, but also of the natural environmental resources that could be found in both the ponderosa and woodland zones.

Several sizes of settlements were prevalent, ranging from large villages of ten or more pit houses to small hamlets of one to three houses. Contrary to popular ideas that social organization at this time was limited to extended family units consisting of two to three generations, large subterranean structures called community rooms, about 25 feet (8 m) in diameter, appear to be Sinagua versions of the Anasazi Great Kiva, and may indicate villages that coordinated or directed the activities of a number of settlements.

Pottery from the Hohokam to the south and the Anasazi to the north indicates that the Sinagua were participating in widespread cultural interaction from their earliest beginnings, in contrast to the long-held idea that they were a fairly isolated population.

By about A.D. 900, most of the population appears to have shifted to the lower flanks of the San Francisco Peaks, except for the Anderson Mesa area, where most of the earlier communities remained in place. This shift occurred about the same time that the climate changed to drier conditions and suggests that the Sinagua moved to areas where water was more readily available. Perhaps in response to this period of drier conditions, we see evidence of the Sinagua manipulating the environment to better control the distribution and storage of water. Check dams can be found along washes, and irrigation ditches were built to divert water from some of the major streams.

Although the major settlements prospered close to the large alluvial parks, smaller pit house clusters and masonry rooms appear farther up the slopes of the Peaks. Some of these, particularly the masonry rooms, were probably used as extensions of the main villages to facilitate farming activities in a variety of different locations. The major fields were likely situated in the parks themselves, where ground moisture and summer rains would have provided the main water source. Other farm plots would have been located on the edges of the parks, where numerous washes entered, while still others would have been scattered behind check dams in the washes farther upslope. Perhaps these different farming situations reflect different ownership or control of farm lands. It is also possible that different kinds of food plants were grown in these different farming locales. Corn and beans may have been grown in the large clan fields, while edible wild plants may have been encouraged to grow in the smaller plots along the washes.

Continued development of social integration, social hierarchies, and religious institutions is also suggested by the size, structure, and location of certain villages. The largest sites are found within a half-mile or so of the parks, while smaller sites occur at farther distances. It has been suggested that settlements along the flanks of the Peaks between major drainages may have been individual communities. Some of the larger villages within these contain either a large community room or, in a few instances, a ball court. Ball courts are usually thought of as being introduced into the Sinagua region by Hohokam immigrants, following the initial Sunset Crater eruption about A.D. 1064; however, more recent analysis suggests they predate this time.

One characteristic common to people around the world is a special reverence for high places, especially high mountains. Such places are often considered to have spiritual power or to be the abodes of gods or other supernatural deities revered by the people. One archaeological site has been found that might suggest the Peaks had religious significance to the Sinagua at this early date, an important bit of evidence relative to Sinagua-Hopi relationships. This site consists of a large community room framed by two rock piles resembling Hopi shrines. Nearby is a single pit house. Such a configuration might be interpreted as a ceremonial center with a resident caretaker-priest or other important person who lived in the pit house. Excavation would be necessary to test this assumption, but it is important to note that no other site of this sort has been found in the Flagstaff area.

## THE SUNSET CRATER ERUPTION(S)

The Preeruptive Period ends in A.D. 1064 with the first Sunset Crater eruption. Just what effects the eruption had on the area is still debated, but some idea of its impact can be obtained from studies of other volcanic eruptions in recorded history, such as that of Mt. Vesuvius on Pompeii, Mt. Thera on Crete, Krakatoa in Southeast Asia, Parícutin in Mexico, and, most recently, Mt. St. Helens and Mauna Loa here in the United States.

In the early 1930s, it became evident to archaeologists working in the Flagstaff area that people lived in the region when the eruptions forming Sunset Crater occurred. Dating the eruption and determining its impacts on the local population became a major project for archaeologists. It was finally decided that there were two separate eruptions, one in 1064 and another between 1066 and 1067. However, recent work by Eugene M. Shoemaker and Duane E. Champion, of the U.S. Geological Survey and California Institute of Technology, has revised our knowledge of this event. Rather than one or two eruptions, their work indicates Sunset Crater had a long history of eruptions, spanning the period 1064–1250.

In the years preceding the initial eruption, several hundred people, living in about 50 pit-house villages, occupied the area around Bonito Park. A half-mile (1 km) to the east, at the foot of O'Leary Peak, was another alluvial park, also surrounded by scattered clusters of houses. The villages were small and consisted of families who probably lived in two pit houses—a deep one in the winter, where the natural insulation of the ground would help retain the heat from the firepit, and a shallow one, which consisted of a more open brush superstructure supported by an outline of rocks around the edge of the pit house. In the spring and summer, most of their time was devoted to planting and tending their fields in the fertile parks. However, in the autumn of 1064, after their crops had been harvested and stored away, the lives of these sedentary Sinagua farmers were permanently altered by the Sunset Crater eruption.

Rather than the surprised and feverish evacuation of their homes as the volcano burst forth behind them, the Sinagua undoubtedly had warnings of the impending doom, such as earth tremors and smoke emerging from the ground. Such highly unusual events may have prompted the people living in the immediate vicinity to pack up and move. Some archaeologists believe they may have had time to dismantle their pit houses and take the logs with them to use in building new homes.

In the aftermath of the initial eruptions, all vegetation within a two-mile (3.2 km) radius of the cone was probably completely destroyed by ash, forest fires, poisonous gases, and highly acidic rains. Although not completely destroyed, other plants up to 15 miles (25 km) away were probably affected as well, and tree growth in the region was restricted for many years after the 1064 eruption. Outside the central zone of devastation, most vegetation probably grew back within a few years.

The cinder fall and lava flows obliterated several areas that had been farmed by the Sinagua in earlier times. The park that had been at the base of O'Leary Peak, and probably numerous villages as well, were completely covered by the Bonito lava flow. Water supplies were probably affected as the ash clogged washes, filled intermittent ponds, and altered surface runoff patterns. While some springs may have been covered over by the cinder fall, new springs may have been developed at the edges of the lava flow from snowmelt and rainfall trickling along the impermeable surface of the lava flow. The destruction of ground cover resulted in increased erosion and arroyo cutting. With nothing to slow it down, water runoff would have raced down washes and gullies, carrying vast amounts of cinders, rocks, boulders, and logs with it, eventually depositing this debris along the sides and mouths of drainages.

An event of this magnitude would certainly have had a profound psychological effect upon the Sinagua and would probably have resulted in the development of supernatural explanations for and associations with the eruption. For many years it seemed curious to archaeologists that the Hopi had no legends that could be attributed to the eruption. That situation has now been changed with the vivid recounting of the eruption in the Ka'naskatsina legend. This account portrays quite effectively how the eruption may have been experienced by the prehistoric Sinagua.

## THE POSTERUPTIVE SINAGUA

It has traditionally been believed that the cinder cover acted as a mulch that prevented evaporation of water from the ground, thus promoting improved crop growing conditions. Because of this, thousands of acres of farmlands became available in areas that could not previously be farmed because of a lack of moisture. Supposedly, news of this spread far and wide throughout the Southwest, causing a prehistoric "land rush" to the Flagstaff area by people of diverse cultural origins. This caused an increase in population as people spread into the ashfall zone, and for a number of years, Flagstaff became a cosmopolitan crossroad of cultures.

From the south, it has been suggested that over 1,000 Hohokam came up the Rim, bringing their red-on-buff pottery, cremation burial, shell jewelry, and ball court concepts with them. From the north, the Anasazi came down, teaching the Sinagua how to build masonry pueblos and bury their dead in a flexed position. On the northwest edge of the Sinagua region, the Cohonina moved into the cinder zone, also introducing the use of masonry architecture and a projectile point form. Other Mogollon relations from the southeast brought new pottery, burial, and pit-house styles into the area. Farther to the east, in central New Mexico, Chaco Anasazi moved west to Flagstaff as their complex culture began to wane, bringing the organizational concept of the Great Kiva with them. Large quantities of pottery from the Prescott area have served as evidence of immigrants from central Arizona joining the hypothesized flood of people.

Such close proximity resulted in dramatic cultural change, which, so it has been thought, altered the Sinagua culture into a totally new and different form. More recent investigations, however, suggest this may not have been the case and that interpretations other than new farmlands and migrations of cultures better explain developments after A.D. 1064 in the Flagstaff region.

When closely examined, the evidence for migrants in the Sinagua area is limited to a few isolated traits, not complete cultural assemblages. Rather than wholesale migrations, it seems more likely that many items and characteristics can be better explained by examining the trade relationships and the development of more complex social organizations within the Sinagua. In addition, archaeologists in the past have tended to overemphasize the amount of change in the Sinagua, relative to the change seen in other prehistoric groups at this time. The 1064 time period is one of rapid and dramatic change over the entire Southwest and is not limited to just the Sinagua region; the change we see in the Sinagua culture after this time is no greater than the degree of change seen elsewhere.

The importance of cinder mulch in forming new, fertile farmlands that influenced the distribution of population has been overemphasized. Some references have been made to the increased fertility of the soil that results from volcanic eruptions. However, in dry climates, it usually takes hundreds or even thousands of years before cinders have weathered to the point where they promote soil fertility. A layer of cinders does act as a mulch to conserve moisture to promote plant growth. Experiments have shown the effectiveness of a light cover of ash to promote corn growth, and even today, ponderosa pine trees grow 1,000 feet (300 m) lower in elevation in the cinder zone than in their normal range. Yet many of these trees are very short, compared with normal ponderosa pine, and have numerous large, crooked and bent branches or multiple trunks—all indications of trees growing under less than favorable conditions.

Reasons other than cinder mulch better explain posteruptive farming practices and population dynamics. The period following the 1064 eruption was one of dramatically increased precipitation over the entire Southwest, not only in the Flagstaff region. Thus, the mulching effects of the cinders were not required to allow the Sinagua to move to lower elevations to farm their crops, although this may have been a factor influencing the settlement of the Wupatki Basin and the Little Colorado River Valley—the driest, most arid portion of the Sinagua region. That the cinder zone was not as important as previously assumed can be seen by examining the distribution of sites in the post-1064 time period. Site densities outside the cinder fall zone are just as great as those inside the zone, indicating other factors than just cinders influenced the settlement of new areas.

It is now thought that the moister climate, rather than the cinder mulch, allowed the Sinagua to settle the pinyon-juniper woodland zone, which, only coincidentally, was partly covered by the Sunset Crater ashfall. In fact, the increased moisture may have prompted population movements by making the area along the base of the Peaks, which normally receives the most precipitation in the region, too wet for successful farming. Also, the fertility of the parklands, after 400 years of cultivation, may have been reduced to the point where crop yields were not as great as in previous times, fostering a move to more fertile areas.

Following the initial eruptions, there was a tentative, seasonal exploration of the pinyon-juniper zone as people investigated its potential for settlement and subsistence. They soon discovered the woodland zone was well suited for their needs and over the next 70 years almost the entire population of the Flagstaff region moved into the pinyon-juniper zone. In so doing, the Sinagua encountered different farming soil situations than had existed in the ponderosa zone. In the woodland zone, limestone bedrock outcrops close to the surface, and soils suitable for farming occur only in the bottoms of broad washes or in small pockets formed by the weathering of the limestone. Consequently, in order to obtain the necessary harvest size, individual Sinagua farmers probably grew crops in a number of soil pockets. Because soils in these pockets were shallow and not subject to annual recharge, they were probably quickly exhausted of nutrients, causing rapid turnover in their use. Chemical tests of soil inside prehistoric fields show that even today, 700 years after their use, they are still depleted of various nutrients.

As the posteruptive population moved into these new zones, both pit-house and pueblo villages became widespread throughout the area. Community centers are still indicated by their greater size and the presence of community rooms. At some of these sites, formalized cemeteries came into being, often marked by earthen mounds. In many cases, these cemeteries are divided into areas that show evidence of two different belief systems concerning burial of the dead—cremation and extended burials. Some have interpreted the cremations as the remains of Hohokam immigrants; however, studies of the cremations suggest they are different from those done in the Hohokam heartland. Except for the use of cremation, the cremation burial population appears identical to that of the more typical, extended, Sinagua burial population. In some places, flexed burials are also found, suggesting another religious concept was also present in the posteruptive Sinagua. Rather than interpreting these different burial styles as evidence for immigrants living in the Flagstaff area, many researchers now believe they reflect Sinagua adaptations of the religious systems of other cultural groups with whom they interacted.

In order to farm their scattered fields, the Sinagua constructed small, one- to three-room structures called field houses. These were used to store tools, process crops, obtain shelter from the sun, and for other seasonal activities required to grow and harvest crops.

Posteruptive pit houses become smaller, suggesting a change in the makeup of family groups living within the structures, and are most commonly lined with stone. Kivas resemble the masonry-lined houses but can be distinguished by having a raised bench across one end. Artifacts from these structures include clay or stone pipes reminiscent of those used by the Hopi in their prayers to bring clouds and rain.

Native tobacco, mixed with a variety of other plant parts, is smoked in the kivas while prayers are said. The smoke is blown through the pipe to emulate the creation of clouds, a ritual referred to as *oomawlawu*, or "cloud making," by the Hopi. The presence of kivas is important, since it is one factor suggesting that societies or clans existed by this time.

The period between A.D. 1130 and 1200 is known as the Elden Phase and is named after Elden Pueblo, or Pasiwvi as it is known to the Hopi, one of the major sites of the Flagstaff area. This can be called the Golden Age of the Sinagua, since it appears to represent the time of their largest population and greatest geographical extent. People lived across the entire region—from the flanks of the Peaks to the eastern edge of Anderson Mesa. While some sites, such as Elden Pueblo and Turkey Hill Pueblo, were located in the ponderosa zone, the majority of them were in the pinyon-juniper zone. This is also the period when cliff dwellings became numerous in the deep canyons, especially along San Francisco Wash and in the vicinity of what is now Walnut Canyon National Monument.

Evidence from site size, village plans, the spacing of villages over the landscape, different treatments of the dead, and unique artifact forms indicate the Sinagua had a complex social and organizational system. A hierarchy of villages can be demonstrated, implying different levels of importance and authority in their culture. At the top of the pyramid is a class of sites that can be recognized from certain formalized characteristics, including a hilltop location, a community room, courtyards, and ball courts. These are believed to be the major, or "chief," villages, where important religious, social, and political leaders lived. Examples of this class of sites include Winona Village, Ridge Ruin, Juniper Terrace, and Wupatki. Of these, Ridge Ruin is unique in being the only site in northern Arizona that has two ball courts.

Evidence of social stratification can best be seen in the burials from this period, particularly from what has been called the Magician's Burial from Ridge Ruin. This was the burial of a very important man who has been recognized as a member of the *motswimi*, or Warrior Society. It has also been suggested that he may have been a *qaleetaqa*, "a strong man," that is, a very important person in the Warrior Society.

Buried with him were a series of carved and painted wands, jewelry, basketry, pottery, and many other items indicative of his importance. The Magician's Burial is a very important find, since it demonstrates the existence of Hopi-like societies in the Sinagua culture by the thirteenth century. Furthermore, it has been suggested that some of the major Hopi societies originated in the Flagstaff area about this time. According to some, the Wuwtsim, Taw, Kwan, and Al societies came into being when the people were living at Pasiwvi, Elden Pueblo. Water from a nearby spring, Pasiwva, was used in performing ceremonies conducted by these societies. Pasiwva may correspond to Oak Spring, or Little Elden Spring, located on the slopes of Mt. Elden above Elden Pueblo.

High status burials have been found at other sites, such as Elden Pueblo, and have been accompanied by other items that may have been used as symbols of authority, such as carved or painted bone hairpins, staffs with elaborate end knobs, wands tipped with a conch shell, or unique ceramic vessels. High-status individuals are also portrayed in a leadership position in several rock art sites and have similar items depicted with them.

Infants were given a unique burial treatment in Sinagua society by being interred in pits below the floors of rooms, as has been found at Elden Pueblo. It has been suggested that this was done so that the soul of the child would be close to the mother, allowing it to be reborn to have another chance at life.

By 1200 there were drastic changes in the population distribution. Much of the pinyon-juniper region around Youngs Canyon and San Francisco Wash was abandoned as populations concentrated in the Anderson Mesa, Mt. Elden, and Wupatki areas. During this time, most of the immediate Flagstaff area was abandoned with only Elden Pueblo, Turkey Hill Pueblo, and Old Caves Pueblo remaining occupied. Some pueblos were built on top of mesas, cinder cones, or at the ends of spurs extending into deep canyons. Usually called forts, these pueblos are thought to indicate a period of friction and stress. However, it has been observed that imported pottery is as common at forts as at contemporaneous pueblos, which would not be expected in a time of strife when activities such as trade were curtailed or stopped. More recent interpretations of such structures discuss the possibility of their being storehouses for food and other commodities, or sites associated with astronomical observations.

By 1300 only Old Caves Pueblo was inhabited in the old Sinagua heartland. The remainder of the Sinagua people apparently moved to join the great pueblos on Anderson Mesa — Grapevine Pueblo, the Pollock Site, Kinnikinick Ruin, and Chavez Pass. It is in sites of this period, dating between 1300 and 1400, that the last of the Sinagua can be recognized, for we can now see them emerging as part of the Hopi. Continuity with past traditions can be seen in site types, pottery, and religious structures.

Chavez Pass, the largest of the Anderson Mesa pueblos, is now known as Nuvakwewtaqa — a Hopi word that literally means "One wearing a snow belt." This term is also used to refer to Anderson Mesa in general because snow along its north side appears as a long white line, or belt, when viewed from the Hopi Mesas. Nuvakwewtaqa continues the pattern of important regional trade centers being situated on a trade route, having courtyard-like areas, and a ball court. It seems that obsidian was a major trade item that was probably made into finished tools at Kinnikinick Ruin and distributed through Chavez Pass. Jeddito Black-on-yellow pottery from the Hopi Mesas was likely distributed to the pueblos in the Verde Valley through Chavez Pass as well. A copper bell has been recovered from Nuvakwewtaqa, indicating far-flung trade relationships that extended as far south as Mexico. Artifacts similar to those found with the Magician's Burial have been found at Chavez Pass, suggesting continuation of the *motswimi*, or Warrior Society.

Certain artifacts, pottery designs, and petroglyphs hint at the existence of the Kachina and Lakon societies at Nuvakwewtaqa. Petroglyphs of masked beings occur at various places in the vicinity of the ruins and may represent kachinas or another class of masked personages present at Hopi today. Other figures of Hopi legend and folklore, such as Pöqangwhoya, one of the Hopi twin brothers, and Kokopelli, the hump-backed flute player, have also been found portrayed in pottery from the site.

Archaeological evidence tends to support Hopi traditions that tell of the abandonment of Nuvakwewtaqa and suggest movement of the people to a group of pueblos located along the Little Colorado River near Winslow. These ten or so large pueblos are well known to the Hopi, and even today, religious pilgrimages are made to shrines at some of these sites. The main concentration of these pueblos consists of four ruins — Homol'ovi II, II, III, and IV — along a four-mile (6.5 km) stretch of the Little Colorado River. Hopi oral traditions suggest that drought and failure of the corn crop, or infestations of mosquitoes and sand fleas, forced the people to abandon the Little Colorado River Valley. Accordingly, Colton and Baxter claim that Shipaulovi, a village settled by some of the clans from Homol'ovi, translates "Place of the mosquitoes," however, linguistically this interpretation is not verifiable. Apache raids, or increased alkalinity of the soil from overirrigation, have also been cited as reasons for leaving the valley. From these ruins, some people probably moved east to the Zuni area and the Rio Grande Valley, while the majority moved through the Hopi Buttes area before arriving at the Hopi Mesas — the final destination in the great ancient clan migrations through the Southwest.

Continuity between the Hopi and their Sinagua ancestors can be seen in the importance of Nuvatukya'ovi, the San Francisco Peaks, to Hopi legend and religion. Many objects required for ceremonial activities, such as Douglas fir boughs, water, and soil, are still collected from the Peaks. Pilgrimages to various places and shrines are still made each year to ensure the harmonious operation of the universe.

Hopi connections with their ancestral homes in the Flagstaff area are evident in the routes various clans take in the early summer, when eagle fledglings are captured and taken back to the villages to be raised as family members. Feathers from the eagles are used to make pahos and for other religious purposes. Eagle-collecting places occur throughout the region inhabited in previous centuries by the Sinagua. One area is located near Sunset Crater. Others occur in Canyon Padre near Ridge Ruin, in Canyon Diablo near Nuvakwewtaqa and Meteor Crater, near Strawberry Crater, on O'Leary Peak, and on the San Francisco Peaks themselves. Routes to some of these areas follow prehistoric trade routes; petroglyphs, shrines, and archaeological sites along these routes further reinforce the Sinagua-Hopi continuum.

Although the prehistoric Sinagua abandoned their homeland centuries ago, the spiritual tie between the Hopi and their *hisatsinom* of this area has never been broken. It is still present in the pueblos, cliff dwellings, artifacts, and rock art sites of the Sinagua—the ancient Hopi ancestors of the Sunset Crater and San Francisco Peaks region.

# EROSION, MESAS, AND VOLCANOES INGREDIENTS OF A DYNAMIC LANDSCAPE

Larry Middleton and Richard Holm

THE SOUTHERN COLORADO PLATEAU is a region of unparalleled natural beauty and an area rich in geology and history. Whether one is viewing gently sloping monoclines, exhumed necks of extinct volcanoes, deeply incised river canyons, or broad, extensive tablelands, the panorama of geologic and scenic features is indeed awe inspiring. Nowhere is this better displayed than in "Navajo-Hopi Country" of northeastern Arizona. Here the landscape is dominated by five major features: Hopi Buttes, Black Mesa, Painted Desert, the valley of the Little Colorado River, and the San Francisco volcanic field. These areas were very important to the way of life of the early inhabitants of the region and appear time and again in their legends.

## HOPI BUTTES

Spectacular buttes rise above the featureless plains north of Winslow and Holbrook, Arizona, and have been named the Hopi Buttes. These dark colored peaks are composed of a variety of volcanic and fine-grained sedimentary rocks. Their geologic history indicates quiescent times, when large lakes developed, punctuated by violent volcanic episodes.

Hopi Buttes consist of slopes of lake sediments capped by volcanic rocks. The sediments exposed on the slopes were deposited during the Miocene and Pliocene epochs, approximately twelve to six million years ago. These sediments and volcanics are referred to as the Bidahochi Formation. This formation consists of three very different groups of rocks, reflecting markedly diverse depositional and volcanic processes.

The basal unit of the Bidahochi consists of gray, brown, and pink mudstone and clay-rich sandstone. Interbedded with these sedimentary rocks are numerous beds of rhyolitic ash. The middle part of the Bidahochi Formation consists of basaltic lava flows, tuffs, and volcanic breccias. The uppermost Bidahochi is composed of silty sandstones as well as beds of volcanic ash.

The lower part of the Bidahochi accumulated in a large lake informally referred to as "Hopi Lake." This lake occupied at least the area north of the present interstate highway (I-40) near Holbrook to Black Mesa. Although its east-west extent is not known, it is believed that the entire lake was on the order of 7,500 square miles (1,200 km²). Within the lake, fine-grained sediments were deposited as well as small amounts of volcanic debris. The lake supported a variety of animal life, the remains of which are preserved as indicated by the fossils of fish, mollusks, and birds.

This serene aquatic setting was short-lived by geologic standards. The demise of Hopi Lake was initiated by the eruption of basaltic tuffs and lava flows through and onto the floor of the lake. Evidence for contemporaneity of volcanism and the lake is the presence of aquatic fossils within the tuff beds. This volcanic material apparently filled large parts of the lake.

The draining of Hopi Lake was largely the result of erosion by the Colorado River. With the opening of the Gulf of California, the Colorado River began to erode headward, towards the north and northeast. This erosion continued until it worked its way through the highlands on the western side of the lake and joined with other west- and south-flowing rivers. Once this outlet formed, the lake quickly drained.

Two major types of volcanic structures are recognized in the area. Circular maar craters were formed when violent eruptions drove magma into water-saturated strata. The mixing of cold water with hot magma resulted in a steam-charged eruption. Fragments of shattered bedrock as well as volcanic particles were extruded through the lake bottom and thrown considerable distances from the vents to form volcanic breccias and tuffs. Lava flowed out on the lake bottom as coherent streams of molten rock. Well-preserved relicts of these explosions can be seen in the Painted Desert of the Petrified Forest National Park in northeastern Arizona. Lava flow domes occur on top of some of these maar craters. Modern erosion of these features has resulted in the formation of large, lava-capped mesas that characterize the landscape of the Hopi Buttes area.

Diatremes, the second major type of volcanic structure, are fragment-filled conduits, or feeder pipes, through which the molten material made its way to the surface. These pipes, now exposed as prominent volcanic necks, are filled with volcanic rocks and broken fragments of vent material that accompanied the rapid and explosive upward movement of the magma. Diatremes offer some of the most spectacular scenery in the region. These dark-colored monolithic structures rise well above the surrounding floodplain of the Little Colorado River system and stand in stark contrast to the tan, gray, and reddish sediments of the lower Bidahochi lake beds, older sedimentary rocks, and modern deposits of rivers and the wind.

The upper part of the Bidahochi represents a return to a less catastrophic period and records the development of an extensive river system that flowed westward parallel to the present course of the Little Colorado River. The deposits laid down by the river system represent a major shift not only in styles of sedimentation but also in direction of drainage for the southern Colorado Plateau.

## BLACK MESA

Black Mesa in northern Arizona is an important geologic and anthropologic area and has been the subject of numerous scientific inquiries in these fields. Black Mesa occurs within the Black Mesa Basin, which is a structural depression, an area where the rocks have been bowed downward in the center and raised on the edges. Black Mesa

Basin dominates the northeastern portion of Arizona and is over 80 miles (130 km) in maximum extent. Black Mesa, which occurs in the northern part of the basin, is a large circular tableland averaging 60 miles (95 km) in diameter. The mesa is between 100 to 200 feet (30 to 60 m) high on its southern and western margins and more than 2,000 feet (600 m) high on the north- and east-facing cliffs. The mesa is largely in Navajo County and is the site of one of the oldest settlements in the United States, the town of Oraibi.

Black Mesa is composed of sedimentary rocks that accumulated in nearshore marine settings as well as on coastal plains, nearby river channels, and associated floodplain areas. The strata exposed are all Cretaceous in age and consist of, in ascending order: Dakota Sandstone, Mancos Shale, Toreva Formation, Wepo Formation, and Yale Point Sandstone—the latter three constituting the Mesaverde Group. Of major economic importance are the thick coal deposits in the Wepo Formation. The coals constitute one of the most productive deposits in the Southwest and are an integral part of the economy in the Four Corners region.

During the late Cretaceous, northeastern Arizona was on the margin of an extensive inland sea. Marine waters were to the northeast and periodically inundated the coastal zones and alluvial plains of northern Arizona in what is now the Black Mesa area.

The three formations that constitute the Mesaverde Group were first described and named for villages and other landmarks on Black Mesa. The Toreva Formation is named for exposures of sandstones and organic-rich mudstones that form prominent cliffs above the Hopi village of the same name. On top of the lowermost sandstone cliff above the village are the pueblos of Mishongnovi and Shipaulavi. The Toreva likely represents deposition in nearshore marine areas as indicated by the presence of shark's teeth and other marine vertebrate fossils. The organic-rich mudstones accumulated on river deltas and in swampy areas.

Above the Toreva Formation are thick sequences of mudstone, sandstone, and coal, which constitute the Wepo Formation. The Wepo was named after Wepo Wash, which occurs in the central part of Black Mesa and drains southwestward to

First and Second mesas. The Wepo Formation is exposed in the center of the mesa where modern erosion has dissected the area into a series of narrow ridges and valleys.

The rim of Black Mesa is held up by resistant sandstone cliffs of the Toreva Formation and the Yale Point Sandstone. The Yale Point Sandstone occurs only along the northeastern side of Black Mesa and represents deposition along a sandy coastline. The Yale Point records the last time that marine waters were present in this part of Arizona.

The Hopi Mesas occur in the southern part of Black Mesa. Here the capping Toreva Formation has been eroded by three major drainages: Dennebito, Oraibi, and Polacca washes. Dissection by stream processes in these washes has resulted in the formation of the three Hopi Mesas, First, Second, and Third.

## PAINTED DESERT

Southward from Black Mesa towards the San Francisco volcanic field, the landscape is relatively flat and covered by the deposits of the Little Colorado River, wind-blown sand dunes, and scattered outcrops of Permian, Triassic, and Jurassic sedimentary rocks. This area forms part of the Painted Desert of northeastern Arizona, which stretches toward the east into New Mexico. There are many interesting natural features within the area that had important meanings to the early inhabitants. Two of these are blowholes and eolian (wind-blown) dune fields.

The blowholes occur in the Permian Kaibab Formation. The Kaibab crops out in a number of places northeast of the San Francisco volcanic field. The unit consists of thin-bedded limestone, dolomite, and sandstone and has been broken into a series of fractures, or joints. Ground waters migrated along these surfaces and dissolved large quantities of the limestone resulting in the creation of large caverns within the Kaibab. Some of these caverns and caves are connected in a complicated fashion, while others are isolated. Air rushes through these caverns, resulting in thunderous drafts of wind, hence the name blowholes. It has been shown that when the atmospheric pressure is very low, air rushes out of these holes; when pressure is high, air is drawn into the caverns. This phenomenon was very significant to the early peoples of the area and figures in their legends.

Other prominent features in the area are widespread dune fields, some of which are actively migrating today and many of which were active during the Quaternary Period. The climate here is dry enough and the wind occasionally strong enough to mold loose sand into a myriad of dune shapes and sizes. The material for these dunes is provided by two main sources: The washes that drain upland areas periodically carry huge amounts of gravel, sand, and silt following major storms. This material is deposited in ephemeral stream channels and is later remobilized by the wind and formed into dunes. A second major source of sand, ironically, is an ancient dune field, the Jurassic Navajo Sandstone, which crops out throughout the mesas in the area. The sandstone is poorly cemented and, hence, is easily eroded. The residue, therefore, is precisely the size of material that the wind can most easily transport. Outcrops of the Navajo Sandstone are typically covered with modern dunes that are extremely similar to their ancient counterparts.

A variety of dune types is present within the area. Parabolic and barchan dunes are identified based on the orientation of the dune crest to the prevailing wind direction. Parabolic dunes have a crest line that is concave into the wind; barchanoid dunes curve in the direction that the wind is blowing. Straight crested dunes, elongated parallel and perpendicular to the flow path of the wind, are also common. More complex dune types occur, such as dome-shaped varieties and dunes classified as reversing, which represent periodic reversals of main wind direction. The latter types attest to the complex wind-flow patterns that have existed for the last 10,000 years.

Perhaps the most fascinating occurrences of wind-sculpted sand are the climbing and falling dune fields. These consist of dunes that climb up and over the mesas (climbing dunes) or migrate down the mesa flanks (falling dunes). The result is a ramp from basin floor to mesa top composed of migrating sheets of dune sands.

The active dune fields (moving sand) occur mostly along dry washes in the Painted Desert and were well established by the time the area was occupied by the first inhabitants. Pottery fragments and pit houses constructed more than 1,000 years ago are associated with dunes that had already become stabilized. The Hopis and their ancestors made great use of the dune fields. The dunes serve as a conduit for rain water, which infiltrates the dune surfaces and seeps into the underlying bedrock only to emerge in lower areas as a series of springs. These springs have long served as a source of water for agricultural purposes. The Hopis have also used the stabilized dunes to plant corn, beans, and fruit trees.

## LITTLE COLORADO RIVER

The Little Colorado River has its headwaters in the White Mountains of east-central Arizona and flows northwestward until its confluence with the Colorado River approximately 32 miles (50 km) west of Tuba City. It is the only major river in northeastern Arizona and as such drains most of the Painted Desert region as well as the region north of the Mogollon Rim. The Little Colorado has characteristics of both meandering and braided streams and experiences periods of maximum discharge alternating with periods when it is nearly dry. As such, the Little Colorado River is an ephemeral river with its water level strongly controlled by melt-water runoff in the White Mountains. In eastern Arizona the Little Colorado River flows through easily eroded sediments of the Bidahochi Formation, its own floodplain sediments, and Triassic-age strata of the Moenkopi and Chinle formations. In this area the river is not deeply incised, and there is little topographic relief between the adjacent floodplain and the main channel. The river becomes more deeply incised, however, towards the west. From Cameron to its junction with the Colorado River, the Little Colorado River has carved deep canyons through the Triassic Moenkopi Formation and the Permian Kaibab Formation. Nowhere is this better seen than in the Little Colorado River Gorge approximately 12 miles (20 km) northwest of Cameron. The history of the river is closely tied to the tectonic history of the southern Colorado Plateau and most importantly to the evolution of the Colorado River system into which it flows.

The Little Colorado River has a complex history of erosion and deposition. The southern Colorado Plateau has undergone periods of regional as well as localized uplifts since the mid-Tertiary. These movements have resulted in periods of channel cutting by the river as well as development of widespread erosion surfaces.

Prior to the uplift of major areas in northeastern Arizona, the ancestral Little Colorado River flowed northward. Once these areas were elevated, the Little Colorado River was confined to areas south of these features and flow was largely to the west. Best estimates of the size of the system indicate a valley between 50 and 124 miles wide (80 to 200 km). This shift in flow was followed by a period of rapid downcutting that entrenched the Little Colorado River at least 1,200 feet (400 m) below its earlier level. The Hopi Lakes developed in this depression. Regional uplift of the entire Colorado Plateau during the latest Tertiary time resulted in the Little Colorado River carving the deep canyon that we see today west of Cameron.

## SAN FRANCISCO VOLCANIC FIELD

Covering a broad region on the southern Colorado Plateau, the San Francisco volcanic field dominates all vistas in northcentral Arizona with its high volcanic peaks and low, rounded cinder cones. Even the flat regions between the volcanic mountains and hills are underlain by nearly horizontal lava flows.

Over 600 separate volcanoes erupted their lavas and cinders in this volcanic field that stretches from the Little Colorado River westward to Ash Fork, and from Shadow Mountain near Cameron southward to the Mogollon Rim. Of course, a volcanic field of this size did not come into existence overnight. Chemical analyses of radioactive elements in the lavas indicate that it took over 8 million years for the field to develop to its present size. If only the 600 or so known volcanoes are considered, the average time span between their eruptions is over 13,000 years; even if there were twice as many vents as are now known, the average length of time between eruptions is immense on a human time scale.

Although the volcanic field appears extinct today, it is regarded as a potentially active one by scientists because the record of the lavas indicates that, on a *geologic time scale*, there has been essentially continuous volcanism from about 8 million years ago to only about 735 years ago. The elapsed time since the last eruption is only a small fraction of one percent of the total amount of time that the field has been active, leading scientists to conclude that the probability of another eruption is very high.

The earliest eruptions occurred southwest of Flagstaff near the present-day Mogollon Rim. These first lavas were of the type that have built the Hawaiian Islands, and when they cooled, dark colored, lava-flow rocks called basalt were formed. These lavas, similar to many that are seen in road cuts along Interstate 17 and Interstate 40 in the Flagstaff area, are dark because they are rich in minerals that contain iron. For reasons that are still unknown, younger vents began to erupt basalt lavas northeast of the earlier ones, and the volcanic field grew and developed as a broad wave of volcanism migrated toward the northeast, reaching the Little Colorado River valley a mere 2.5 million years ago. Sunset Crater, although not on the leading edge of the wave, last erupted about 735 years ago in the eastern part of the volcanic field, in conformity with the overall pattern.

Beginning about 4 million years ago, lavas of different compositions began to erupt in a few volcanic centers that appear to be located along major breaks or weaknesses in the earth's crust. These localized lavas (andesite, dacite, and rhyolite) formed thick, stubby lava flows and built up prominent, steep-sided volcanic mountains over their vents.

The andesite and dacite lavas first began to extrude in the area around Bill Williams Mountain on the southwest side of the volcanic field about 4 million years ago. During the next 2.5 million years, the volcanic locus shifted northeast and erupted the prominent volcanoes of Sitgreaves Mountain and Kendrick Peak. When the volcanic locus reached Kendrick Peak just under 3 million years ago, it jumped eastward to another, but parallel, crustal fracture and initiated the long-lived volcanism that eventually saw San Francisco Mountain grow to become the highest peak in Arizona by about 400,000 years ago. The andesite and dacite lavas of San Francisco Mountain erupted as alternating layers of lava flows and cinders to construct a classic cone-shaped composite volcano that must have originally resembled the modern volcanic peaks of the Cascade Mountains.

At the base of San Francisco Mountain, thick, pasty lavas piled up on top of each other to construct the complex of lava domes of the Dry Lake Hills, and the steep, protruding, bulbous flows of Elden Mountain, some of which were so viscous that they stopped flowing before reaching the bottom of the volcano. Eventually, the volcanism shifted northeastward again and the dacite lavas of O'Leary Peak erupted just north of the present-day Sunset Crater National Monument, only 200,000 years ago.

Sometime between 400,000 and 200,000 years ago, after San Francisco Mountain had reached an elevation of over 15,000 feet (4,600 m), a series of catastrophic land-slides, probably volcanically generated, decapitated the volcano and created a large bowl-shaped valley in its center, known as the Inner Basin. Debris from the land-slides was deposited on the lower flanks of all sides of the mountain, but most of it slid out to the northeast where it forms a broad apron sloping gently down toward Deadman Flat.

During the Ice Ages, glaciers occupied the Inner Basin and the higher elevations in the valleys on the outside of the peaks. Sculpting by the glaciers carved the Inner Basin even deeper and created the precipitous cliffs that surround it. Even today, local patches of snow in sheltered places may survive a summer that follows an especially heavy snowfall winter.

The relatively young basaltic volcanism in the eastern part of the volcanic field produced a landscape dotted with dozens of cinder cones. The older cones have been eroded down to low mounds, whereas the younger ones present smooth, steep sides that converge upward to well-preserved craters at the summits. Many of the cinder cones appear to be random in their locations, as if the earth's crust could be penetrated almost anywhere with liquid basalt rising from depths, but some cones can be connected along lines, which implies that the lava moved up in local areas along weak zones or fissures.

Two and a half million years of volcanism and erosion in the Little Colorado River valley created a landscape of cinder cones, lava flows, mesas, and canyons.

Lava appears to have been available from an almost inexhaustible source deep within the earth for many hundreds of thousands of years. Volcanism was certainly not a newcomer to northern Arizona when the latest supply of lava started its way upward in the eleventh century.

## SUNSET CRATER

Sometime during the late fall or winter of A.D. 1064–65, basalt lava that had been forcing its way up from great depths along a fissure over six miles long finally reached the surface just east of Bonito Park. If the events that led to the birth of Sunset Crater were at all similar to those that accompany recent, fairly well-documented eruptions of basalt lava, like at Parícutin in Mexico, it is probable that earthquakes were felt in the region for a few days or even weeks prior to the first opening of the vent. As the ground began to crack open, escaping steam and volcanic gases were probably the first visible signs of the volcanic drama that was beginning and that was to continue, intermittently, for over 200 years.

Bubbles in the gas-charged lava that was approaching the surface began to expand and burst violently, creating explosions that ripped open the vent and tore the molten lava into jagged, frothy, incandescent pieces that were ejected high into the air. Cooling in the atmosphere turned most of the lava fragments into cinders, irregular particles of solidified lava, but larger masses that retained heat longer were molded by surface tension into spherical volcanic bombs. A large eruptive column of cinders and volcanic gases may have risen thousands of feet into the atmosphere above the crater, and the eruption was probably accompanied by frequent lightning flashes and a tremendous roaring sound. Rapid, upward displacement of the atmosphere by the outrushing volcanic material may even have set strong winds in motion that blew in toward the base of the eruption column.

Many of the cinders and practically all of the bombs fell back down around the vent, and as the eruption progressed, the growing deposit began to take on the characteristic shape of a cinder cone type of volcano. At night the explosive rise of incandescent volcanic bombs above the crater and their subsequent fall back onto the slopes of the growing volcano must have presented a spectacular fire-work display.

The smaller cinders in the eruption column and volcanic ash and dust drifted away from the volcano on air currents and were blown by winds generally toward the east. As these smaller particles settled out of the air, a mantling blanket of volcanic cinders and ash began to cover the landscape, including the houses and fields of the Indians living in the area. Over 800 square miles (2,070 km²) were covered with the blanket of ash, which extended in a broad ellipse eastward beyond the Little Colorado River; very fine volcanic dust probably reached as far east as the Hopi Mesas. According to scientists who have studied the history of Sunset Crater, this early, highly explosive stage may have lasted for over 25 years, and when it ended, the new cone was several hundred feet high, and a large region surrounding it lay under a thick deposit of black cinders and ash.

About 85 years after the first cinders erupted from the new vent at Sunset Crater, lava with relatively less gas contained within it emerged from the fissure and pushed its way up into the cinder cone. Because the gas-poor lava was much denser than the weak, unconsolidated cinders, the cone could not contain it and a stream of lava broke through on the east side and started flowing down Kana-a Wash toward the Little Colorado River. As the lava extruded from the base of the volcano, loose cinders collapsed down on top of the flow and were carried away; a slight indentation of the east side of Sunset Crater remains today as subtle evidence of the force with which the cone was disrupted.

The northeastward-flowing stream of lava, named the Kana-a flow, continued down Kana-a Wash for about four miles to where it split into two streams around an older volcano, and continued to flow for another two miles. All of this early stage of the Kana-a flow was covered by the blanket of cinders, which is so thick near Sunset Crater that the flow is completely buried. The Sunset Crater–Wupatki road follows the northwest side of the Kana-a flow and crosses it in two places; to the traveler, the flow presents dark, jagged outcrops of disjointed slabs of basalt that poke up through the cinder blanket. At the northeast end of the lava flow, where the cinders are much thinner, its edge consists of a jumbled mass of irregular, spiny fragments called *aa* clinkers, named after a common feature of Hawaiian lavas that forms when the lava flow is cooler and becomes stiffer.

At some time after the extrusion of the Kana-a flow, the character of the eruption from Sunset Crater's vent changed. As a result of less gas in the lava, and possible hotter temperatures, the explosions became weaker and formed larger cinders and volcanic bombs that were not ejected as high above the vent. Because many of the cinders and bombs were still hot and sticky when they landed back on top of the cone, they became welded together. As some of the layers of welded cinders and bombs became thicker, they started to ooze down the side of the volcano, much like a lava flow. These so-called rootless lava flows never reached the bottom of the volcano, but because the flow movement blended the cinders and bombs together, their appearance is very much like true lava flows. Surrounding these rootless lava flows are layers composed of pieces of volcanic spatter (small, irregular pieces of lava torn apart by weak explosions) that are very weakly welded together.

The rootless flows and layers of welded spatter formed a black to red carapace on the upper slopes of the cone around the crater. These welded layers are no longer visible on the slopes of Sunset Crater because younger deposits of unconsolidated black and red cinders cover them. We can infer their existence within the cone, however, because the youngest eruptions from Sunset Crater tore out a few blocks of the buried layers and scattered them in a disoriented manner around the present crater.

The most spectacular occurrences of the welded layers, however, are large mounds on top of a basalt lava flow, named the Bonito flow, that extruded from the northwest base of Sunset Crater. The mounds, some over 30 feet (10 m) high, are strung out like beads in a chain for almost three-quarters of a mile (1.2 m) in a north-westerly direction from the extrusion point of the lava flow. How could deposits that originally formed around the summit of Sunset Crater very near the vent get scattered across the top of a lava flow up to several thousand feet away from the volcano? Although the layers appear to be tilted differently in each mound, their general lack of internal disruption would seem to rule out a gigantic explosion that blew them out; also, Sunset Crater lacks a large hole or crater that should be present if a large explosion took place. A probable scenario follows.

Sometime around 70 years after the Kana-a flow extruded, gas-poor lava welled up again inside Sunset Crater, and again, the cinder cone could not contain it. This time, however, the lava broke out on the northwest side and started flowing into a basin bounded by the deposits and lava flows of older volcanoes. As the Bonito lava flow pushed its way out of the base of Sunset Crater, the welded layers at the top were undermined and started to slide down. On reaching the bottom, they were carried off to the northwest, piggy-back fashion, on the top of the extruding Bonito lava. Although a scar was probably produced on the cone when the layers slid down, it was healed by subsequent reconstruction of Sunset Crater during later eruptions.

Although much of the molten rock extruded from the volcano as a lava flow, lava still exploded out of the crater, and a shower of black ash and cinders covered the newly extruded Bonito flow and added to the thickness of the deposits already on top of the previously erupted Kana-a flow. Most cinders landed back on Sunset Crater and helped to rebuild the cone that was disrupted by the Bonito flow. The welded layers still in place around the summit were buried completely, and the volcano grew higher and wider during the continuing eruptions.

As this latest explosive phase started to ebb, almost 200 years after the eruption of the first cinders, and the outrush of escaping cinders and volcanic gases began to slow down, more air was stirred into the eruption column. Reacting with particles of iron in the hot cinders, the oxygen in the air turned them red. When these oxidized cinders landed, the familiar sunset glow at the top of the volcano was formed. Even after the eruption ended, hot volcanic gases escaped at the top. As the gas flowed around the uppermost cinders, yellow and red minerals were deposited that added to the colorful cap on this long-lived cinder cone.

The last volcanic activity at Sunset Crater occurred as gas-poor lava was injected again into the cone. Some of the lava found its way to the summit and blew out a small crater nestled against the east side of the main crater. Black volcanic bombs were ejected and landed on top of the red cinders around the edges of the newly formed vent.

Most of the lava, however, quietly extruded from the base of the volcano on its east and northwest sides and was added to the Kana-a and Bonito lava flows. Lava that extruded on the east side appears to have followed an old lava tube inside the Kana-a flow, because the lava did not emerge to flow on the surface until it was about 5 miles (8 km) from the volcano. This latest addition to the Kana-a flow is easily recognized near the northeast end as a patch of lava, free of overlying cinders, on top of the older, cinder-covered lava flow.

The Bonito flow probably was still molten on the inside when the last pulse of lava was added. The resurgence of the basalt liquid spread the flow farther on all fronts and filled in the small basin just east of Bonito Park. Low areas between older volcanoes were inundated, and on the south side of the basin, the lava overtopped a low divide and flowed down into the crater of an older, extensively eroded cinder cone. The force of the extruding lava broke up the solidified and cinder-covered crust of the Bonito flow and floated the massive plates away like pack ice. The violent ejection of cinders from Sunset Crater's vent must have died down by this time, because the newly advanced part of the Bonito flow created a wide margin that lacks the typical cover of cinders mantling the older part.

The cinder-free part of the Bonito lava flow presents a savage, inhospitable appearance with its black, jagged, and tumbled slabs of basalt lava. Anyone who ventures out on the flow is immediately struck by its stark, impenetrable appearance; plants have had difficulty in getting established, even though the lava is now over 700 years old. Although the flow is dominantly slab *pahoehoe*, named for a common variety of lava on Hawaii characterized by chaotically tilted crustal slabs, a wide variety of surface structures occurs: some are smooth and massive, others have the appearance of coils of rope, and elsewhere the crust is composed of thin shells where it was puffed up by expanding gas. Locally, the internal gas pressure was high enough to break open the flow's crust and eject blobs of lava that built up small steep-sided volcanoes, called hornitos, on its surface. At some places, only volcanic gases escaped from the interior, and as they passed through the mantle of cinders, the iron particles were oxidized, creating local spots of red cinders in a sea of black cinders. Expanded gas bubbles that were trapped by the solidifying lava left smooth, round openings called vesicles, some of which are several inches in diameter. Common around the edges of the flow are spiny *aa* clinkers that add to the flow's complexity.

As the flow's molten interior continued to spread outward, stresses exerted on the solidified crust opened up large cracks, one of which is over a half-mile long. Although some are just gaping, open cracks with steep walls, others contain knife-edged "squeeze-ups" marked with vertical grooves that formed as stiff, pasty lava welled up in the opening fissures. Other cracks and depressions in the flow's crust and inside caves resulted when the molten interior was able to break out the edge of the flow and drain away, allowing the crust to subside in some places but leaving elongated cavities elsewhere.

Caves in lava flows, called lava tubes, are commonly like long tunnels, and many are high enough to stand up in and walk through with relative ease. They may, however, branch and converge like a complicated catacomb, and in constricted places become too narrow to pass through. Water that enters the lava tubes may freeze during the winter as cold air sinks in, and because rocks are such good insulators, the ice may survive the next summer. Undoubtedly, many lava tubes are unknown because their ends are sealed with lava, but where the roof is thin, collapse may form a sinkhole that provides access. One well-known lava tube in the southeast part of the Bonito lava flow is over 225 feet long.

Although most of the lava that surged toward the surface from depths within the earth on the order of 35 to 50 miles (55 to 80 km) erupted from the vents at Sunset Crater, some escaped from the six-mile-long (9.6 km) fissure at other places to the southeast. After the eruptions began at Sunset Crater, lava broke through to the surface at many points in a mile-long (1.6 km) segment of the fissure located at its southeast end and erupted with fairly weak explosions that ejected incandescent volcanic spatter and bombs. This activity probably resembled the well-known "curtain of fire" eruption style on Hawaii, and when it ended, dozens of small round spatter cones and elongated spatter ramparts dotted the surface along the fissure. These small volcanic structures must have still been hot and emitting oxidizing vapors when they were covered by the cinders from Sunset Crater because the black cinder blanket has spots of red cinders where it overlies each structure. Eventually, a lava flow over four miles long (6.5 km) extruded from this elongated vent.

Gyp Crater, about at the midpoint of the fissure in the volcanic zone, is an impressive vent: it is only about 1,100 feet (335 m) long and 600 feet (180 m) wide, but it is over 200 feet (60 m) deep. The early explosive stage of its eruption produced thick deposits of red cinders along the edges of the fissure, but soon, with the exhaustion of much of the gas from the lava, the eruption style changed and volcanic spatter and bombs were deposited in layers that mantle the inner and outer slopes of the crater. That Gyp Crater was constructed during the eruptive episodes of Sunset Crater can be inferred by its cover of cinders that blends into the widespread cinder blanket that mantles the surrounding countryside.

Along the fissure between Gyp Crater and Sunset Crater, gas-rich lava erupted at numerous points to construct two rows of small cinder cones. These mile-long rows of cones, easily seen to the southeast from the cinder hills view point on the east side of Sunset Crater, stand out because their bright red cinders were deposited on top of the blanket of black cinders that had erupted previously from the main Sunset Crater vent. These small cones are so closely spaced that their deposits coalesce into continuous red strips, but each vent can be identified by its own mound of cinders, and the tops of many were turned into cemented crusts by red and yellow minerals deposited from escaping vapors.

The lava that escaped from the earth's interior during the Sunset Crater eruptive episodes is less than one-tenth of one percent of the total lava that makes up the San Francisco volcanic field. This small quantity of lava, however, changed forever the landscape in this young volcanic province.

Approximately three-fourths of the lava erupted explosively as cinders and was deposited in nearly equal amounts in the cinder cone of Sunset Crater and as its surrounding blanket of black cinders. The cinders that accumulated near the vent piled up for almost 200 years to construct a nearly symmetrical cone about 1,000 feet (300 m) high and almost exactly one mile (1.6 km) in diameter. The main crater at the summit is over 400 feet (120 m) deep; it originated during the last stages of the explosive eruptions as the cinders piled up deeper around the periphery of the vent that was ejecting gas and cinders at high velocities.

Only about one-fourth of the lava was extruded as coherent streams of liquid, and most of this flowed into the basin between Sunset Crater and Bonito Park to bury nearly two square miles (5 km²) of land, some of which was probably under cultivation in more tranquil times. The Bonito lava flow is only about six to ten feet thick (1.8 to 3 m) at some places around its edge, but in the center it could be over 100 feet (30 m) thick. The cool and dry climate of northern Arizona retards the natural weathering processes of rocks, with the result that the Bonito flow appears so fresh that it might have extruded yesterday, rather than over 700 years ago.

No one can say for certain when and where the next eruption will occur, but if we base our prediction on sound geological knowledge of the history of the San Francisco volcanic field, it probably will be an eruption of basalt lava within the next few hundred to few thousand years in the valley of the Little Colorado River. Ultimately, volcanism is a constructive activity, as it adds to and builds up the landscape with its erupted products.

# THE HOPI ALPHABET

## Ekkehart Malotki

Hopi, an American Indian language spoken in northeastern Arizona, is a branch of the large Uto-Aztecan family of languages, which covers vast portions of the western United States and Mexico. It is related to such languages as Papago, Paiute, Shoshone, Tarahumara, Yaqui, and Nahuatl, the language of the Aztecs, to mention only a few. Navajo, Apache, Havasupai, Zuni, Tewa, and many other languages in the American Southwest are completely unrelated to it, however. At least three regional Hopi dialects, whose differences in terms of pronunciation, grammar, and vocabulary are relatively minimal, can be distinguished. No prestige dialect exists.

While traditionally the Hopi, like most Amerindian groups, never developed a writing system of their own, there today exists a standardized—yet unofficial— orthography for the Hopi language. Langacker has presented a "simple and linguistically sound writing system" (Milo Kalectaca, *Lessons in Hopi*, edited by Ronald W. Langacker, Tucson, 1978) for the Second Mesa dialect of Shungopavi (Songoopavi).

My own generalized Hopi orthography is equally phonemic in nature and is based on the dialect habits of speakers from the Third Mesa communities, of Hotevilla (Hotvela), Bakabi (Paaqavi), Oraibi (Orayvi), Kykotsmovi (Kiqötsmovi), and Moenkopi (Munqapi), who constitute the majority of Hopis. Speakers from the First Mesa villages of Walpi and Sichomovi (Sitsom'ovi) as well as from the communities of Shungopavi (Songoopavi), Mishongnovi (Musangnuvi), and Shipaulovi (Supawlavi) simply need to impose their idiosyncratic pronunciation on the written "image" of the preponderant dialect, much as a member of the Brooklyn speech community applies his brand of pronunciation to such words as "bird" or "work."

Hopi standardized orthography is thus truly pan-Hopi; it is characterized by a close fit between phonemically functional sound and corresponding symbol. Unusual graphemes are avoided. For example, the digraph *ng* stands for the same phoneme that *ng* represents in English si*ng*. Symbols like *ṅ*, as the translator of the New Testament into Hopi elected to do, or *ŋ*, which is suggested in the symbol inventory of the International Phonetic Alphabet, are not employed. In all, twenty-one letters are sufficient to write Hopi, of which only the umlauted *ö* is not part of the English alphabet. For the glottal stop, one of the Hopi consonants, the apostrophe is used.

Hopi distinguishes the six vowels, *a, e, i, o, ö,* and *u,* the last of which represents the international phonetic symbol *ɨ*. Their long counterparts are written by doubling the letter for the corresponding short vowel: *aa, ee, ii, oo, öö,* and *uu*. The short vowels are found in combination with both the *y-* and *w-* glide to form the following diphthongs: *ay, ey, iy, oy, öy, uy* and *aw, ew, iw, öw, uw*. Only the diphthong *ow* does not occur. The inventory of consonants contains a number of sounds that have to be represented as digraphs or trigraphs (two or three letter combinations): *p, t, ky, k, kw, q, qw, ', m, n, ngy, ng, ngw, ts, v, r, s, l*. The two semi-vowels are the glides *w* and *y*. Notably absent are the sounds b, d, and g, to mention only one prominent difference between the Hopi and English sound inventories. Because Hopi *p, t,* and *k* are pronounced without aspiration, speakers of English tend to hear them as *b, d,* and *g*. This accounts for many wrong spellings of Hopi words in the past.

The following table lists all the functional Hopi sounds, with the exception of those characterized by a falling tone — a phonetic feature not shared by First and Second Mesa speakers. Each phoneme is illustrated by a Hopi example and accompanied by phonetic approximations drawn from various Indo-European languages.

## THE HOPI ALPHABET

| Phoneme | Sample Word | | Sound Approximations English (E), French (F) German (G), Russian (R) |
|---------|-------------|--|----------------------------------------------------------------------|

1. Vowels:
   (a) short vowels

| | | | |
|---|---|---|---|
| a | p*a*s | very | E *cut*  F *patte* |
| e | p*e*p | there | E *met*  F h*e*rbe |
| i | s*i*hu | flower | E h*i*t  G m*i*t |
| o | m*o*mi | forward | F *col*  G *soll* |
| ö | qötö | head | F n*eu*f  G L*ö*ffel |
| u | t*u*wa | he found it/saw it | R  B*b*|Tb  E j*u*st (when unstressed) |

   (b) long vowels

| | | | |
|---|---|---|---|
| aa | p*aa*s | carefully/completely | F p*â*te  G St*aa*t |
| ee | p*ee*p | almost | F *ê*tre  G M*äh*ne |
| ii | s*ii*hu | intestines | F r*i*re  G w*ie* |
| oo | m*oo*mi | he is pigeon-toed | F r*o*se  G B*oo*t |
| öö | q*öö*tö | suds | F *feu* G T*ö*ne |
| uu | t*uu*wa | sand | G B*üh*ne (but lips spread without producing an [i] sound) |

2. Diphthongs:
    (a) with y-glide

| | | | |
|---|---|---|---|
| ay | ts*ay* | small/young | E fl*y*   G Kl*ei*der |
| ey | *ey*kita | he groans | E m*ay* |
| iy | yaap*iy* | from here on | E fl*ea* |
| oy | ah*oy* | back to | E t*oy*   G h*eu*te |
| öy | hö*y*kita | he growls | F *oe*il |
| uy | *uy*to | he goes planting | G pf*ui* |
| | | | (but with lips spread |
| | | | instead of rounded) |

    (b) with w-glide

| | | | |
|---|---|---|---|
| aw | *aw*ta | bow | E f*ow*l   G M*au*s |
| ew | p*ew* | here (to me) | E m*et* + E *wet* |
| iw | p*iw* | again | E h*it* + E *wet* |
| ow | nonexisting | | |
| öw | ngöl*öw*ta | it is crooked | G L*ö*ffel + E *wet* |
| uw | p*uw*moki | he got sleepy | R B*b*|Tb + E *wet* |

| Phoneme | Sample Word | | **Sound Approximations** |
|---|---|---|---|
| | | | English (E), French (F) |
| | | | German (G), Russian (R) |

3. Consonants:
    (a) stops

| | | | |
|---|---|---|---|
| p | *p*aahu | water/spring | F *p*ain |
| t | *t*upko | younger brother | F *t*able |
| ky | *ky*aaro | parrot | E *c*ure |
| k | *k*oho | wood/stick | F *c*ar |
| kw | *kw*ala | it boiled | E *qu*it |
| q | *q*ööha | he built a fire | G *Kr*aut |
| | | | (but *k* articulated farther back |
| | | | in mouth) |

| | | | |
|---|---|---|---|
| qw | yang*qw* | from here | E *w*et, added to pronunciation of *q* |
| ' | pu' | now/today | G Ver'ein |

(b) nasals

| | | | |
|---|---|---|---|
| m | *m*alatsi | finger | E *m*e |
| n | *n*aama | both/together | E *n*ut |
| ngy | yu*ngy*a | they entered | E ki*ng* + E *y*es E si*ng*ular (casually pronounced) |
| ng | *ng*öla | wheel | E ki*ng* G fa*ng*en |
| ngw | kookya*ngw* | spider | E ki*ng* + E *w*et E pe*ng*uin (casually pronounced) |

(c) affricate

| | | | |
|---|---|---|---|
| ts | *ts*uku | point/clown | E hi*ts* G Zunge |

(d) fricatives

| | | | |
|---|---|---|---|
| v | *v*otoona | coin/button | E *v*eal G *W*inter |
| r | *r*oya | it turned | syllable initial position: E lei*s*ure (with tongue tip curled toward palate) |
| r | hin'u*r* | very (female speaking) | syllable final position: E *sh*ip F *ch*arme |
| s | *s*akuna | squirrel | E *s*ong |
| h | *h*o'apu | carrying basket | E *h*elp |

(e) lateral

| | | | |
|---|---|---|---|
| l | *l*aho | bucket | E *l*ot |

4. Glides:

(a) preceding a vowel

| | | | |
|---|---|---|---|
| w | *w*aala | gap/notch | E *w*et, how |
| y | *y*uutu | they ran | E *y*es, hay |

(b) succeeding a vowel see diphthongs

# GLOSSARY

## ALIKSA'I

A storyteller usually begins with *aliksa'i*. In reply to this introductory formula the listeners utter, "Oh." As the narrator continues with his story we keep acknowledging his story with this same response. But not all Hopis begin their tales in this manner. We, who trace our ancestry to Orayvi, follow this custom, while some living in the distant villages of the other mesas commence by saying, "*Haliksa'i*, it is my story."

## APPLYING CORNMEAL TO SKIN

Grinding corn is a very arduous task. Small wonder then that a woman perspires when engaged in this work. For this reason a woman prone to perspiring takes a little bit of cornmeal and daubs it on her face so she does not feel so hot. As a rule, any woman grinding corn smears corn flour on her face, for with it she keeps herself cool.

Corn flour is also used on the twentieth day after the birth of a child when the female, who is attending the newborn, and her relatives hold a naming ceremony. On this occasion they wash the infant's hair and pat its face with white corn flour. In addition, they rub some on the baby's back and on the chest over the heart area.

## ALIKSA'I

Tuutuwutsniqa sutsep aliksa'it akw yaynangwu. Noq hakim put aw tuuqayyungqam hu'wanayanik hakim, "Oh," kitotangwu. Pu' pay aapiy pam tuutuwutsqw paapiy pu' hakim put pay piw an hu'wantiwisngwu. Niikyangw pay qa soosoyam hopiit pan tuuwutsit yaynayangwu. Itam orayngaqwyaqam pay tuwat pan tuwi'yyúngqw pu' imawat kiyavaqsinom peetu, "Haliksa'i, yaw kur ituwutsi," yan tuuwutsiy yaynayangwu.

## NGUMANQÖMATOYNA

Ngumantaniqwqw pi a'ni tumalaningwuniqw oovi himuwa pantsakye' pam paasivukuwkyangw pantsakngwu. Noq oovi himuwa palvonen, pam it ngumniy angqw qömate', pu' paasat qa pas an utuhu'mokiwkyangw pantsakngwu. Oovi ngumantaqa pay pas son put qa angqw qömatangwu, pam put akw naahukyanangwuniiqe oovi.

Pu' himuwa tiposhoyat tiiqatsni'ytaqa sunattaqat aqw pituqw, ep pu' puma put tungwayaniniqw, paasat pu' puma put asnayat pu' put tiposhoyat qötsangumnitwat akw qömatoynayangwu. Pantotit pu' puma piw put hotpanit pu' unangwpe put akw enang lelwiyangwu.

## BAKED SWEET CORN

*Tuupevu* is sweet corn baked in a pit oven. After removal from the underground oven it is strung up and then dried in the sun. Once the *tuupevu* is thoroughly dehydrated and people want to eat some, they need only boil it for it to return to its moist state. A kachina always includes *tuupevu* when he comes bearing gifts.

## BEGRUDGE/ENVY THE POSSESSION OR ENJOYMENT OF SOMETHING

Whenever a Hopi does something spectacular or acquires something valuable or good, another person is bound to be envious. The person will begrudge the former his good fortune, because he is not the one who has been blessed with it. In such a case the person who is jealous will almost always put the other down in some way. He may label him a sorcerer, or even claim that he sold a corpse to gain his things of value. In these ways Hopis typically slander one another.

## CICADA

The cicada is a small insect that, along with other creatures, has its habitat in Hopiland. The insect's singing is distinctly audible in midsummer, but where exactly the noise is located is often hard to discern.

According to the Hopi the cicada knows how to

## TUUPEVU

Tuupevu pay i' tawaktsi tuupep'iwpuningwu. Put hak koysömiq tuupengwu. Noq pu' hakim put pangqw ipwaye' pu' put hotomnayat pu' put taplakni'yyungngwu. Paasat pu' pam pas lakqw, pu' hakim hisat piw tuupevutyanik, hakim pay put panis ahoy kwalaknayaqw pay pam piw ahoy antingwu. Noq i' katsina pay pas son piw put enang qa na'mangwu'yvangwu.

## QA NAANI

Himuwa hiita ep pay sen kyaahintini, sen hiita neengem nukngwat sen lolmat himu'yvaniqw, hak put aw qa kwangwatayte' hak pan qa naaningwu, qa pam hapi pantiqe oovi. Noq pu' himuwa panhaqam hintiqw, mi'wa ayangqw aw qa kwangwatay- taqa pay put pas son hinwat qa sasvingwu. Epha- qam pam put powaqsasvingwu. Pu' ephaqam hi- muwa pangqawngwu pam mashuyi'ytaqe oovi put hiita nukngwat aw pituuqat. Pay yanhaqam pam put naap hin sasvingwu.

## MAAHU

I' maahu pay himu hiisayhoya taytaqaningwu. Pam nuutum yangqe hopiikivaqe qatu. Noq pu' suutala'tiqw pam susmataq leelenngwuniikyangw pam haqam leelenngwuniqw hak put qa tuwa'y- tangwu.

Noq itamuy hopiituyniqw pam it mumkiwuy

produce heat. Hence the weather usually gets hot when it sings. One clan, before arriving at Orayvi, actually tried to melt the ice high in the north by drawing on the knowledge of the cicada. The insect failed, however, so the northern portion of this continent is still frozen solid.

## CORN

Corn is ever present in the life of a Hopi. At birth a perfect ear of white corn represents the symbolic mother of a child. From corn a variety of items are made: food, sacred cornmeal, flour. Wherever a special event is going on, corn or its byproduct is never missing. Corn is so precious that whenever it is incorporated into a Hopi's song it is spoken of as his mother. At death a trail of cornmeal is made along which the deceased travels wherever he is destined to go.

## CORNMEAL

Cornmeal was once used by the Hopi on an everyday basis. Each morning as he went out to pray toward the rising sun he made it a habit to pray with *hooma* (cornmeal).

The kachina father, the man who tends the kachinas, also uses it as he takes care of them during their dances. When the kachinas are to change dance positions the father makes a cornmeal path for them. He ceremonially feeds them with the

tuwi'ytaqe oovi pam leelenqw pu' utuhu'tingwu. Noq oovi ima himungyam naat pay qa oraymi ökikyangw puma yepeq pas kwiningyaq it patusngwat as paalalwa, put maahut tuwiyat akwa'. Noq pay pam put qa angwutaqw oovi pam naat pepehaq huur patusungw'iwta.

## QAA'Ö

Hopit qatsiyat ep i' qaa'ö pas qa sulawningwu. Hak tiitiwe' tsotsmingwut mooti enang yu'ytangwu. Pu' itam put angqw hiita yuykuya, nöösiwqat, hoomat, ngumnit. Himu haqam hintsakqw i' qaa'ö, sen put angqw himu yukiltingwuqa, pam qa hisat pep qa sulaw. Noq oovi pam it hopit aw pas himuniqw oovi antsa hiita taawi'ewakw ep hiitawat qaa'öt tungwani'yte' pay piw pam put yu'ytangwu. Pu' hak mokq pu' pay piw putakw hakiy engem homvöötotaqw pu' hak paasat haqaminiqey put angningwu.

## HOOMA

It hoomat akw i' hopi as hisat pas naaqavo hintsakngwu. Aasakis talavay pam kuyvate' pam naat piw putakw talpumiq naawaknangwu.

Pu' i' katsinmuy na'am pumuy tumala'yte' pay naat pam piw putakw pumuy tumala'ytangwu. Naalakyaniqw pu' amungem pöötapngwu. Pu' pumuy nopnaqw pu' puma tiivantivayangwu. Pu' tapkiqw yukuyaqw, pay naat pam piw put enang pumuy yuwsinaqw, pu' puma ninmangwu.

cornmeal, whereupon they commence dancing. In the evening, at the conclusion of their performance, sacred cornmeal is again an ingredient in ritually preparing the kachinas for their journey home.

On the occasion of a wedding, after the ceremony is completed and the bride is to return home, a cornmeal path is once more marked on the ground for her. Again when there is a ritual in progress and prayers are being conducted, cornmeal is involved. On *astotokya*, the climactic night of the Wuwtsim initiation, a member of the Kwan society seals off the paths leading into the village with cornmeal. Finally, when one goes to deposit a *paaho* one always takes cornmeal along. Before the *paaho* is deposited, one first prays to it using the cornmeal. This accounts for the expression *hom-'oyto*, "he is going to deposit cornmeal."

## CORNMEAL ROAD MARKER

A cornmeal road is usually made for such beings as the kachinas. They move along the marker in the direction in which it has been laid out. It is employed either as they move from one dance location on the plaza to another, or when they return home upon completion of their performance. A cornmeal path is also made for a new bride by her mother-in-law when the bride is ready to return to her home. Upon this path she travels home. The person making this road marker actu-

Pu' mö'öngna'yat yukiltiqw pu' pam mö'wi nimaniniqw paasat pu' piw put engem homvöö-totangwu. Pu' hiitu yungiwte', pavasiwye', puma piw naat hoomat akw enang hintsatskyangwu. Pu' i' kwaani'ytaqa piw astotokpe put hoomat akw ha-qe' pöhut utatangwu. Pu' himuwa paahoy oyate' pam piw sutsep it hoomat enang kimangwu. Nen pu' pam haqam put oye', pam piw naat hoomay akw put aw naawaknat, pu' paasat put oyangwu. Paniqw oovi himuwa hom'oytoqat pangqaqwa-ngwu.

## PÖÖTAVI

I' pöötavi pay imuy hiituy katsinmuy'ewakw amungem yukiltiqw pu' puma put anawit haqami nankwusangwu. Sen kiisonve haqamiwat naalak-ngwu, sen ahoy ninmangwu. Pu' i' mö'wi piw nimaniniqw, ep pu' i' mö'wi'ytaqa put engem piw pöötapqw, pu' pam piw put ang nimangwu. Pu' himuwa pan pöötapninik pam it hoomat akw tuts-kwava puma, sen hak haqamiwat nakwsuniqat, pangsoqwat pam put engem it hoomat akw tuu-wuungwu.

ally draws a line on the ground with cornmeal. It is generally drawn in the direction in which a group or individual intends to journey.

## DRUM

The drum is one of the musical instruments the Hopi has employed for a long time. Whenever a Hopi performs a ceremony that requires a drum accompaniment, he beats the drum. During the month of Kyaamuya (approximately December) there must not be any drumming. According to Hopi custom, pounding a drum at this time would signify to those living in the underworld that there is life here above.

Drums are usually fashioned from cottonwood trunks. Being hollow inside, each open end is covered with horsehide, which is believed to give the drum a loud "voice." Occasionally cowhide is also used. Long ago, of course, when hides from horse or cow were not available, other animal skins were employed.

Manufacturing a drum also requires creating a heart for it. Since the heart is located inside the resonator it is not visible. The heart consists of a piece of sinew stretched across the inside of the drum with a turkey feather attached in the middle. Just before closing up the drum, the kiva member reputed to have the deepest bass inserts his voice into it by coughing or clearing his throat into the resonator. That done, the drum is considered to possess a deep tone.

## PUSUKINPI

I' hopi pay hisat it pusukinpit akw enang hintsaki. Pam hiita wunime' kur pusukintotaniqw pam put aqw pususutoynangwu. Niikyangw pam it kyaamuyat ep pay put qa aw hintsakngwu, itaanavotiniqw hak ep qa hiita aqw pususutoynangwuniqw oovi. Hak yaw pantsakye' imuy atkyayaqamuy nanvotnangwuniqw oovi.

Noq i' pusukinpi it söhövit angqw yukiwtangwuniikyangw pam aasonva hötsiningwu. Pu' pam nan'ivaqw it kawayot puukyayat'ewakw akw aqw uutsiwtangwu. Pam yaw pavan töna'ytangwuniqw oovi pu' put angqw pusukinpilalwa. Pu' pay ephaqam hakim piw it wakasvukyat angqw piw put yukuyangwu. Hisat pi pay sonqa hiitawat puukyayat angqw pantsatskya, naat qa himu haqam kawayo pu' waakasiningwuniqw.

Pu' hakim put yuykuye' haqam piw put engem unangwat yukuyangwu. Noq pam pay aasonngaqw pakiwtangwuniiqe oovi qa susmataqningwu. Pu' put piw aasonngaqw i' tahu naahoy laana'iwtaqw, pu' put aw i' koyonghomasa suusunasave wiwtangwu. Pam put unangwa'atningwu. Pu' hakim put aqw uutayaniqw, pu' i' hakimuy kivaptuy amungaqw sus'a'ni töna'ytaqa put aqw tönay panaqw, pu' hakim put aqw uutayangwu. Pam put aqw tönay pananinik pam pangsoq öhömtingwu, pu' ephaqam pay natönvastangwu. Pantiqw pu' yaw pam a'ni töna'ytangwu.

Pu' pam pusukinpi piw ephaqam pay sumtsovuningwuqat pangqaqwangwuniqw, oovi himuwa

It is held that at times a drum may easily get chilled. For this reason the drummer will first place it adjacent to the stove and not use it until it has warmed up.

Naturally, a drum must also have a drumstick, which is occasionally referred to as its "husband." Perhaps the drumstick is labeled this way because it is always together with the drum and actually resembles a penis. As a rule, drums are also given a name, usually that of a female.

## ENEMY

An enemy is someone who causes another person harm or grief or is not friendly toward him. In a war the enemy is the one who raids for the other side. Of course, even one's own tribesman or relative can be one's enemy. Long ago such tribal groups as the Navajos, Apaches, Comanches, Kiowas, Chemehuevis, and Yavapais came to raid the Hopi villages and, consequently, were the Hopis' enemies.

## EXTREMELY POWERFUL BEING

A being may have greater than human powers for a variety of reasons. Sometimes these powers are rooted in evil. Other times, exceptional powers may be based on the capability to achieve great things. The kachinas are extremely powerful beings in this sense because they know how to produce rain. All those beings who exist invisibly and aid the Hopi with their knowledge are considered

pusukintaniqa put mooti qöpqöt aqlap tavi'yte' pu' paasat ason pam mukiitiqw pu' pam put aqw pusukintangwu.

Pu' pam pi son piw qa maawiki'ytangwuniqw pay ephaqam put pangqaqwangwu pam koongya'atniiqat. Noq pay pi pam sutsep pusukinpit amumningwuniikyangw pu' pay pam antsa kwasit aw hayawtaqw oovi pay kya paniqw put pangqaqwangwu. Pu' put pusukinpit naat piw tungwayangwuniqw pam maanat tungwniyat makiwngwu.

## TUWQA

I' haqawa hakiy hiita akw yuuyuynaqa, hakiy qa aw yan unangwa'ytaqa, tuwqa'atningwu. Pu' it naaqöyiwuy ep hakiy aw kiipokqa pam mitwat tuwqa'atningwu. Pu' hikis himuwa hakiy naap sino'at hakiy tuwqa'ytangwu. Noq hisat ima himusinom tasavum, payotsim, yotsi'em, kumantsim, kaywam, tsimwaavam, kooninam, puuvuma himusinom hisat yukiq hopiikimiq kikiipokyangwuniiqe oovi puma paniqw hopiituy hisattuwqamat.

## A'NI HIMU

Hak a'ni himunen pay naap hinwat pantangwu. Noq ephaqam himuwa pay soq nukpanvewat pantangwu. Pu' pay hak piw a'ni himunen hak hiita pavanniiqat tuwi'ytangwu. Noq oovi ima katsinam a'ni hiituniiqe oovi puma it yooyangwuy tuwi'yyungwa. Pu' ima qataymataq yesqam puma piw it tuwiy akw hopit pa'angwantotaqe oovi piw a'ni

creatures of superhuman strength. Many of them, such as Old Spider Woman and her grandsons, Pöqangwhoya and Palöngawhoya, Pavayoykyasi, Maasaw, and the Sun god appear in many myths and tales and perform many feats. Since the Hopi cannot perform these feats, they constantly plead to these beings to support them in their lives, each being using its own special methods.

## FAMINE

A famine is a very tragic event, causing people terrible suffering whenever it occurs. Its initial phase is usually marked by crop failure. As time passes, all the stocked corn and other food reserves are slowly depleted. At the point when nothing is left to consume anymore, the famine is on. Not until a god has compassion for the people and rights the wrong committed by them can recovery begin. The Hopi have experienced famines on many occasions.

## FIRE MAKING

Before the advent of matches, the Hopis had to produce fire on their own. Consequently, they had special instruments devised for this purpose. Actually, there were two types. One method employed a flint. While holding the flint close to shredded cedar bark or some other material that ignites easily, one constantly struck the flint. When struck just right, a spark flew off. The instant the spark fell on the tinder one blew on it without let-

hiitu. Noq pay puma it tuutuwutsit ang pas sonqa tangawtangwuniiqe puma hiita tuhishintotingwu, kyaahintotingwu. I' kookyangwso'wuutiniqw pu' put mömatniqw, pu' i' pavayoykyasiniqw, pu' i' maasaw, pu' taawa, pay ii'ima puma hiitu. Noq i' hopi pumuy tuwiyamuy son naap hintiniqe oovi pam pumuy amumi put hiita tuwiyamuy tuuvingtimakyangw yep qatu.

## TSÖNGÖSIW

I' tsöngösiw himu qa lolmaningwuniqw, hakim put aw ökye' hakim kyaananaptangwu. Mooti hakimuy uuyi'am hintaqat akw qa aniwtingwu. Paapiy pu' pay i' tuu'oyi, tunösmaskya'iwtaqa soosoy sulaw'iwmangwu. Paasat pu' hakim pay paapu kur hiita nöönösaniqw pam paasat pu' pep i' tsöngösiwningwu. Pas ason himu hakimuy ookwatuwe' pu' hakimuy hiita qa'antipuyamuy ep amungem aw antsanqw, paasat pu' hakim piw angqw ahoytotingwu. Noq pay hopi put qa suus aw pitu.

## QÖQÖHA

Hisat naat qa haqam himu kohotövuningwuniqw ima hopiit nawus naap hiita akw qööyangwu. Niiqe puma oovi piw paas put engem hiita awiwa'yyungngwu. Noq pam lööpwa. I' suukyawa pilakinpiniqw put akw himuwa hiita laaput'ewakw, paas sisngyiwtaqat, pu' pay piw hiita suu'uwikngwuqat put aw himuwa it pilakinpiy iitsi'ykyangw put aw pilakintangwu. Put pantsakqa it pilakinpit hisatniqw su'an pilakna, pu' put

ting up. As soon as one got the tinder to catch fire and to flame up, one could use it to start a fire.

A second fire making method employed a fire drill. The entire apparatus consisted of a hard stick and a piece of cottonwood root. The drill stick was placed atop the cottonwood and then rotated rapidly between the palms. Soon the spot on the board became very hot and finally turned into glowing embers. A small chunk of crushed cedar bark or a piece of cotton was then placed on top of the cottonwood. Once more, the drill spindle was twisted back and forth steadily until the tinder caught fire. The embers could then be placed on whatever one wished to burn.

## FIREPIT

Within a kiva the firepit is always situated just beneath the entrance ladder. It is in the area north of this firepit that most activities take place. The ancient firepits were usually square and slightly dug into the floor. Its side walls consisted of flat rocks. The fuel was always kept underneath the ladder. The person who looked after the fire was known as *tsoylan'aya* or "fire tender."

angqw i' töövu tsalamte' pu' pam töövu put hiita uwikngwuqat aw posq, pu' pam put aw pooyante' pas qa matavi'ymangwu. Pas ason pam put taqtsokye', pavan uwikne', paasat pu' pam put akw qööngwu.

Pu' hisat piw ayanwat qööyangwu. Pam i' himu pilakho himu huru kohoningwuniqw pu' put enangningwuqa paakoningwu. Put paakot atsmi hak it hurut kohot tavi'ykyangw pu' hak put hurut kohot pavan öqalat may akw muriwantangwu. Noq pu' pam hisatniqw kya pi a'ni mukiite' pu' pam paasat töövutingwu. Pu' hak put paakot atsmi pay hiisakw laaput paas sisngiwtaqat, pu' pay sen pösövit, tavi'ykyangw pu' put muriwantaqw pu' ason pam pas taqtsokq paasat pu' hak put hiita uwiknaniqey aw tavingwu.

## QÖPQÖ

I' qöpqö pay sutsep kivaapeq it saaqat su'atpipningwu. Noq put akwniwi hakim hiita hintsatskyangwu. Pu' pam hisatqöpqö hisat pay nevewvutsqaningwuniikyangw pu' pam aqw atkyamiqwat pay hiisavo hötsiningwu. Noq pam it tusyavut akw angqe ngöyakiwtangwu. Noq pu' puma hiita qööqööyaniqey put saaqat atpik maskya'yyungngwu. Noq pu' i' hak put aw tunatyawtaqa pam tsoylan'aya'amningwu.

## FLINT/ARROWHEAD

Before the introduction of matches, the old people used flint to ignite a fire. Generally, the stone was struck with another hard object to produce a spark. When landing on something like shredded cedar bark or cotton, the spark caused the tinder to catch fire.

A flint arrowhead is said to be the weapon of the rains. When a Hopi finds one, he tends to think, "Lightning must have struck this place; that's why this arrowhead lies here." An arrowhead should never be kept inside a home. Occasionally though, when a person comes across one, he will take it home, smoke ritually over it, and then take it back. Medicine men usually have one among their paraphernalia.

## FLYING SHIELD

In stories powerful beings, such as gods, are bound to own a *paatuwvota* or "flying shield," that they employ as a mode of transportation. With it they reach any destination in no time because they can fly about with the shield. The shield is made from cotton and is woven in the manner of a Hopi wedding robe. The owner of such a vehicle needs only to climb aboard, tug on something and utter a command, whereupon the shield rises in the air and takes him wherever he says. When the being wishes to descend, he goes through the same procedure.

## YOYSIVA

Naat hisat qa haqam himu kohotövuningwuniqw ima hisatsinom qööyanik puma it hiita hurut akw it yoysivat aw pilakintotangwu. Noq pu' put angqw i' töövu hiita laaput sen pösövit aw wukumte' paasat pu' pam put uwiknangwu.

Noq pu' i' yoysiva yaw imuy yooyoyangwtuy tunipi'amningwu. Noq oovi hak put haqam tuwe' hak pan wuuwangwu, "Kur pew it hisat yooyoyangwt mu'ayaqw oovi i' yep yanta." Noq pu' yaw hak piw qa kiy ep put tavi'ytangwu. Niikyangw pay himuwa ephaqam put tuwe', pam put kiy aw yawme', pu' pam put aw tsootsongkt pu' paasat put pay ahoy haqami tavitongwu. Noq pu' haqawat tuutuhikt piw put yoysivat himu'yyungwa.

## PAATUWVOTA

It tuuwutsit ep i' himuwa pay pas a'ni himunii-qa pay pas son it hiita paatuwvotat qa pooko'yte' pam putakw waynumngwu. Noq pam putakwnen pam haqami suptungwu, pam yaw putakw puuyawnumngwuniiqe oovi. Noq pam yaw it pösövit angqw yukiwkyangw pay it oovat an pöqniw-tangwu. Pu' pam put pooko'ytaqa put aqw wuuve', pu' hiita langangaykinat pu' aw pangqawqw, pu' pam oomi hölölte' pu' put haqami wikngwu. Pu' pam hawninik pay piw antingwu.

## GOING OUT TO SPEAK THE EARLY MORNING PRAYER

Since people hold a variety of beliefs, we each pray to different gods. Thus, we Hopi address our heartfelt wishes to "one who lives unseen." But we do not really address our prayers directly to this being. Rather, we turn early in the morning towards the rising sun and pray for all beneficial things concerning ourselves, our relatives, our children, and people in general. The sun, upon receiving these prayers, takes them to a place unknown. The appropriate time for this prayer ritual is just before sunrise.

## GRINDING CORN

When a woman or girl is to grind corn she first shells the amount of dried corn she wants and then winnows it so that the chaff and worm-eaten kernels can be separated. Next, she puts the corn kernels into the coarse grinding stone and there begins to crush them, coarse-grinding everything. This done, she heaps the corn back up in the slanted metate and grinds it repeatedly to make it finer. Finally, the corn becomes cornmeal, and when the desired texture is reached, it is scooped from the grinding bin. Next, the woman builds a fire under a roasting pot, and dry-roasts the cornmeal until no trace of moisture is left. Then she places the corn in a finer metate, spreading it out to

## KUYVATO

Pay pi itam sinom qa sun tuptsiwni'yyungqe oovi itam nanap hiituy amumi naanawaknangwu. Noq itam hopiit pi tuwat it hakiy hiita qataymataq qatuuqat aw itaa'unangwvaasiy oo'oyaya. Niikyangw pay itam qa put pas aw put oo'oyaya. Hak talavay naat pay pas su'its talpumiq neengem, pu' piw sinomuy, timuy, sinmuy amungem hiita lolmatniqat pangsoq naawaknangwu. Noq pu' pam taawa put ömaate' pu' pam put haqami kimakyangw tuwat yang oova nakwsungwu. Pu' hak piw pan kuyvate' pay naat taawat qa pas yamakqw hak pantsantongwu.

## NGUMANTA

Wuuti, maana ngumantanik pam mooti hiisa'niqey paasa' huumit pu' paasat put wuwhingwu. Pu' pam put pantiqw pu' i' tsiipu'atniqw pu' i' aavu'iwyungqa ang ayo' löhökngwu. Paasat pu' pam put hakomtamiq oye' pu' pam put pangqe haakokintangwu. Ephaqam put hakomtat mataaki'at pööngalaningwu. Pu' hak putakw put tuqyaknangwu. Tuqyaknat pu' pam paasat piw ahoy oomiq kweete' paasat pu' pam put angqe piw pan ngumantangwu, angqe haanintakyangw pu' pam hihin tsaatsakwtangwu. Paasat pu' pam put hakwurkwakyangw pu' kur pay pangsayniniqw pu' pam ahoy put intangwu. Inte' pu' pam haqam tulakinsivut atpipoq qööhe' pu' pam put aqw tulaknangwu. Pangsoq pu' pam put laknat paasat

cool off, at which time she fine-grinds it. This accomplished, she sifts the cornmeal to remove any remaining chaff and, if she wishes, grinds it once more.

## HAHAY'IWUUTI

According to Hopi belief Hahay'iwuuti is the mother of all kachinas. Appearing only at special ceremonies she accompanies, for example, the So'yoko ogre group and also comes during the performance of the two Sa'lako puppet girls. She has her own peculiar song that she keeps singing over and over. Characteristically, she has a very high pitched voice in which she both talks and sings. She always carries a small water vessel and a perfect ear of corn. From the vessel she pours a small amount of water into the palm of her hand and pats it on people's heads. With this gesture she symbolizes the hair washing ritual.

A female infant always receives a flat Hahay'i as her first kachina doll. A new bride is also presented one on the occasion of the Niman ritual. This doll she slides down her body for the purpose of bearing many children.

The Hahay'iwuuti who appears in Orayvi wears a *nasomhoya* or "little knotted hairdo of the non-marriageable girl" on each side of her head, whereas the one appearing in the villages of the other mesas has a *torikuyi* or "braid," a married woman's hairstyle. The front of Hahay'iwuuti's

pu' put angqw ahoy tsaame' pu' pam put pingyamtamiqwat oyangwu. Pu' pam put pangqe möyikni'ykyangw put hukyani'ytaqw pu' pam ason hukyaqw paasat pu' pam put angqe piingyantangwu. Pu' pam put paas piingye' pu' pam paasat put tsaatsayat pu' ang tsiipuyat ayo' maspat pu' paasat piw angqe haananik pantingwu.

## HAHAY'IWUUTI

Hopitniqw i' hahay'iwuuti pay soosokmuy katsinmuy yu'am. Pu' pam pay hiitasa ep piw pitungwu. Ephaqam pam imuy sooso'yoktuy amumum waynumngwu, pu' pam piw imuy manawyatuy ngumantaqw ep pam piw pitungwu. Pu' pam oovi pite' pam piw pas naap taawi'ytaqe oovi pam put tawlawngwu. Niikyangw pu' pam piw tötönawyaniiqe oovi pas oova yu'a'atikyangw pu' piw pang tawmangwu. Pu' pam piw it kuywikorot angqw kuuyiwtaqatnit pu' it tsotsmingwut enang yawnumngwuniiqe, pam put kuywikorot angqw mapqölmiq hiisaq kuyt, pu' pam paasat put akw hakiy qötöyat aw palalaykinangwu. Pan pam hakiy tuwat asnangwu.

Noq pu' manawya tihut susmooti makiwe', pam it hahay'it putsqatihut mooti makiwngwu. Pu' i' naat pu' löökökqa aapiy nimantikive piw put makiwe', pu' pam put naapa siroknangwu, pam hapi ti'o'oyniqey oovi.

Noq pam yepeq orayveqniiqa nan'ivaqw qötöveq nasomhoya'ytangwu, pu' pam kiyavaqkiva

forehead is adorned with a fluffy eagle breast feather. In addition, she has bangs of red hair. Each of her cheeks is marked with a circular red spot. Her mouth is painted in the fashion of an upside-down crescent moon with a small black dot, directly above it. The configuration of the eyes is exactly like that of the mouth.

## HAW!

When a man wants to let something be known to another person, he first announces his presence with, *"Haw!"* and then tells him what he wants to say. Thus, long ago it used to be customary that when a man approached someone else's home he first shouted, *"Haw!"* Following that he might have added, "Is anyone at home?" Or on a different occasion today, if a man is to fetch another person at a kiva, he will first climb to the kiva's roof and call, *"Haw! Is he down there?"* In the case of a woman, the appropriate exclamation is, *"Hawaa!"*

## HEHEY'A

There is one particular kachina whose name is Hehey'a. One type, known as Kuwanhehey'a or "Colorful Hehey'a," is very handsome. *Hehey'amuy taaha'am*, the "Uncle of the Hehey'a," on the other hand, is very homely and speaks backwards. He has hair consisting of lamb's wool and adorns his head with a bunch of red peppers. His face is black with a distorted mouth. For a nose he has a corn cob in whose top is inserted a turkey wing

torikuytangwu. Pu' pam suukw suuqalpeq kwavöönakwa'ykyangw pu' paalangput qalmongwa'ytangwu. Pu' pam piw taywave nan'ip paalangput pongokput qöma'ytangwu. Pu' put mo'a'at it puhumuyawuy supatangqatsqat su'an pe'ytakyangw pu' atsve pay hiisayhoya piw qömvit akw tsookokiwtangwu. Pu' poosi'at pay piw antangwu.

## HAW!

I' taaqa hakiy hiita navotnanik mooti, "Haw!" kitat pu' paasat hiita pangqawniqey pangqawngwu. Meh, hisat kya pi himuwa hakiy kiiyat aw pite' mooti aqw pangqawngwu, "Haw!" Pu' pay paasat angk sen ayangqawngwu, "Ya qa hak qatu?" Pu' paasat himuwa haqami kivami hakiy sen wikte', pam mooti kivats'omi wuuve', pu' piw aqw pangqawngwu, "Haw! Ya pam qa pepeq pakiwta?" Noq wuutinen pu' tuwat, "Hawaa!" kitangwu.

## HEHEY'A

I' suukya katsina antsa piw hehey'a yan maatsiwa. Noq peetu, ima kuwanhehey'am, puma pay pas suhiituniqw pu' pumuy taaha'am pay tuwat okiw hin'ewayniikyangw pu' piw ahoytuqayta. Noq i' hehey'amuy taaha'am mangpukqötö'ykyangw pu' tsiilit nakwa'ytangwú. Pu' pam qömvit taywa'ykyangw pu' toritsangwtangwu. Pu' pam piw sööngöt yaqa'ytaqw put ooveq it koyongot masa'at aqw tsööqökiwtaqw pu' put poosi'at qa

155

feather. His eyes are sad-looking. Kaolin is used for his body paint, and red deer hoofs are depicted on both sides of his arms and thighs. His whole upper torso is clad with a goat skin, and his waist is girdled with a silver concho belt. In addition, the uncle wears a kilt and footless black stockings that go up to the knee and are tied to the shin by means of narrow woven belts. His brown-colored moccasins are decorated with embroidered ankle bands, and from his hips dangles a rattle made of antelope hoofs. Wherever the uncle arrives in the company of the Kuwanhehey'a, he acts as their side dancer and mimes the words of their chants. During the performance of the Sa'lako puppet drama, a pair of Hehey'a uncles participates who tote on their backs the grinding stones of the little puppets. During the actual dance of these two marionettes, the two uncles act out the words of the song in pantomime and also check the fineness of the sweet cornmeal the puppets are grinding. More than one *hehey'a-muy taaha'am*, also come with the So'yoko ogre kachinas. In this role, they carry ropes.

## HOMINY STEW

Any meat served in stewed form is known as *nöqkwivi*. In days past cottontail, jackrabbit, or deer meat was the primary ingredient, which accounts for such specific names as rabbit stew and venison stew. Nowadays mutton and beef are used. In addition, hominy stew contains *paatsama* or

haalayqat an soniwngwu. Pankyangw pu' pam tumatsöqa'asi'ykyangw pu' paalangput akw maynit pu' qaspe nan'ip sowi'ingwtanat peeni'ytangwu. Pu' pam piw it kapir'aapat torikiwkyangw pu' atsva sipkwewtangwu. Pankyangw pu' pam it pas pitkunat kurivaqe pitkuntangwu. Pu' pam piw hokyanavankyangw pu' put angqe kwewawyat akw namoy ang somi'ytangwu. Pankyangw pu' pam lomasawkototskyangw pu' honhokyaasomkyangw pu' pam piw it tsöptanat pi'alhaytangwu. Pu' pam imuy hehey'amuy amumum pite' pam pay pumuy amuqle' wunimantinumkyangw pu' paasat pumuy hiita taawi'yyungqw pam put maasantangwu. Pu' piw imuy manawyatuy ngumantaqw, ep puma lööyöm piw pumuy amumum pite' puma pumuy matayamuy iikwiwnumngwu. Pu' pumuy manawyatuy wunimaqw, puma pumuy nan'ivaqw qatuwkyangw pu' piw taawit an maasankyangw pu' pumuy manawyatuy toosiyamuy aw pingvoptangwu. Pu' puma pay qa suukya imuy sooso'yoktuy amumum ökingwu, wikpangwa'ykyaakyangw.

## NÖQKWIVI

Nöqkwivi pay naap himu sikwi kwangwqa, kwiiviwtaqa, pamningwu. Niikyangw hisat ima hopiit pay imuy taataptuy, sowiituy, sosowi'yngwamuysa pas nönöqkwipyangwuniqw oovi pam sowinöqkwiviningwuniikyangw pu' piw sowi-'ingwnöqkwiviningwu. Noq pu' itam pay imuy kanelmuy pu' piw waawakastuysa sikwiyamuy nö-

"shelled corn kernels." Long ago when people were hired for a specific task, their only remuneration was hominy stew. Such a stew is also served at any communal work party as well as on the final day of many major ceremonies.

HOPI

We Hopi settled here ages ago and we are still here. But the land is not ours. We are here only as tenants. We emerged from the underworld at the Grand Canyon with many races of people and then migrated in all directions.

The being who first inhabited this upper world gave us explicit instructions, and we are the only people that still adhere in some ways to these instructions. Tradition has it that we first undertook a long migration before arriving here in Hopi country. Along the way we left many structures that still exist as ruins. It is as if in this way we marked out the land area that is ours. Some of those participating in the migration were Hopi just like us, but when they arrived at certain places they settled permanently for some reason. Yet our destination was a place called Tuuwanasavi or "Earth Center," and only after reaching this place were we to settle for good. These were our instructions, though they were not followed by other men.

It seems as though a Hopi does not do any evil, hence the name Hopi, which means "good, well-behaved, civilized." But some of us are evil.

nöqkwipya. Noq i' nöqkwivi piw paatsama'yta-ngwuniqw pam paatsama it humitat angqw yuy-kiwa. Noq pu' hisat himuwa hiita aya'yte' pam pay nöqkwiviysa akw hiita aya'ytangwu. Noq pam nöq-kwivi pay pas sutsep na'yat epningwu pu' piw tiikive.

HOPI

Itam hopiit pay pas kyaahisat yepeq yesva-kyangw pay itam naat yepeqya. Noq i' pay qa itaatutskwa, itam pay naat yep haakyese. Nii-kyangw itam yaw pay soosok hiituy sinmuy amu-mum as öngtupqaveq nöngakkyangw pay itam pangqw naanan'i'voq nankwusa.

Noq i' hak mooti yep qatuuqa itamumi hin tutaptaqw pay itamsa naat pay put tutavoyat hihin anhaqam yeese. Noq itam yaw mooti angqe' haqe' wuukonankwusat pu' peqw hopiikimiq öki. Niiqe itam yaw angqe' a'ni kiiqötotaqw naat pam angqe' hongya. Niiqe itam oovi songyawnen angqe' hiisaq tutskwa'yyungqey put akw itam angqe' tuvoyla-tota. Noq pu' peetu piw pay as angqe' nankwusa-qam pay as piw itamun hopiitniikyaakyangw pay puma haqamiwat ökye' pay puma hiita akw pep pas huruyesva. Noq itam hapi as naat yuk yaw ha-qami tuuwanasami mooti ökit pu' paasat pep pas suus yesvaniqat yan as i' itamumi tutavoniqw pay pumawat qa pantoti.

Noq pu' i' hopi as hiita qa nukpanat himuyat suupan hintsakqe oovi pan natngwaniy'ta. Noq pay peetu itamungaqw nuunukpant.

## KACHINA

A kachina is very special to a Hopi. Although the kachinas live unseen, they appear in person when someone calls them from Hopi country. On arrival they entertain us all day long. They visit us with the intention that all will be well, and they bring us gifts consisting of food prepared by their sisters. At the conclusion of their dances we present them with *paaho* and pray that they take our messages in all directions so that we may be constantly visited by rain. But a Hopi does not pray solely for himself; he prays for everyone who is thirsty, including animals and plants. He prays to the kachinas for rain for all things.

The kachinas inhabit a variety of places. They usually reside where springs surface. They travel about by way of clouds and visit us in that guise. Way back in the past the Hopi did not carry out kachina ceremonies on their own. At that time it was the actual kachina gods who came to the Hopi. Because some Hopi were evil, however, and began to show disrespect for the kachinas, the kachinas abandoned them. Before departing they turned over their secrets to the Hopi. From that time forward the Hopi had to carry on the kachina cult by themselves.

## KATSINA

I' katsina it hopit aw pas himu. Noq pam katsina pay as qataymataq qatuqw pay haqawa hopiikiveq pumuy wangwayqw pay puma pepeq pas naap ökingwu. Noq pay hakim paasat pumuy oovi tuwa'yyungngwu. Nen pu' puma piw hakimuy taawanawit songyawnen tiitaptotangwu. Niikyangw pay puma soosok hiita lolmatniqat enang tunatyawkyaakyangw hakimuy pootayangwu. Pu' hakimuy amungem na'mangwuy siwamuy noovayamuy oo'oyayangwu. Noq pu' puma tiitso'nayaqw pu' hakim piw pumuy yuwsinayat pu' pumuy amumi okiwlalwangwu. Puma hapi naanan'i'vo tuu'awwisqw pew yooyangw piptuniqat oovi. Niikyangw hopi pay qa neengemsa it yan naawaknangwu; pay pam sopkyawatuy sinmuy paanaqso'iwyungqamuy amungem enang naawaknangwu, pu' piw imuy popkotuy amungem, pu' uuyiy piw engem. Pay pam soosok hiita hiihikwqat engem pumuy amumi yoynawaknangwu.

Pu' puma pay haahaqe' piw ki'yyungwa. Haqam paahu yamakiwtaqw pay puma pang tuwat yeese. Niikyangw pay puma imuy oo'omawtuy akw yaktaqe oovi puma putakw hakimuy poptayangwu. Noq hopi hisat as it katsinawuy qa naap hintsakngwu. Hisat ima pas katsinam pas naap imuy hopiituy amumi ökiwtangwuniqw pay pi i' hopi nukpananiiqe oovi pay pumuy haqaapiy qa kyaptsi'ymaqw pu' puma pay son pi put ep haalaytotiqe pu' pay puma pumuy pas suus maatatve. Niikyangw pay puma pumuy piw put

## KIVA

Many different kachinas hold their dance performances in the kivas. But they are not the only ones who make use of the kiva. When the initiates of a secret society are to hold their ceremonies they also assemble within these underground structures. For example, the men stage their religious activities here during Wuwtsim. In addition, the Powamuy, the Flute, and the Snake societies, to mention only a few, congregate here for their secret endeavors.

Social dancers, too, use the kivas to practice. In winter, men and boys occupy the kivas engaging in whatever activities are assigned to them. Thus, one may bring his weaving to the kiva and set up his loom there. For Powamuya, kachina dolls, bows and arrows, and other items of this nature are manufactured. Since the women, too, have rituals of their own, the Maraw and Lakon societies also carry out their ceremonies in a kiva. So these religious chambers are not occupied solely by men. A kiva is off limits only to uninitiated children. It is not until the month of Paamuya, and the night dances following the Powamuy rites, that these children, accompanied by their mothers or grandmothers, are allowed to witness the dances. On these occasions they watch, together with the women, from the raised area at the south end of the kiva's interior. At one time even young girl initiates were not permitted to go witness dances unaccompanied. The same was true when they

tuwiy mooti amumi no'ayat pu' haqamiya. Paapiy pu' pay hopi nawus naap put katsinawuy hintsaktima.

## KIVA

Yang kivanawit pay hiihiitu katsinam tiilalwangwu. Niikyangw pay qa pumasa it kivat akw mongvasya. Pay hiituywatuy wiimiyamuy aw pituqw puma piw pang yungiwta. Ima taataqt it wuwtsimuy ang puma pang hintsatskyangwu. Pu' ima popwamuyt, leelent, tsuu'tsu', pay puuvuma haqamwat yungiwtangwu.

Pu' ima tsetslet tuwanlalwe' pay puma piw kivanawit pantsatskyangwu. Noq pu' hakim taataqt, tootimnen yangqe' tömölnawit piw hakim kivaapa yesngwu. Pu' hakim pay pang hiihiita pay taqahiita tumala'yyungngwu. Ephaqam himuwa tuulewniy pangso yawme' pam pep put langakni'ytangwu. Pu' hakim piw it hiita tihut, awtat, puuvut hiita powamuymi pang kivanawit yuykuyangwu. Noq ima momoyam piw naap wiimi'yyungqw oovi ima mamrawt, lalkont piw haqamwat put aw pituqw pep kivaape yungiwtangwu. Niiqe oovi pay qa taataqtsa pang yesngwu. Pay ima tsaatsayomsa qa wiiwimkyam pangso qa yungtangwu. Pas ason paamuynawit pu' piw angktiwqat ep ima katsinam pang yungiwmaqw pu' pam tsay pangsoq yuy, soy amum tiimaytongwu. Pu' puma pangsoq ep tiimaywise' puma pay tuuwingaqwsa tiitimayyangwu, imuy momoy-

went there to practice for a social dance.

The ancestors of the Hopi all lived in kivas once. Thus, in the eyes of the Hopi, the kiva is also a home. However, it was not like the dwellings we inhabit today, but rather was simply a hole dug in the ground with a cover on top. Entering the kiva was only possible by descending a ladder.

## KOOYEMSI

The Kooyemsi is a kachina for both the Hopi and the Zuni people. His head is painted with reddish-brown ochre; small globes are attached in place of his ears and on the top and back of his head. This accounts for the appellation *tatsiqtö* or "ball head" occasionally applied to him. From the balls hang turkey feathers. The kachina's mouth and eyes can take on various shapes. Around his neck some sort of cloth is usually tied. For a kilt he wears a folded woman's dress and his waist is adorned by a silver concho belt. On his legs and feet he wears footless black stockings and brown (sometimes white) moccasins. At times he may also go barefooted. In his right hand the Kooyemsi carries a rattle that has its own distinctive style, and in his left hand he holds an eagle wing feather with which he motions while dancing. A second feather is tucked into his kilt on his back.

A Kooyemsi can fulfill more than one function. While not considered a clown, the kachina will perform in funny ways similar to a clown. In the past

muy amumum. Hikis ima mamant naamahin wii-wimkyamniikyangw hisat qa nanalt pangsoq tiimaywisngwu, pu' piw tsetsletuy tuwantawise'.

Noq ima hisatsinom as soosoyam kivat ang yesngwu. Niiqe oovi i' kiva hopitniqw pay piw kiihuningwu. Niikyangw pam pay itamuy pu' hinyungqat ki'yyungqw qa pantangwu. Pam hisat pay yaw tutskwat aqw hangwniwkyangw pu' ki'amiwtangwu. Niiqe oovi himuwa pangsoq pakininik pam pay it saaqatsa ang pangsoq pakingwu.

## KOOYEMSI

I' kooyemsi itamuy hopiituyniqw pu' si'ootuyniqw pay piw katsina. Noq put qötö'at pay it sutat akw lewiwtaqw pu' hak haqam naqvu'ytangwuniqw pam pepnit pu' koopaveqnit pu' qötöy aakwayngyaveq tatsi'ytangwu. Niiqe pay ephaqam oovi himuwa put tatsiqtö kitangwu. Noq pu' pam haqam tatsi'ytaqw put angqw i' koyongvöhö piw enang haayiwtangwu. Niikyangw pu' pay pam naap hintaqat poosi'ykyangw pu' mo'a'ytangwu. Pantakyangw pu' pam pay hiita tsatsakwmötsaput ngöntangwu. Pu' pam tuwat it kanelmötsaput nömökput pitkunkyangw pu' sipkwewtangwu. Pu' pam piw hokyanavankyangw pu' paasat sawkototskyangw pu' ephaqam pay piw qötsatotstangwu.
Pankyangw pu' pam putngaqw aaya'ykyangw pam pay piw pas naap hintaqat aaya'ykyangw, pu' suyngaqw kwaawukit yawtangwuniiqe, pu' pam

he acted in this role only during dances performed by kachinas classified as *taqkatsinam* or "powerful, manly kachinas" such as the Hoote, Hooli, and Tsa'kwayna. Today, he no longer clowns for the *taqkatsinam* in any of the villages. Only at Zuni does he still carry out this function. Whenever a kachina group requires a drummer, the Kooyemsi will also take on this task.

In the days when the Hopi men still herded sheep, a shepherd participating in a kachina dance might once in a while not have the time to prepare an elaborate mask. He would then simply put on a Kooyemsi mask and join the dance group. A Kooyemsi could therefore appear in conjunction with such diverse costumes as those worn by the Long Hair kachina or the Hoote. The dancer would dress exactly like the other kachinas except for the head, which would represent a Kooyemsi.

There are occasions when a large group of Kooyemsi will sing as a chorus for the other nonchanting kachinas. Also, each time clowns are part of a kachina plaza dance, a few Kooyemsi always act as *kipokkatsinam* or "Raider kachinas." Hence they are named *kipokkokoyemsim* or "Raider Kooyemsi." Also in the past they used to arrive in the village during the month of *Ösömuyaw* (approximately March) to challenge the girls to all sorts of guessing games in the dance court. Occasionally, they would also come during kachina night time performances for this same reason.

putakw maasankyangw wunimangwu. Pu' aakwayngyangaqw pam piw sukw pitkunay aqw tsurukni'ytangwu.

Pu' pam pay tuwat qa suukw hiita aw awiwa. Noq pam pay as qa tsukuniikyangw pay pam piw tsukut an kunalawngwu. Niikyangw pam hisat as pay piw pas imuy tsutskutuy amun tsukulawngwu-niikyangw pam tuwat imuy pas taqkatsinmuy, imuy hootemuy, hoolimuy, tsaatsa'kwaynamuy, pumuy hiituy amumi tsukulawngwu. Niikyangw pu' pam pay qa hisat haqam hopiikiveq pumuy amumi tsukulawngwu. Niikyangw pam yepwat si'ookiveq pay naat pumuy katsinmuyatuy amumi tsukulawngwu. Pu' pam piw pay hiituywatuy pusukintotaqamuy amungem pusukintangwu.

Pu' hisat ima taataqt naat kanelvokmu'yyungngwuniqw ephaqam himuwa nuutumnen naat laalaye', qa qeni'yte', pam pay putsa ang pakit pu' pay hiituywatuy amumumningwu. Noq oovi ephaqam pay suukyawa piw koyemos'angaktsinaningwu, pu' pay sen hooteningwu. Pam pay pumuy amun yuwsi'ykyangw pay qötöveqsa koosemsiningwu.

Pu' ephaqam piw puma kyaysiwqam hiituywatuy amungem tawvongya'yyungngwu. Pu' piw katsinmuy amumi tsukulalwaqw, ima peetu pay pas kiipokninik ökingwuniiqe puma oovi kipokkokoyemsimningwu. Pu' piw puma hisat as ösömuyvahaqe' navö'ökye', puma kiisonve imuy mamantuy amumum nanavö'yangwu, pay naap hiita akwa'. Pu' puma ephaqam pay piw mihikqwtikive paniqw ökingwu.

## LARGE BELT ("RAIN SASH")

The *wukokwewa* or "large belt" has been woven by Hopi men for a long time. It belongs to any dancer's outfit and is worn by certain types of social dancers as well as certain kachinas as an integral part of the dance costume. Above all, this belt must be provided to every daughter-in-law. The central portion of the belt consists of a wide band that has a long fringe on each end. The beginning sections of the individual cords making up the fringe contain ball-shaped objects referred to as *siipölö* or "flower buds." The belt is slung around the waist in such a way that the fringe falls downward, symbolizing rain. Because a Hopi forever desires rain, the strands imitate this weather phenomenon.

## LEFTHANDED KACHINA

The Suyang'ephoya, literally "lefthanded person," differs from the other kachinas in that he carries his rattle in his left hand and the bow in his right. His body decoration is identical with that of Eewero, that is, his left arm has alternating black and white stripes. The same goes for his right leg that is striped in this manner. Wrapped about the kachina's upper torso is a piece of buckskin, and a quiver is slung across his back.

## WUKOKWEWA

It wukokwewat pay hopi hisat yuuyuwsi. Hak pay hiita wunimaninik put enang yuwsi'ytangwu. Noq oovi ima peetu tsetsletniqw pu' piw ima peetu katsinam put enang yuwsi'ykyaakyangw tiivangwu. Pu' i' hopi it mö'wiy pas as son put engem qa yukungwu. Noq pam pöqniwtangwuniikyangw pu' sunasava pay wuuyaqaningwu. Niikyangw pam nan'ivoq qalavoq wuuwupat tsona'ykyangw pu' haqam tsona'at yayngwa'ytaqw pep i' sipölö'at pakiwtangwu. Noq put pi hak kwewte' hak put kwewtaqva kwewtangwuniqw, put tsona'at oovi atkyamiq siwukiwtangwuniqw pam it yooyangwuy tu'awi'yta. Pay pi hopi sutsep yooyangwuy naawaknangwuniqw paniqw pam oovi piw put tututskyayna.

## SUYANG'EPHOYA

I' suyang'ephoya pay piw suukya katsinaniikyangw pam tuwat suyngaqwwat aaya'ytangwuniikyangw pu' putngaqw awtay yawnumngwuniiqe oovi paniqw pàn maatsiwa. Pu' pam it eewerot an tsöqa'asiy'tangwu. Put maa'at suyngaqwwat qömvitnit pu' qöötsat akw naanatsva kwikwilvuningwu. Pu' pam hokyay ang putngaqwwat pay piw antangwu. Pu' pam it sowi'yngwat torikiwkyangw pu' hotngat piiw.

## LIGHT-COMPLEXIONED PERSON

Because in the past the Hopi carried out most of their activities in the sun, their skin was usually dark-pigmented. Hence, when a person had fair-complexioned skin, he or she was usually admired because of it; this is especially true of a female. Light-colored skin, therefore, enhances the beauty of a Hopi girl or woman.

## LONG HAIR

In the past the Hopi never cut their hair. They wore it in long tresses, which added to their handsomeness and beauty. As a rule, when young boys and girls wore their hair long in this manner, they let it flow down their backs. During adolescence a girl wore her hair rolled up and tied to the sides of her head. Later, as she reached marriageable age, she dressed it in large whorls resembling the wings of a butterfly. A young man used to fold his long hair and tie it into a bun on the back of his head.

## LÖHAVUTSOTSMO
(Volcanic hills northeast of Flagstaff)

Shortly before reaching Nuvatukya'ovi (the San Francisco Mountains) as one comes from Hopi, there is an area with a series of hills and mounds in close proximity to each other. These elevations are known to the Hopi as Löhavutsotsmo or "Testicle Hills." When looking at these hills on one's way from Kaktsintuyqa, they closely resemble testicles, hence the name.

## SIKYAVU

Hisat hopi pi pay sutsep taavitsa ep hiita hintsakngwuniiqe pam oovi pay hisat qa pas kwangw'ewakw toko'ytangwu. Niiqe oovi himuwa haqam sikyavuniqw put hopi aw kwangwa'ytuswangwu, tis oovi maanat. Himuwa maana, wuuti oovi pan sikyavunen pam putakw son'ewakoy aw hoyokni'ytangwu.

## ANGA

Hisat hopi höömiy pay qa tukungwuniiqe pam oovi hisat wuuwupat anga'ytangwu. Noq pam piw pay itakw enang naasuhimu'ytangwu. Pu' hisat tiyoniqw pu' manawya wupa'anga'yte' puma pay angaapuyawtangwu. Noq pu' maana wuuyoqte' pu' pam naasomkyangw pu' pam kongtanisayte' pu' pam poli'intangwu. Noq pu' tiyo pay pas ason taaqate' pu' paasat hömsomngwu.

## LÖHAVUTSOTSMO

Hak yangqw hopiikingaqw yuk nuvatukya'omiqniikyangw pay naat hak qa pas aw pituqw, pang i' naanaqle' tsotsmo. Noq put pang tsotsmot i' hopi pan tuwi'yta, löhavutsotsmo. Pay hak naat pu' kaktsintuyqangaqwniikyangw hak put tsotsmot aw yorikqw, pay pam put löhavut anhaqam soniwngwuniiqe paniqw oovi pam pang pan maatsiwa.

## MAASAW

Maasaw was the first inhabitant of the land when the Hopi emerged into this upper world. He is its overseer for another being who is the true owner of our world. Permission for the Hopi to settle here was given by Maasaw. Due to his grotesque features it is said that he will never reveal his real face to anyone. Should he approach someone, however, he will do so in human form and as a very handsome man.

After being granted permission to inhabit his land, the Hopi entreated Maasaw to be their leader, but he refused. He told them that they had arrived here with great ambitions that must be fulfilled before he would become their leader. He added that it was true he was the first being on this earth, and he would also be the last. After these words he disappeared from sight.

## MASK

Whatever someone wears over his head to hide his face constitutes a *tuviki* or "mask" for the Hopi. Another term for such a device is *kwaatsi*, which literally translates as "friend." Although merely a mask, it becomes alive the minute it is prepared for use. And when the living mask detects something negative about its wearer, it will take revenge on him. Thus, during a particular ceremony, a dancer may become weary before the day is over. Another may complain that the mask is hurting him. He

## MAASAW

I' hak himu maasaw yaw susmooti yep it tuuwaqatsit ep qatuqw ima hopiit pew nönga. Noq pam yaw hak it yep tutskwat hakiy engem pas himu'ytaqat aw tunatyawta. Niiqe pam oovi imuy hopiituy hu'wanaqw pu' puma yep yesva. Noq pu' pam hak pay yaw son hisat pas hin soniwqey pankyangw hakiy aw naamaataknani. Pi yaw pam nuutsel'ewakw pitsangwa'yta. Pu' kur pam hakiy aw pituninik, pam yaw suhopiniikyangw suhimutaqaniikyangw yaw hakiy aw namtaknangwu.

Noq pu' pam antsa imuy hopiituy hu'wana yep yesniqatniqw pu' puma as put aw ö'qalya put mongwi'yyungwniqeyniqw, pay pam qa nakwha. Pay yaw itam naat a'ni hin tunatyawkyaakyangw pew öki. Ason yaw itam put aw antsatsnaqw paasat pu' yaw pam sen pantini. Pay yaw as pam antsa mooti yepniikyangw, pay yaw pam naat nuutungktatoniqey pumuy amumi yan lavaytit pu' haqami naatupkya.

## KWAATSI

Pay hak hiita ang pakiwkyangw hiita akw naatupki'ytangwuniqw, pam itamuy hopiituyniqw tuvikuningwu. Pu' pay itam piw put kwaatsi yan tuwi'yyungwa. Niikyangw pay pam naamahin as pamsaniikyangw hak put yuwsinaqw pam taatayngwu. Niiqe pu' pam oovi piw hakiy aw hin hiita nukusnavote', pam hakiy put ep songyawnen ahoy aw naa'oyngwu. Noq oovi ephaqam himuwa

may feel fine in the morning but then all of a sudden the mask may turn on him. If the wearer of the mask then changes his attitude, the mask quickly ceases to cause him pain. Consequently, a mask must not be upset or toyed with under any circumstances, and it is imperative to have a pure heart when engaging in a kachina ceremony.

Traditionally, the kachina impersonator wishes for various foods while adding the various attachments to the bare mask. Typically, he will say, "Let this, its ear, be a peach as it goes on here. Let this, its eyeballs, be grapes as it gets tied on here. Let this, its snout, become a squash as it is attached here." Thoughts of this kind cross the impersonator's mind while he is mounting all the pieces that form part of the mask.

Generally, masks are kept at home out of sight. Sometimes they are also stored at a kiva. On *totokya*, the day before a dance ceremony, the masks are first assembled properly and then fed with honey. A drop of honey may be placed right into the mouth hole, or at times, people may put the honey in their mouth, mix it with saliva and then spray the mixture over the mask.

Long ago, when the kachinas did not wear masks, they used to hide their faces with Douglas fir. As a result, children never attended a dance performance in those days. Today, *tuutukw-nangwt* or "Cumulus cloud" kachinas still do not don masks but conceal themselves behind an array

naat pay tiikive qa tapkinat pay maangu'yngwu. Pu' himuwa oovi piw pangqawngwu put kwaatsi'at tuuholawqat. Naat as pu' talavaynenhaqam qa aw hin nanvotq, pu' pay naat yankyangw pam put pantsanngwu. Pu' kur pam hak put ang pakiwtaqa naa'alöngtaqw, pay pam paasat piw put qa tuuholawngwu. Yaniqw oovi hak put qa hinwat yuuyuynangwu. Pu' piw hak oovi as sonqa suyanis'unangwa'ykyangw put katsinawuy hintsakngwu.

Pu' yaw hak it hiihiita nöösiwqat tungla'y-kyangw put kwaatsiy aw hiita kwaplawngwu. Niiqe oovi hak unangwngaqw pangqawngwu, "Nam i' naqvu'at sipalaniikyangw yep it aw yantani. Nam i' posvölö'at oovaniikyangw yep it aw somiltini. Nam i' motsovu'at patnganiikyangw aw piw yantini." Yaayan hak wuuwankyangw hak hin hakiy kwaatsi'at nuumi'ytaniqat pan aw hiita kwaplawngwu.

Noq ima pay hakiy kiiyat ep haqaqw qa susmataqpungaqw tangawtangwu. Pu' pay ephaqam piw kivaapeningwu. Noq pu' totokpe hakim pumuy yuwsinaye', pu' hakim piw pumuy it momospalat nopnayangwu. Pu' haqam pam mo'ahötsiniqw pangsoq put hiisakw tsakwangwu. Pu' ephaqam hakim pay amuupa pavoyayangwu.

Pu' ima katsinam naat pay pas hisat qa kwatstangawtangwuniiqe puma it salavit akw naatupki'yyungngwuniqw oovi ima tsaatsayom yaw hisat qa tiimaywisngwu. Noq pu' pay ima tuutukw-nangwt piw qa kwatstangawkyaakyangw puma it

of turkey feathers held together with twine. Others, such as the *paavangwt* or "Mountain sheep" kachinas may do the same at times. In the eastern pueblos along the Rio Grande, kachinas still disguise their faces with Douglas fir. Such kachinas are termed *piniitom* by the Hopi. To this day, the Hopi kachina known as Tsito covers his features in this manner with fir branches.

## METATE

A Hopi woman utilizes corn flour on a daily basis. Consequently, in the past it was a must for her to possess her own grinding stone or metate. There are two types of grinding stones. One is a coarse-grained slab, the other is a fine-grained one. Sometimes the coarser metate is equipped with two handstones or manos, implements with which the grinding is carried out. Generally, the woman first shells her corn, then grinds it down to the proper size in the coarse grinding bin. By repeating this process she produces flour with a coarse texture. After she removes the flour from the bin, she dries it in a hot kettle. Next, she places it on the finer stone slab where she regrinds the entire amount two or three times.

The metate proper forms an enclosure with four sides of thin flat stone slabs. In the front of the grinding stone is a narrow channel referred to as *matavuva*. A similar channel runs along each side. These channels, about equal in width to the front

koyongvöhöt qek'iwtaqat akw naatupki'yyung-ngwu. Pu' ima hiituwat sen pi paavangwt piw ep-haqam panyungngwu. Pu' hopaqkivaqe puma pee-tu pay naat salavit akw naatupki'yyungngwu. Noq ima hiitu yanyungqam yaw hiitu piniitomningwu. Pu' i' tsito piw pay naat pan salavitsa akw naatupki'ytangwu.

## MATA

I' hopiwuuti pay sutsep ngumnit hintsakngwu-niiqe oovi pam hisat pay pas sonqa naap mata'y-tangwu. Noq pam mata lööpwaningwu. Suukya-wa hakomtaniqw pu' mi'wa pingyamtaningwu. Noq i' hakomta ephaqam lööqmuy mataaki'ta-ngwu. Pam wuuti susmooti huumit pu' pam put hakomtavaqe hingsakwniqat put qayaknangwu. Pu' pam piwnen pu' pam put hakwurkwangwu. Paasat pu' pam put pangqw matangaqw ipwat paasat pu' pam put tulaknangwu. Paasat pu' pam put pingyamtamiqwat tangate' pu' paasat pangqe put lööš, paayishaqam haanangwu.

Noq pam hongni'at naanan'i'vaqw matamiq i' tusyavu ki'iwtangwu. Pu' put matat mookyaqe hiisaq puutsi pam put matavuva'atningwu. Pu' pam nan'ikyaqe aqw oomiq pay piw an puutsin-ngwuniikyangw pu' angqe oovaqe pay piw an hii-saq puutsit matavuva'ytangwu. Noq i' mata ooveq-wat pay atkyaqniiqat ep hihin ooveningwuniqw oovi ngumantaqa put atkyamiqwatsa haaninta-ngwu. Noq pu' himuwa angqw aakwayngyangaqw

one, are sloped upward. Along the top there is still another channel that is also termed *matavuva*. Overall, the top end of the metate is positioned somewhat higher than the bottom part, so that the person grinding is compelled to make downward strokes only. The place behind the grinding bin where the grinding is carried out in kneeling position is referred to as *mataptsö* or "metate corner."

As the process of fine grinding the corn goes on, the finished flour is placed into a pottery vessel where it is firmly packed down. Not all the flour can be removed from the slab, however; a small amount always remains. So the person grinding takes a brush, licks it in order to moisten it, and with spittle removes the small amount remaining by touching it with her brush. In this way all the flour is cleaned off the metate.

People are told not to step inside the grinding bin. Should someone do so, according to a saying, one's colon will protrude from one's anus.

## MIXED KACHINA DANCE

When an assortment of various kachinas stages a dance together, they are referred to as *Soyohimkatsinam* or "all types kachinas." Mixed kachina groups of this kind traditionally sing during performances of the Water Serpent drama and the puppet play of the two Sa'lako girls. However, they can also dance on their own at just about any time.

möyiqtuwkyangw ngumantangwuniqw, pangqw pam put mataptsö'atningwu.

Paasat pu' pam put ngumniy piingyankyangw pangsoq tsaqaptay aqw inlawngwu. Pu' pam put aqw huur ngungu'ytikyangw put pangsoq inlawngwu. Pu' pam put pantsakkyangw pay qa soosok intangwu. Pu' pam qa soosok intaqw, pam angqw hiisa'hoya peetingwu. Pu' pam matawsiy ang lengitsmiqw pu' pam mowatingwu. Nen pu' pam put tutsvalay akw put hiisa'hoyat peetiqat, put matawsit akw aw tongongoykinaqw, pu' pam put aw huurtiqw pan pam put pangqw soosok ipwangwu.

Pu' yaw hak pangsoq matamiq qa pakingwuqat hakimuy amumi pangqaqwangwu. Hak yaw pangsoq pakye', hak yaw pakoymakngwu.

## SOYOHIMKATSINAM

Ima katsinam pay soosoyam hinyungqam neyngawtaqam tiive' puma soyohimkatsinamningwu. Niikyangw puma pay pas sutsep imuy lölöqangwtuynit pu' piw imuy sa'lakwmantuy amungem tawlalwaqw puma tiivangwu. Pu' puma pay piw naap hisat pas naap tiikive'yyungngwu.

## MUSANGNUVI (Second Mesa village)

When the Musangnuvi people arrived here they first settled on the west side of Kwangwup'ovi. In due course, when they expressed a desire to become integrated members of the village of Songoopavi they approached the *kikmongwi* to ask his permission. Tradition has it that they were very loquacious and that they spoke quite aggressively. Whenever the *kikmongwi* said something they were quick to give a negative reply. But the *kikmongwi* of Songoopavi spoke to them as follows: "There is no way that you can live with us here in Songoopavi. We have become quite numerous here. If your heart is indeed set on living here with the Hopi, build your own settlement at that butte off to the east. There I have my seeds stored. If you really want to settle here among us, go to that place, establish a village, and guard my seeds." The Musangnuvis consented and did exactly that.

## NORTHWIND

The Hopi dread *kwingyaw* "the northwind," because it is a malevolent wind that freezes the crops and peach orchards. The wind always comes from the north and is ice-cold.

## NUMBER "FOUR"

A Hopi always does things either four times or in multiples of four. Thus, when a group of people engage in a ceremony which is planned to run its

## MUSANGNUVI

Pam musangnuvi pi pay susmooti peqw pituuqe pam yep kwangwup'oviy taavangqöyveq mooti kitsokta. Kitsoktat pu' pam as songoopaviniwtiniqe pu' pam oovi pangso kikmongwit aw maqaptsita. Pu' yaw pam piw a'ni lavayi'yta, a'ni yaw nukpantuqayta kya pi pam musangnuvi. Noq yaw kikmongwi hingqawqw pay yaw pam piw naap hin put aw sulvaytingwu. Noq pay yaw pam put aw pangqawu, "Pay kur uma hin yep songoopave itamum yesniy," yaw kita. "Pay itam wuuhaqti yep'e. Pu' uma pas antsa yep itamum hopiituy amumum yep yesninik, uma pep hoop tuukwive naap kitsoktotani. Pep hapi nu' ivoshumiy hiihiita tanga'yta. Kur uma pas antsa yep itamumyaninik uma pangsoye', uma pep kiitote', pu' uma pep ivoshumtangay tuuwalayaniy," yaw amumi kita. Pu' yaw pay musangnuvi nakwhaqe pu' panti.

## KWINGYAW

It hiita kwingyawuy hopi pay mamqasi, pam himu pay qa lomahintaqw oovi. Pam it uuyit pu' it sipal'uyit soq tuusungwtangwuniqw oovi. Niikyangw pam pay sutsep yangqw kwiningyaqwsa pitungwuniikyangw pam piw pas iyoho'ningwu.

## NAALÖS

Hopi pay pas sutsep naalössa aqw hiita hintingwu. Pu' pam pay piw nanalsikisniikyangw pu' piw suukop enang akw hintsakma. Noq oovi hiitu-

entire length, they will be in session for the full sixteen days. At other times they may go on for only
eight or even four days. By the same token, when a
Hopi seeks a response to his inquiry, he will ask up
to four times only and then quit. At that point he
will be given an answer if he did not receive one
right away. Thus there is not a single aspect of
Hopi culture that does not require the number
four. Likewise, the creator has now purified us
thrice. If he cares to repeat this purification and
cleanses us once more, we will live thereafter as we
should.

## NUVATUKYA'OVI (San Francisco Mountains)

The mountain range to the southwest of Hopiland is known by the name of Nuvatukya'ovi. The
Hopi go there during the Home dance, and occasionally at Powamuya, to gather evergreens. Since
shrines are located there, those who go to gather
these evergreens deposit *paaho* at these sites. It is
Hopi belief that the mountains are one of the
homes of the kachinas; therefore, there is a kiva at
the summit of the peaks. Nuvatukya'ovi also constitutes one of the traditional boundary markers of
Hopiland.

## ORAYVI (Third Mesa village)

According to some, the Hopi first settled at
Songoopavi. There the *kikmongwi* and his
younger brother are said to have differed over

wat sen hiita yungiwte' kur puma pas aqwhaqami
pan yungiwtaninik puma suukop taalat ang aqw
yungiwtangwu. Pu' puma ephaqam pay panis nanalsikis sen naalös yungiwtangwu. Pu' oovi piw
himuwa hiitsa sen aw maqaptsitaninik, pam piw
naat naalös pantit, pu' pay paasavoningwu. Ason
pepeq pu' pam hinwat put aw lavaytingwu, kur
pay qa aapiy hu'wananinik. Pay oovi qa himu
hopit hiita himu'at qa naalöq aqw tuwani'yta. Pu'
pay i' hak itamuy it hikwsit maqaaqa pu' pay
paayista itamuy powataqe, oovi pu' yaw pam kur
piw naat itamuy hiitawat akw powataniniqw,
paapiy pu' yaw itam pas hin yesniqey pas pan
yesni.

## NUVATUKYA'OVI

Nuvatukya'ovi pay it hopiikit aatavang tuukwi
pan maatsiwa. Pangso itam tuwat it itaahintsakpiy
nimaniwuy ep pu' piw ephaqam powamuyve
uymokwisngwu. Pu' pang piw tuutuskyaniqw
pang piw puma uymokwisqam it paahoy oo'oyti-
wisngwu. Pu' pam pep piw itamuyniqw imuy katsinmuy kii'amniqw oovi yaw pepeq ooveq piw pas
kiva. Pu' i' hopi hiisaq tutskwa makiwa'ytaqw pam
piw put qalalni'at.

## ORAYVI

Peetuyniqw hopi yaw songoopave susmooti
kitsokta. Noq pu' yaw puma hakim pep naatupkom, i' kikmongwiniqw pu' tupko'at, kya pi hiita

some matter. As a result, some believe the younger brother left, headed north and started his own community at Orayvi, while others claim that the Hopi, after their emergence at the Grand Canyon, first embarked on a migration before establishing their first settlement at Orayvi.

. More recently, the people of Orayvi clashed due to differing views regarding the white man's way of life, in particular, schooling. This led to the banishment of the faction that rejected the Anglo way of life. It, in turn, founded the village of Hotvela. After renewed conflicts there, some people settled at Paaqavi. Next, several of those who wanted to adopt the way of the whites, and who had remained at Orayvi, moved below the mesa and established another village where they worked for the government. Today that place is known as Kiqötsmovi. Yet others, for some reason, migrated to Munqapi, a place the Orayvians had already been going to on foot for ages because of the farming land they owned there. Thus, as a result of the banishment, several villages now exist north of Orayvi.

## PAIRED PAAHO

The *neveqvaho*, literally "side-by-side *paaho*," is made by the Wuwtsim initiates. It consists of two sticks, one of which is painted blue-green, the other black. The blue-green stick represents a female and is beautiful; the latter represents a male.

ep neepewtiqw, pu' i' tupko'atwa yaw pangqw naakopanqe pu' pam kwiniwiqniiqe pu' orayve tuwat naap kitsokta. Noq pay pi qa soosoyam it sun navoti'yyungqw, peetuyniqw hopi pay öngtupqaveq yamakkyangw pu' angqe' mooti nakwsukyangw pu' paasat orayve mooti kitsokta.

Noq pu' hayphaqam puma pep it pahanqatsit, tutuqayiwuy ep piw neepewtotiqw, pu' paasat puma pep naahonayaqw, pu' ima qa pahannanawaknaqam pu' pangqw nöngakqe pu' oovi hotvelpeq tuwat kitsoktota. Pu' pay puma piw tuwat hiita ep neepewtotiqw, pu' puma peetu paaqavitwat ep yesva. Noq pu' ima peetu pay pahannanawaknaqam orayve huruutotiqam atkyami hanqe pu' piw pepwat tuwat yesva. Pay puma pep tumalyesva. Noq pam pepeq pu' kiqötsmovi yan natngwani'yta. Paasat pu' piw peetu munqamiqwat hintiqw pi oovi tuwat nönga. Niikyangw pangsoq pay ima orayvit hisat sasqaya. Puma pepeq paasa'yyungngwuniiqe oovi pangsoq naap hisat sasqayangwu. It naatsikiwuy akw pu' oovi orayviy kwiniwiqwat pu' qa suukya kitsoki.

## NEVEQVAHO

It neveqvahot ima wuwtsimt tuwat yuykuya. Noq pam sutskyaqe sakwawsaniikyangw pu' pam ayangqewat qömviningwu. Noq put neveqvahot tsotsokpi'at nan'ikyaqe pantangwuniqw, pam suukyawa wuutiningwuniiqe oovi pam pas lolmaningwu. Noq pu' aqle'niiqa, i' qömviwa, pam

The rear of the *neveqvaho* is covered by a turkey feather. The *mösi* or "pouch" attached is fashioned from dried cornhusk. It contains food consisting of all the various kinds of seeds and is usually daubed with honey. In addition, sprigs of mountain sagebrush and snake weed are tied to the *paaho*. Also attached is a fluffy eagle down feather on a piece of string that is termed its "breath." Both the female and the male stick have faces drawn with corn pollen at the tip. Others claim that the faces are painted with *pavisa*, the yellow clay collected at the foot of the Sipaapuni. Thus, while both *paaho* sticks have the same face, the male is stained black in the lower portion in contrast to the female stick whose stem is blue-green. Both sticks are sharpened to a point at their bottom end; these points represent the legs. Since the ends are also painted black, the male *paaho* is almost always entirely black.

## PAIUTES

The Paiutes are a native people with a culture quite different from that of the Hopi. For ages they sought out the Hopi country on their raids. Generally, they arrived from a northerly direction. Today, during the event of a social dance, the Hopi also disguise themselves to resemble other tribes, including the Paiutes.

yaw taaqaningwu. Noq puma it' koyongvöhöt ustangwu. Noq pu' pam mösi'ytangwuniqw pam it silaqvut angqw yukiwtangwu. Pu' pam angqe put paahot atkyaq tsotsokpiyat aw somiwtangwu. Pu' put mösiyat ep put tunösmoki'at mookiwtangwu. Pep pay i' soosoy himu poshimu mookiwtangwu. Pu' put piw it momospalat akw lelwiyangwu. Noq pu' i' kuungyaniqw pu' i' maa'övi piw put aw somiwtangwu. Pu' put aw i' kwavöhö hikwsi'ytaqa somiwtangwu. Noq pu' pam wuutiniqw pu' taaqa puma taywa'ytangwuniiqe oovi puma piw talasit akw ooveq lewiwtangwu. Pu' pay piw pangqaqwangwuniqw pam it pavisat akw pep tayway ep lewiwtangwu. Pu' pay puma as suntaqat taywa'ytaqw i'wa taaqa atkyamiq qömviningwuniqw pu' mi'wa, wuuti, atkyamiq sakwawsaningwu. Pankyangw pu' puma atkyaq piw aqw tsuku'ytaqw pam yaw hokya'amningwu. Noq pepeq pam piw qömvit akw lewiwtangwu. Noq oovi pam taaqaniiqa pay pas peep soosoy qömviningwu.

## PAYOTSIM

Ima payotsim pay piw tuwat himusinom, niikyangw puma pay hisat hopiikimiq ökiwtakyangw, puma pangsoq kiipokye' pu' pangsoq ökingwu. Puma pay tuwat kwiningyahaqaqw pangsoq ökiwtangwu. Noq pu' hakim tseletikive piw imuy himusinmuy enang yuuyaangwuniiqe oovi hakim imuy payotsimuy akw tsetselyangwu.

## PEACHES

The Hopi acquired the peach from the Spaniards, who brought this fruit with them when they arrived at Hopiland. Ever since that time peaches have been part of the Hopi diet. As a result the Hopi now own many peach orchards. As soon as the peaches are ripe, they are carried home and large quantities of them are spread out to dry in various places. They need to be split and pitted before they can be dehydrated in the heat of the sun. At times special structures are erected solely for this purpose. Peaches dried by this process will last indefinitely. Rations of dried peaches can easily be taken on short trips or on long journeys. The traveler is in this way not burdened down by a great bulk of food. When the peaches are boiled, *piiki* can be dunked into their juice. Peaches are also consumed when people undergo a purification rite and are forbidden to partake of certain other foods.

## PIIKI (Hopi dish)

*Piiki* is an ancient food of the Hopi. When a woman plans to make it she begins by heating up her stone griddle. She then boils some water and pours it on the blue flour. That accomplished, she adds wood ashes mixed with water, giving the batter its hue. As soon as her stone griddle is hot enough, she gathers ground melon seeds, burns them and then rubs the remains into the surface of the griddle to make it smooth again. Next she

## SIPALA

It sipalat pay i' kastiila peqw hopiikimiq pitukyangw pam put enang hinvaqw, pu' i' hopi paasat put angqw put himu'yva. Niiqe paapiy pu' pam put pay enang sutsep tuumoytangwu. Noq pu' pam oovi it sipaltsokit qa suup himu'ytaqe pam oovi put kwangwtiqw, pam put kiy aw oye' pu' pam put haqe' wukomöyni'ytangwu. Niikyangw pam mooti put putsimnat, pu' angqw poosiyat ayo' tuuvat, pu' paasat pantaqat taplakni'ytangwu. Pu' ephaqam pam piw pay pas put engem haqam sipalmöyankitangwu. Noq pu' i' sipala pan laakye' pam wuuyavotingwu. Pu' hak put pan lakput pay ephaqam haqaminen, hak put nitkya'yme', pay hak put angqw moylawngwu. Nen pay hak qa pas hiita nöösiwqat enang naasos'onmangwu. Pu' hak put piw kwalakne' pay hak piw put aqw pikqentangwu. Pu' piw hakim naanapwale' hakim ep piw pay pas putsa pas noonovangwu.

## PIIKI

I' piiki pas it hopit hisatnösiwqa'at. Wuuti piktanik pam mooti tumay aqw qööngwu. Qööt pu' pam tuupatangwu. Tuupate' pu' kwalakqw pu' pam put sakwapngumniy aw wuutangwu. Ngumniy aw wuutat paasat pu' pam qötsvit aqw piw kuyqw pu' put paqwri'at put qöötsapkuyit akw kuwantingwu. Pu' put tuma'at mukiitiqw pu' pam put sivostosit sumitsovalat paasat pu' pam put ang taqtsokt pu' paasat put akw tumay ang maamapringwu. Pam pantiqw pu' put tuma'at ahoy talviti-

spreads the liquid batter on the griddle. When the batter is done she removes the *piiki* sheet and spreads a new layer of batter over the griddle. The previously made *piiki* is now placed on top and becomes moist from the steam of the new batter. The completed *piiki* can then be rolled up and set aside for storage. From that point on she continues rolling and stacking one *piiki* on top of another.

It is said that Old Spider Woman is skillful and talented in many things, so someone eager to learn how to make *piiki* prays to her. Old Spider Woman also resides somewhere west of Orayvi. Thus, whenever a girl wishes to learn the art of *piiki* making, she takes some wood to her abode and leaves it there for Old Spider Woman along with some sacred cornmeal.

## PLAZA

The plaza is usually situated somewhere near the middle of a village, hence it is used as the dance court if a ceremonial activity is taking place or kachinas have come. Various other non-kachina dances are also performed in the plaza. The Snake, Lakon, and Kwan societies, for instance, carry out their dance performances there.

Houses are erected on all four sides of the plaza, and alleys lead into it. In the past, when certain items were to be traded, someone would make a public announcement on behalf of the vendor, who would then sell his things at the plaza.

ngwu. Pu' pam paasat pik'oyqw pu' pam paasat kwasingwu. Put pam sukw ang ayo' hölöknat pu' pam piw ep lelwingwu. Pu' pam put mootiniiqat put naat pu' ang lelwiqey atsmi taviqw pu' pam pay söviwangwuy akw mowatingwu. Paasat pu' pam put muupat pu' ayo' tavingwu. Nit paasat pu' pam pay piw antikyangw pu' pay pansa put aapiy yuykungwu, put muupankyangw pu' put naanatsva oo'oyngwu.

Pay it kookyangwso'wuutit pangqaqwangwuniqw pam yaw tuhisaniikyangw pu' piw nawiso'aniqw oovi himuwa piktuwi'yvanik pam yaq put aw naawaknangwu. Noq ayam orayviy taavangqöyve pep atkyahaqam pam kur piw kiy'ta. Noq oovi hak pan piktuwiy'vanik hak pangso put kiiyat aw kohot kimangwu. Pu' hak hoomat enang put aw oyangwu.

## KIISONVI

I' kiisonvi pam pay haqamwat kitsokit ep pay sunasavehaqamningwuniqw oovi pam pan natngwani'yta. Noq himu hintsakqw sen katsina pite' pam pep wunimangwu. Pu' pay piw aapiy hiihiimu tiitikive pep hintsakiwa. Meh, pay ima tsuutsu't, lalkont, kwaakwant, pay ii'ima pep tiikive'yyungngwu.

Pu' pay pangqw naanan'i'vaqw kiikihu aqwwat hongyangwu. Pu' pay angqw piw aw kiskya'yyungngwu. Pu' hisat himuwa hiita huuyaniniqw, haqawa put engem pan tsa'lawqw, pu' pam paasat piw ephaqam pep huuyangwu.

## PÖVÖLPIKI (a Hopi dish)

To prepare *pövölpiki* a woman first boils water that she then adds to a bowlful of blue flour. Into this she pours water mixed with ashes, blending everything again. If desired she can add sugar to make the mixture sweeter. In the past, women used to add pulverized prickly pears as a sweetener. This recipe was then known as *yöngövövölpiki*. If the batter is still too watery, she adds more flour to thicken it. When it finally has the right consistency, she takes small amounts at a time and rolls them into little balls. Then the balls are boiled.

## PRAIRIE DOG

Prairie dogs exist in great numbers on Hopiland and form part of the Hopi diet. Whenever one is out hunting for small game, one also considers this rodent as possible prey.

## PRAYER FEATHER

A *nakwakwusi* is fashioned to the accompaniment of a prayer. Then smoke is exhaled on it. This type of prayer feather has more than one function. It can be the symbol of a path laid out, but it can equally well be worn on the head. It also serves to represent symbolically the breath of life. A *nakwakwusi* is produced from the downy breast feather of an eagle, together with hand-spun cotton twine.

## PÖVÖLPIKI

Pövölpikit yukuniqa pay kuuyiy kwalaknat pu' paasat ngumniy tsaqaptat aqw oyat pu' kuuyit kwalalataqat ngumniy aqw wuutangwu. Pu' pam piw qöötsapkuyiy aqw wuutakyangw pu' put enang qöqringwu. Pu' pay pan naawaknaqa pay aqw piw kwangwa'öngat oyangwu akw kwangwtaniqey oovi. Noq hisat ima momoyam it yöngöt tos'iwput akw put kwangwlalwangwu. Noq pam i' yöngövövölpikiningwu. Kur put paqwri'at pas paakuypuniqw pu' pam put ngumnit akw huruutangwu. Pu' pam hihin huruutiqw, paasat pu' pam put may akw angqw hingsakw tutkilawkyangw pu' put pölölantangwu. Pu' pam put yukye', pu' pam pay piw kuuyit piw aqw kwalaknangwu.

## TUKYA

Ima tukyaat hopiikivaqe kyaastaqw, ima hisatsinom pay piw pumuy enang noonova. Pay himuwa hiita tsaakw maqnume', pay pam pumuy enang wuuwankyangw angqe' maqnumngwu.

## NAKWAKWUSI

Nakwakwusit hak pay piw aw okiwlawkyangw put yukungwu. Pu' hak piw naat put aw tsootsongngwu. I' nakwakwusi pay qa suupwat engem. I' suukya pöötaviningwu, pu' paasat pay hak piw put nakwa'ytangwu. Pu' ephaqam hak hiita put hikwsitoynangwu. I' nakwakwusi pay it kwavöhötnit pu' pösöptonit angqw yukiwta.

## PRAYER STICK

A *paaho* is not only made from a variety of items, but it is also fashioned in many different ways. While it is never made from the breast feather of the eagle, it can be made from turkey feathers. *Paaho* can be found hanging from the ceilings of kivas. When kachinas are to return to their homes they are given *paaho*. The members of the Kwan, Al, and Wuwtsim societies each fashion their own unique *paaho*. A great diversity of *paaho* is made at the time of Soyalangw. It is said that those for whom the *paaho* is intended are elated upon receiving it. A *paaho* carries with it a person's most intense wishes and prayers. A medicine man who has treated you takes what ails you along with a *paaho* and goes to deposit it. In fact, there is nothing that the Hopi does not make a *paaho* for. He makes it for the sun, the moon, deities who exist unseen, and all the other beings that he relies upon for his existence.

## RAIN

The Hopi are forever praying for rain. By drinking the moisture of rain-bearing clouds their plants will grow. With the resulting crops the Hopi sustain themselves. Whenever a serious ceremony is conducted, longing for rain is always on the minds of the participants. Also, whenever the kachinas are about to return home, prayers for rain

## PAAHO

I' himu paahoniqa pam pay hiihiita angqw yuykiwkyangw pu' piw qa sun yuykiwa. Niikyangw pam pay qa hisat kwavöhöt angqw yukilti. Pu' pay piw it koyongvöhöt angqw enang paaholalwa. Meh, pay kivaapa panyungwa, haqaqw kyeevelngaqw haayiwyungngwu. Pu' pay imuy katsinmuy ninmaniniqw pu' pumuy put huytotangwu. Pu' pay piw ima hiihiitu kwaakwant, aa'alt, wuwtsimt, puma piw qa sunyungqat paaholalwa. Pu' piw soyalangwuy ep qa suukya paaho yukiltingwu. Pay imuy hiituy amungem put yuykuyaqw, puma tuwat put ömaatote' yaw tuwat haalaytotingwu. Pu' pay piw pam hakiy unangwvaasiyat, okiwayat enang yawmangwu. Pu' pay himuwa tuuhikya hakiy aw mamkyaqa piw paahot enang hakiy hiita tuuyayat enang hom'oytongwu. Pu' pay hopi qa hiita qa engem paahotangwu. It taawat, muuyawuy, pu' imuy qataymataq yesqamuy, pu' pay aapiy soosok hiituy amumi enang tatqa'nangwqey pumuy amungem pam piw paahotangwu.

## YOOYANGW

Hopi sutsep it yooyangwuy oovi hiita aw okiwlawu. Put uuyi'at hapi imuy oo'omawtuy paalayamuy hiihikwkyangw pu' nawungwni'ymangwu. Noq pu' paasat itam hopiit putakw enang nayesni'yyungwa. Aasakis himu pas pavanniqa hintsakqw, hakim it yooyangwuy oovi enang wuuwankyaakyangw put hiita hintsatskyangwu.

175

are uttered so that they may carry these petitions with them.

## RATTLE

Rattles are fashioned from gourds. They contain small pebbles that give them their "voice." Whenever a Hopi dances, he carries a rattle. This applies to both kachina and social dancers. Kachinas, as a rule, have unadorned rattles. However, should a kachina wish to have a painted rattle, he usually colors it a uniform blue-green, or occasionally white. Sometimes the rattles of social dancers and kachinas have flowers depicted on them. Almost all the kachinas' rattles are flat on each side. Only the Kooyemsi have round ones. However, once in a while a kachina or social dancer will carry a small, round rattle. The members of the Antelope society carry white roundish rattles. In former times some rattles were manufactured from the scrotums of antelope or other game animals. Normally, the women used these rattles when putting their infants to sleep.

The rattles given to children at the occasion of Powamuya are not at all decorated in the same manner. And while a little girl ceases to receive a rattle at a certain age, little boys will always get one during Powamuya. The small rattle given to an infant is painted blue or green and decorated with bird tracks. Together with the rattle, a little boy

Aasakis ima katsinam ninmaniqw, pay naat hakim piw put amumi tuuvinglalwangwu, itaalavayiy angqe' tuu'awvayaqw yokvaniqat.

## AAYA

I' aaya pi pay sutsep tawiyat angqw yukiwtangwuniqw pu' put aasonngaqw i' qalavi tangawtaqw put pam akw töna'ytangwu. Noq i' hopi hiita wunime' pam it aayat yawkyangwningwu. Noq oovi ima tsetsletniqw pu' katsinam pay pas sonqa aaya'yyungngwu. Pu' puma katsinam pay qa pe'ytaqat aaya'yyungngwu. Pu' pe'ytaqat aaya'ytaniqa pay soosok sakwawsat akw lelwingwu. Pu' himuwa piw pay qöötsatsa akw lewiwtaqat aaya'ytangwu. Pu' pay imuy tsetsletuynit pu' katsinmuy aayayamuy ephaqam pay ep piw himu sihu'eway pe'ytangwu. Noq pay katsinam peep soosoyam it nan'ivaqw putsqat aayat himu'yyungwa. Pu' ima kookoyemsim tuwat pölangput aaya'yyungngwu. Pu' ephaqam hiituwat katsinam sen tsetslet piw ayawya'yyungngwu, niikyangw pölangput. Pu' ima tsöötsöptsa it pongokput, qöötsat aaya'yyungwa. Noq pu' hisat i' peehu aaya pay it hiita tsööviwuy pu' pay pan tuutuvosiptuy löhavuyamuy yaw angqw yuykiwa. Pu' ima momoyam put akw aayankyaakyangw timuy puupuwvitsnayangwu.

Pu' powamuyve ima tsaatsayom it aayat makiwyangwuniqw, pam pay qa sun pe'yyungngwu. Niikyangw i' manawya pay haqaapiy aayat qa makiwngwu. Niikyangw i' tiyooya pay sutsep

annually receives a bow until the time he is initiated into the Kachina or Powamuy society.

One of the rattles he may receive has a blue-green mark in its center and a white background. The blue-green marking consists of a fairly large-sized spot that is said to represent the earth. After all, when it rains for a long time, the earth is green throughout just like this color. In the middle of the rattle and radiating out from the navel of the gourd into the four cardinal directions are four lines with hooks. Some say they symbolize the migratory routes the Hopi took before arriving at Orayvi. After this migration, they claim, the Hopi gathered back at Tuuwanasavi, the "Center of the Earth." The blue-green patch is encircled by a black line decorated with dashes of white. From the top of this configuration, little red crooked lines that are supposed to represent the sun branch in a multi-directional pattern. Around the edge of the rattle, dividing the gourd in half, is a design resembling barbed wire. It is said to depict the Milky Way. At the top of the rattle is attached a bunch of eagle down feathers, all of them sticking upward, except for one that dangles down and resembles a prayer feather worn on the head.

aayat makiwngwuniikyangw pay piw powamuy-vesa. Pu' i' tiposhoya it sakwawsatsa ang tsirokukve'ytaqat makiwngwu. Noq pu' tiyooya pay pas wimkyatiniqey aqwhaqami put awtay enang makiwngwu.

Noq i' suukyawa aaya sunasave sakwawsat akw pe'ytaqa qöötsatsa tutskwa'ytangwu. Pam pay su'awwuyaqat sakwawsat akw pep pongokiw-tangwu. Noq pam yaw it yep tutskwat tu'awi'ytaqe oovi yan yooyoklawqw, i' yang tutskwa pan sa-kwatalngwu. Noq pu' put aasonve tawiyat sipna-yat angqw naanan'i'voq naalöyöm ngölöshoyat an-taqa paalangput akw angqw pe'yyungngwu. Noq pay peetu pangqaqwaqw pam yaw imuy hopiituy angqe' kuktotakyangw pu' pew oraymi ökiqw put yaw pam tu'awiy'ta. Pan yaw puma angqe' nan-kwusakyangw pu' piw ahoy pangso tuuwanasami ahoy tsovalti. Noq pu' pam put sakwawsat angqe qömvit akw uutsiwkyangw pu' qöötsat akw ang longna'ytangwu. Pu' put atsva i' paalangpu angqw oomiq naanan'i'voq ngölöwyungngwuniqw, pam yaw it taawat tu'awi'yta. Noq put aayat angqe qalavaqe piw siva'uutsi'eway pe'ytaqw, pam yaw pangqe it soongwuqat tu'awi'yta. Pu' put aayat ooveq i' kwavöhö piw angqw oomiq tsomikiw-kyangw pu' suukya angqw ayo' haayiwtangwu. Pam pay it kwavöönakwat su'antangwu.

## SIKYAQÖQLÖ KACHINA

The Sikyaqöqlö is another type of Qööqöqlö except that his head is yellow, hence the name Siyaqöqlö or "Yellow Qöqlö." The crown of his head and the sides where the ears are normally located are adorned with the complete wings of a medium-sized bird. At the village of Songoopavi a pair of Sikyaqöqlö usually appears during the Powamuy ceremony. This is also true at Orayvi and the other villages of Third Mesa where, during the ceremony, the pair goes about delivering bean sprouts at times. Once in a while the two Sikyaqöqlö may also join the large kachina procession taking place in the same afternoon. At that time, the Sikyaqöqlö constantly shake their rattles and incessantly chat with one another. They have their own distinct song that they chant as they walk about. They wear two buckskins sewn together in the fashion of a woman's dress and turquoise blue moccasins. Therefore, they are not dressed very elaborately.

## SMALL WEDDING ROBE

During the wedding ceremony two bridal robes are woven for the female in-law. One is large, the other, which is smaller in size, is called ovawya or "little wedding robe." Previously sacks were manufactured from these garments; they also served people as seats.

## SIKYAQÖQLÖ

I' sikyaqöqlö pay piw as qööqöqlöniikyangw put qötö'at sikyangpuningwuniqw paniqw oovi pam tuwat pan natngwani'yta. Pu' pam qötöveq, koopaveqniikyangw pu' hak haqam naqvu'ytangwuniqw pam pepeq it hiitawat pay wuukoq tsirot puukyayat nakwa'ytangwu. Noq pam songoopave tuwat powamuyve pitungwuniikyangw puma lööyöm pitungwu. Pu' pay orayve puma piw pan lööyöm pitungwuniikyangw pay piw powamuyveningwuniiqe oovi puma ephaqam haru'o'oytinumngwu. Pu' pay puma ephaqam piw ep nuutum qöqöntinumngwu. Pu' puma ayayatoyni'ynumngwuniikyangw pu' piw naami hiita yu'asvekiwnumngwu. Pu' puma piw naap taawi'ytaqe oovi puma piw put taatawtinumngwu. Pu' puma it lööqmuy sowi'yngwat namitskiwtaqat kwasa'ykyangw pu' sakwatotstangwu. Puma pay oovi qa pas hiihin yuwsi'ytangwu.

## OVAWYA

It mö'öngna'yat ep hakim mö'wiy engem lööq oovat yukuyangwuniqw i' suukya wuuyaqaningwu. Noq pu' suukyawa, pay qa aasaqaniiqa, pamwa ovawyaningwu. Pu' hisat put pay angqw tukput yuykuya. Pu' piw pay put atsvewlalwa.

## SOMIVIKI (a Hopi dish)

*Somiviki* is made from the batter of blue corn flour. It is wrapped in a cornhusk and then tied in two places with yucca strips. After being packaged this way it is boiled.

## SONGOOPAVI (Second Mesa village)

Songoopavi lies southeast of Orayvi. According to the traditions of some, the Hopi established their first settlement there. However, they did not settle on top of the mesa then, but migrated there much later. Tradition also has it that two brothers, the *kikmongwi* and his younger brother Matsito, had differences of opinion that resulted in the latter's moving to Orayvi. He took some people along and founded Orayvi. For some unknown reason the people of Songoopavi and the people of Orayvi do not speak the same dialect, even though they are both Hopi.

## SORCERER/SORCERESS

A sorcerer is the equivalent of an evildoer. For this reason we, the Hopi, did not inform the sorcerers that we wanted to ascend to this upper world. Somehow, however, the sorcerers found out about it and made the emergence with us. They are reputed to congregate at a place called Palangwu. How they convert people into their ranks is not known. Sorcerers and witches do not live on their own. They increase their life spans at the expense of their relatives. Whenever one of them

## SOMIVIKI

Somiviki pay it sakwapngumnit paqwri'iwtaqat angqw yuykiwa. Pam it angvut ang mookiwkyangw pu' löökye' it moohot akw somiwtangwu. Put pan mokyaatotat pu' paasat put kwalaknayangwu.

## SONGOOPAVI

Songoopavi pay orayviy aatatkyahaqam. Noq peetuy navoti'amniqw pep yaw i' hopi susmooti kitsokta. Niikyangw pay qa pep oove, pay puma aapiy wuuyavotiqw pu' pangso yayva. Noq pu' piw peetu navoti'yyungqw yaw puma hakim pep naatupkom, i' kikmongwiniqw pu' put tupko'at matsito yan maatsiwqa, hiita ep pay neepewtiqw, pu' pam tupko'atwa oraymiqniiqe pu' pepeq tuwat peetuy sinmuy tsamkyangw pu' qatuptu. Noq pay hintaqat akw pi puma songoopavitniqw pu' orayvit qa sun tuuqayyungwa, naamahin as puma sun hopiitniikyaakyangw.

## POWAQA

I' powaqa pi pay songyawnen nukpananingwuniqw oovi itam hopiit as pumuy qa awini'ykyaakyangw pewwat atkyangaqw nöngakniniqw, pay puma hin pi nanaptaqe oovi pew antsa itamum nönga. Noq pay puma haqam yaw palangwuy epeq tuwat tsovaltingwuqat pay yan lavayta. Pu' pay hin pi puma tuwat sinot naanami tuuwiklalwa. Pu' pay puma qa naap yep yeese. Puma yaw naap sinomuy qatsiyamuy akw yaaptotingwu. Pu' pam

seeks to extend his life he extracts a relative's heart with a spindle. All witchcraft activities are carried out at night. Sorcerers are also said to go about disguised as animals.

Sometimes when a Hopi acquires something through his own hard work another person, who is envious and looks upon the former with disfavor, will label him a witch. If he is one he will never admit it, of course. A witch who is caught red-handed performing acts of witchcraft will try to entice the person who finds him or her to accept some valuable object, such as a possession (in the case of a sorcerer) or even her own body (in the case of a sorceress). This is to keep the person from revealing their identity.

## SOYALANGW

Soyalangw is a ceremony that takes place during the winter, not long after the Wuwtsim ritual. The entire event lasts sixteen days. During this time the *sosyalt* or "members of the Soyal society" carry out esoteric rites in their kiva and fashion prayer feathers of various kinds for everything from which the Hopi benefit. It is also at this time that the sun reaches its winter home. From that point on it journeys towards its summer home, and the days grow increasingly longer. In addition, Soyalangw marks the beginning of the new kachina season with the appearance of the Soyal kachina. Somewhat later the Qööqöqlö kachinas arrive to ceremonially open all the kivas so that the other kachinas, too, are now able to make their visits.

yaw hakiy akw yaaptinik, pam yaw hiita patukyat akw hakiy unangwhoroknangwu. Pu' pay puma tuwat mihikqwsa put hiita tuwiy hintsatskyangwu. Pu' pay puma piw yaw imuy hiituy popkotuy akw enang yakta.

Noq pu' piw himuwa haqam pay as naap maqsoniy akw hiita haqamniqw pay himuwa qa naane', hakiy aw qa kwangwatayte', pam hakiy a'ni powaqsasvingwu. Noq himuwa pam himunen son put nakwhangwu. Pu' yaw hak put panhaqam hintsakqat nu'ansanqw, pam yaw hakiy hiita nukngwat akw uunatoynaniqey antingwu, it hiita himu'ytiwngwuqat sen tokoy, hak yaw put qa lalvayniqat oovi.

## SOYALANGW

Soyalangw pay tömölnawit it wuwtsimuy panis yukiltiqwningwu. Niikyangw pam suukop taalat ang pan soyalangwningwu. Noq ep ima sosyalt yungiwtangwunen pu' puma ep soosokmuy pu' piw soosok hiita akw mongvasyaqey, soosok hiituy, amungem paaholalwangwu. Ep pu' i' taawa piw tuwat tömö'kiy aqw pite', pu' pam paasat paapiy tala'kiywat aqw hoytangwuniqw, pu' paapiy i' taawa wup'iwmangwu. Noq ep i' soyalkatsina susmooti pitungwu. Noq pu' paasat aapiy pantaqw, pu' ima qööqöqlöm ökye', pu' puma paasat it kivat pas soosok ang hötaatotaqw, pu' mimawat katsinam ökimantani.

## SPIDER

For some Hopi the spider constitutes a clan totem. To those who are not of the Spider clan a spider has no significance whatsoever. Thus, when a person comes across a spider in his home he will kill it. It is also commonly believed that if a spider urinates on you, you will break out in sores.

There exists an old woman in Hopi mythology who assists the Hopi in many ways. She is very compassionate and very powerful. The giver of all life created her before the animals were created, even before this world was made. The woman is known as *kookyangwso'wuuti* or "Old Spider Woman" by the Hopi. But it is not known for sure why she is referred to in this way.

## TORCH

A torch consists of either finely shredded cedar bark or other sticks that are bound together. Hence its Hopi name *kopitsoki*, literally "upright things bundled together." To light a torch one uses a flint on material such as cotton. Once the cotton is ignited, one can take the light from it. In the days when matches were not yet available to the Hopi and someone's fire went out, one simply took a torch to somebody else's house and used it to borrow fire there.

## KOOKYANGW

I' kookyangw pay tuwat peetuy hopiituy wu'ya'am, pu' pay mimuywatuy put qa wu'ya'yyungqamuy amumi pam pay qa pas himu. Noq oovi himuwa kiy ep put waynumqat pay niinangwu. Pu' pam yaw piw hakiy aw sisiwkuqw hakiy yaw aapa u'ya'yvangwu.

Noq pu' i' so'wuuti pam hopit a'ni hiita akw pa'angwankyangw pu' piw nu'okso'wuuti. Pu' pam piw a'ni himu. Naat i' himu pooko, pu' hikis i' tuuwaqatsi naat qa yukiltiqw, pay put i' hikwsit himu'ytaqa mootihaq yuku. Noq itam hopiit put so'wuutit kookyangwso'wuuti yan tuwi'yyungwa. Noq pay kya qa hak put pas suyan navoti'ytani hintiqw pam tuwat pan maatsiwqw.

## KOPITSOKI

I' kopitsoki pam pay i' laapu paas sisngiwtaqa pu' pay sen koho kop'iwtangwu. Niiqe oovi pam paniqw pan maatsiwngwu, kopitsoki. Noq pu' hak put uwiknanik hak put it pilakinpit hiita pösövit'ewakw akw taqtsoknat, paasat pu' hak put angqw paalatangwu. Noq pu' hisat naat qa kohotövu'yyungngwuniqw, hiitawat qööhi'at tokq pu' pam it kopitsokit akw pangso hakiy kiiyat aw kookoste', pu' paasat put kopitsokit pangso yawme', pu' pam paasat pep neengem put qööhiyat angqw kookostangwu.

## TURDS (derogatory label for sorcerers)

Since the beginning of time the Hopi have been speaking of certain people as "turds" or "feces." They represent sorcerers and witches and are almost a necessary force in a narrative. Sorcerers frown upon benevolent people and for this reason conjure up schemes to harm or destroy them. They particularly dislike a man who marries an exceptionally beautiful girl in their village. They then plot how to take his wife away from him. Eventually, however, the man harmed by them overcomes his evil opponents with the help of a more powerful being. Nevertheless, these turds are said to be very potent themselves, for they have at their disposal a multitude of ways and means of doing things.

## TSUKUVIKI (a Hopi dish)

*Tsukuviki* consists of blue corn flour. To make it one first produces a batter which is subsequently wrapped in the green leaf of the cornstalk. This small loaf is then given a pointed shape at each end. Hence the name *tsukuviki* or "loaf with a point." It is not bound anywhere. The ends of the corn leaf are merely tucked back into the *tsukuviki*. When the dough is properly enclosed it is boiled. This dish is especially prepared by a *mö'wi* or "female in-law."

## KWITAVIT

Ima hopiit pay imuy hiituy kwitavituy ayang-qaqw yu'a'atotangwu. Puma pay it hiita tuuwutsit pay pas son ep qa nuutumyangwu. Noq himuwa haqam hiita nukngwat hintiqw, puma pay put qa hisat ep tsuyti. Niiqe puma oovi tuwat pay put lolmat hintsakqat pas sonqa hinwat put haqami hintsatsnaniqey pansa engem pasiwnayangwu. Pu' piw himuwa ephaqam pumuy kitsokiyamuy ep pas hakiy lolmat nukngwat nöömataqw, pu' puma qa naaniye', pay puma piw paasat put hin nömanaw-kiyaniqey engem yukuyangwu. Niikyangw pay hi-muwa hin hinmakyangw ephaqam pas pavanniiqat pa'angwniyat akw pay pumuy sonqa pö'angwu. Noq pay yaw puma piw hiitu a'niya. Puma yaw a'ni hiita tuwi'yyungwa.

## TSUKUVIKI

Tsukuviki pay sakwapngumnit angqw yukilti-ngwu. Niikyangw put yukuniqa mooti paavaqwrit pu' put it sami'uyit naapiyat mangwnit ang mokyaatangwu. Pu' pam löövoq nan'ivoq tsuku'y-tangwuniiqe oovi pam paniqw tsukuviki yan maa-tsiwngwu. Pam pay qa haqe' somiwtangwu. Noq put mangwnit so'ngwa'at pay ahoy put tsukuvikit aqw paysoq tsurukiwtangwu. Paasat pu' pam put yan yukye' pu' pam put kwalaknangwu. Noq tsu-kuviki tuwat mö'wit noova'atningwu.

## STORY

The *tupatsa* is a building structure erected on the ground floor of a house. Older Hopi residences occasionally had one or more additional stories. The bottommost structure housed the living quarters, but featured no entranceway of its own. In order to enter, it was necessary to climb to the rooftop first by means of a ladder or stairs; only then could one descend to the ground floor. The upper story, as a rule, held the corn stacks, the grinding bins, and also a fireplace. In the olden days it was customary for girls to grind corn on this upper story.

## URGE TO DEFECATE

Often in a story, when the hero or heroine is either on the way to an unfamiliar destination or is being taken somewhere by an evil being, Old Spider Woman knows about it. If she then intends to show herself to them, she will in some magical way cause in them the urge to defecate. As soon as the urge is felt, the male or female protagonist will step aside, and before they can empty their bowels, Old Spider Woman will speak to them. She typically begins by saying, "Phew! Can't you move farther away and then defecate?" Next she instructs them to enter her abode after they have finished with their business. The reason that Old Spider Woman employs this method to reveal herself to a mortal only at a time like this may be that at that moment one is all alone.

## TUPATSA

I' tupatsa pay kiihut atsveq piw suukyawa kii'iwtangwu. Ephaqam i' hisathopiki pay suukw pu' ephaqam hoyokput tupatsa'ytangwu. Noq put sus'atkyaq kii'iwtaqat epeq pi yeyespi'amningwuniikyangw pam hisat qa atkyaveq aw hötsiwa'ytangwuniqw, oovi puma pangso yungninik, puma pas aqw kits'omiq saaqat sen tutuvengat ang yayvat pu' ahoy saaqat ang aqw yungtangwu. Noq pepeq tupatsveq i' pay tuu'oyi, mata, pu' pay piw qöpqöningwu. Pu' hisat maana tupatsveqsa ngumantangwu.

## KWAYNGYAVOMOKI

It tuuwutsit ang himuwa haqaminiqw sen himu pay nukpana'eway haqami hiitawat wikqw, i' kookyangwso'wuuti pay put paas navoti'ytangwuniiqe oovi pam put hakiy aw naamaataknaninik, pam piw put hin kwayngyavoniqat unangwtoynangwu. Noq pu' oovi pam hak kwayngyavomokye', pu' pam put wikqat angqw ayo'nen, pu' pep haqam kwayngyaptaniqw, paasat pu' pam kookyangwso'wuuti put aw mooti hingqawngwu. Niiqe pam pay oovi sutsep hakiy aw pangqawu, "Itse, hak yaavonitningwu!" Paasat pu' pam put aw tutaptangwu ason pam kwayngyaptat pu' put kiiyat aqw pakiniqat. Yan pam put aa'awnangwu. Noq pay pi hak kwayngyaplawe' pay hak sunalaningwuniqw, pay kya pam oovi paniqw hiitawat aw paasatsa naamaataknangwu.

183

## VILLAGE

Whenever the Hopi established a village, they settled there with the intention of staying permanently. As soon as some sort of disaster struck the community, however, they usually moved on in search of a place with better living conditions where they could found another village. Unlike some other Indian groups, the Hopi were not nomads. Homes were built using only stone and mortar except for the roof, which was constructed from log beams covered with brush and mud. Wherever a village was erected, a village center or plaza had to be part of it. In general, the northern end of the plaza was occupied by members of the Bear clan who constituted the Hopi elite. The three remaining sides of the plaza were open for anyone who wished to build there. Within the village were several rows of houses that were often multi-storied. They consisted of rooms especially built to store corn and other crops, a chamber where *piiki* was made, and, of course, an area which served as living quarters.

## VILLAGE LEADER

The *kikmongwi* or "village leader" of old came from the Bear clan. In a given village he is supposed to be the father of all. Therefore, in the olden days, he was the first to rise in the morning and the last to retire at night. The *kikmongwi* never gives orders. Nor is he selfish when he does things. On

## KITSOKI

I' hopi haqam kitsokte' pam pay pas pepsa qatungwu. Ason pay pam pas hiita qa antaqat aw pite', pu' pam pangqw kitsokiy angqw haqamiwat qatsiheve', pu' pam piw supwat kitsoktangwu. Niiqe oovi pam qa imuy peetuy himusinmuy amun angqe' nanaalaktinumngwu. Pu' pam piw it owatnit pu' tsöqatsa angqw kiitangwuniqw, pay i'sa kii'ami'at-sa pay lestavitnit himutskitnit pu' tsöqat akw kii'amiwtangwu. Noq pu' pam haqam kitsokte' pam piw it kiisonvit pas sonqa enangningwu. Noq put kiisonviy akwningyaqw ima honngyam, kii-kyam, pas sonqa ki'yyungngwu. Pu' aapiy pay naap himuwa haqam kiitaniqey pan wuuwe', pu' pep kiitangwu. Niikyangw pep kitsokive piw qa suukya kiletsiningwu. Pu' hopi piw qa suup natsve ki'ytangwu. Haqamwat pam hiita qaa'öy pu' hiita natwaniy oyi'ytaniqey put engem piw paas kiita-ngwu. Pu' hopiki piw oovi tumtsokki'ykyangw pu' piw yeyespi'ytangwu.

## KIKMONGWI

I' hisatkikmongwi imuy honngyamuy angqwni-ngwu. Pam yaw pay haqam kitsokive soosokmuy na'amningwu. Pu' pam oovi hisat piw susmooti taytangwu, pu' pam piw nuutungk tuwat puwto-ngwu. Pu' pam pay qa hisat pas hakiy hiita pas nu'an ayalawu. Pam qa naamisa wuuwankyangw hiita hintsakngwu. Pam imuy timuy amungem

the contrary, his only concern is that his children the villagers will benefit. Therefore he is not alone when he takes on a task. He seeks advice from his fellow leaders as he works on it. Obviously, a white man's "chief" and the *mongwi* of the Hopi are not synonymous.

## WALPI (First Mesa village)

Walpi is an old village. The people of Walpi may have settled at this location at about the same time as the people of Orayvi and Songoopavi. However, it is uncertain where they came from. Just like the Songoopavi residents, they used to live below the mesa, but due to continual raids by enemy groups they moved to a site above the original settlement, where they were better off. In time, some relocated at a place east of Walpi and founded a new village known at Sitsom'ovi. Finally, people from a Rio Grande pueblo arrived and settled at the easternmost end of the mesa, just west of the place called Waala. That village is termed Hanoki by the Hopi.

## WEDDING BOOTS

When a Hopi prepares wedding garments for his female in-law, he also makes wedding boots for her. They are fashioned from tanned buckskin and cowhide. Cowhide is used for the soles, and the uppers are produced from a piece of supple white

nukngwatiniqat put wuuwankyangw hiita hintingwu. Pu' pam oovi piw qa naala hiita aw yukungwu. Pam naat piw imuy mongsungwmuy amumi maqaptsitikyangw hiita aw antsani'ymangwu. Noq oovi it pahaanat mongwi'atniqw pu' hopit mongwi'at puma qa sunta.

## WALPI

Walpi pay pas hisatkitsoki. Pay puma walpit son oovi qa imuy orayvituy pu' piw imuy songoopavituy amuusaqhaqam pepeq tuwat yesvakyangw, haqaqw pi puma tuwat pangsoq öki. Noq pay puma piw imuy songoopavituy amun as atkya yesngwuniqw, pu' pay i' himu tuwqa pas peqw hopiikimiq kikiipoklawqw, pu' pay puma haqam kitsoktotaqey put aa'omi yayvaqe pu' pepwat pay ngas'ewya. Noq pu' walpiy angqw hoopowat puma peetu naakwiipayat pu' pep piw it sukwat kitsoktotaqw pamwa pep sitsom'ovi yan natngwani'yta. Pu' pepeq sushopaq it waala'ytaqat aatavang piw ima hopaqkingaqwyaqam piw hisat peqw ökiiqe pu' pepeq yesva. Pay pam navoti qa sunta. Noq pepeq put kitsokit i' hopi hanoki yan tuwi'yta.

## MÖ'ÖNGTOTSI

Hopi mö'wiy engem mö'öngyuyuwse' pam put engem piw it mö'öngtotsit yukungwu. Noq pam it sowi'yngwatnit pu' it wakasvukyat angqw yukiwtangwu. Put aatöqavi'at it wakasvukyat angqw yukiwtaqw, pu' put oongaqwvi'at it paas pöhiw-

buckskin. It takes a while to put these boots on. The uppers are usually quite long, so that the woman putting them on must wrap them around her legs several times. Extremely long uppers almost reach up to the knee and wind around the leg in several coils. But these boots are not for everyday wear.

Although termed wedding boots, they can also be worn by other than brides. On some occasions teenage girls, and even little girls will wear them when they participate in a ceremony.

## WEDDING ROBE

The *oova* or "wedding robe" comes in two sizes, one being quite a bit larger than the other. The large one is woven for the bride so that she can journey to Maski, the "home of the dead." As the robe constituted a married woman's vehicle to make her descent to the underworld, she was not supposed to sell it. In previous times when the *oova* was never sold, the woman would sometimes fashion a sack from it. People also used the garment as a sitting mat. It was also not supposed to be decorated. Embroidery would have added weight to it and not permit the dead woman to ride it down the Grand Canyon on her way to the underworld.

The bridal robe is further said to function as a

niwtaqat qöötsat sowi'yngwat angqw yuykiwa. Pu' himuwa put totsvakqa pay pas wuuyavotat pu' put ang pakingwu. Put oongaqwvi'at pas wuupaningwuniqw, oovi put ang pakiiqa put hokyay akw angqe qa suus nömngwu. Noq pam pas wuupanen hiitawat peep tamömi pitukyangw pu' piw pam oovi qa suus hiitawat hokyayat angqe nöömiltingwu. Niikyangw it pay himuwa qa sutsep ang pakiwtangwu.

Pu' pam as naamahin mö'öngtotsi yan maatsiwkyangw pay i' qa pas mö'wisa put ang pakiwtangwu. Ephaqam pay ima mamant, mamanhooyam hiita pantaqat tootsi'ytaqat tiive', puma piw put ang tangawkyaakyangw nuutumyangwu.

## OOVA

I' oova lööpwaningwuniqw i' suukyawa pay qa mitwat aasaqaningwu. Noq i' oova it mö'wit engem yuykiwa. Noq pam tuwat yaw putakw haqami maskimiqningwu. Niiqe pam oovi it wuutit hahawpi'atningwu. Noq pam oovi as put qa huyangwu. Pu' himuwa hisat put qa huye', pam pay ephaqam put angqw it tukput yukungwu. Pu' pay puma piw put atsvewlalwangwu. Pu' yaw piw hak put as qa peenangwu. Hak yaw put pantiqw, pam yaw a'ni putuute' hakiy öngtupqamiq qa hawnangwu, hak maskimiq hoytaqw.

Pu' pam yaw piw i' paatsayanpiningwu. Putakw yaw ima oo'omawt paalay tsaayantotangwu. Noq hak yaw mookye', hak yaw oomawnii-

water sieve. With its help the clouds sift their moisture to produce very fine rain. In Hopi belief, upon one's demise a mortal is transformed into a cloud personage, and whenever a woman checks on the people she left behind, she employs the *oova* as a sieve. By using the *oova* to sift the rains a fine drizzle is produced instead of hail. Hail is dreaded by the Hopi because it ruins the corn and smashes holes into muskmelons and watermelons.

One of the corners of the wedding robe is embroidered with sixteen stitches of red yarn. They symbolize a young woman's menstruation. Also attached at this corner is an ear of corn. This ear of corn is not a real corn but is made from varicolored yarn. However, it closely resembles a corn.

## WIND

Winds can be classified in more than one way. One is referred to as whirlwind, another as northwind, yet another as blizzard. Since none of them is distinguished by any positive attributes, no Hopi ever prays for these winds. Only an evil person or a sorcerer will wish them upon the Hopi, because when the wind arrives, it desiccates the plants and blows away the clouds. For this reason the members of the Kwan society practice a ritual that is supposed to "lock out" the wind.

. kyangw pan sinmuy ahoy popte', putakw yaw hak put yooyangwuy tsaayantangwu.' Pam it yooyangwuy tsaatsayaqw pam qa lemowa yokvangwu. Pam i' suvuyoyangw paasat yokvangwu. It lemowat pay hopi qa naawakna, ispi pam hakiy uuyiyat aw yokve' pam put nukushintsanngwu. Pu' pam it meloonit, kawayvatngat piw soq poromnangwu.

kip paalangput tonit akw angqe tuu'ihiwtangwu. Pam yaw put maanat ungwayat tu'awi'ytangwu. Noq pu' pepeq i' qaa'ö put aw wiwtangwu. I' pay qaa'ö qa pas it tuu'oyit angningwuqa. Pam pay it hiita nana'löngöt tonit angqw yukiwtangwu. Niikyangw pay pi antsa qaa'öt an soniwngwu.

## HUUKYANGW

I' huukyangw pay qa suupwa. I' suukyawa tuviphayangwniqw, pu' suukyawa kwingyawniqw, pu' piw suukyawa nuvahukyangw. Noq pay i' qa himuwa lomahintaqw, oovi i' hopi pay qa hisat put hiita oovi naawakna. Put pay i' himu nukpana, powaqa, hakimuy amungem naawaknangwu. Pam hapi huukyangw pite' pam it uuyit laknangwu. Pu' pam piw imuy oo'omawtuy naap haqamiwat huhukhoynangwu. Noq oovi paniqw piw ima kwaakwant hiita ep huk'uutayangwu.

## YUCCA ROOT

The Hopi word *moovi* refers to the root of the yucca. The person intending to use it digs up the entire plant and takes it along. Upon severing the root from the leaves, the root is pounded with a heavy object, such as a rock. To use it as a shampoo, it is first soaked in water in a container set aside for this purpose. As soon as the pulp becomes really sudsy, one can cleanse one's hair with it.

Some people also say that dreaming of yucca root signifies nearness to death. This belief is based on the custom of washing the deceased's hair before burying.

## YUCCA SIFTER

Sifter baskets are still being produced by the Hopi in every village, by both women and men. The weaving material consists of spliced yucca, and the basket is woven while the yucca is still green. The basket owes its name to the fact that it is used to sift things. Because its weave is not tight, chaff from various agricultural products, as well as sand, will easily filter down through the bottom of the basket.

## MOOVI

I' moovi pay it moohot nga'atningwu. Noq oovi hak put hintsanniqa put yaahat pu' paasat put pas pantaqat yawmangwu. Paasat pu' hak put moovit it moohot angqw tukye' pu' hak put moovit pay owat'ewakw, hiita pututt akw tatpamangwu. Pu' hak oovi put akw asninik, hak mooti put moovit hiita aqw qeeni'ytangwu. Noq pu' pam pangqw pankyangw pu' hisatniqw pas pavan qöttiqw, pu' hak paasat put aqw asngwu.

Noq haqawat piw pangqaqwaqw hak yaw mokhaykyawte' moovit tuumoklawngwu, ispi hak mokq hakiy pay piw putakw asnayat pu' hakiy taviyangwuniqw oovi.

## TUTSAYA

I' tutsaya pay naat hopiikivaqe yuykiwa. Put pay soosovik kitsokinawit tuwi'yyungwa. Pu' ima taataqt pay piw put enang yuykuya. Noq pam it moohot tsiitsikvut angqw yukiwtangwu. Naat pam mooho sakwawsaniqw, himuwa put tutsayat pantaqat angqw yukungwu. Pu' pay putakw pi himuwa hiita tsaatsayangwuniqw oovi pam pan maatsiwa. Pam pay qa huur pöqniwtangwuniqw, oovi put ang hiita tsiipu'atniqw, pu' i' tuuwa ang atkyamiq suunöngakngwu.

# BIBLIOGRAPHY

Baars, Donald L. *The Colorado Plateau: A Geologic History.* rev. ed. Albuquerque: University of New Mexico Press, 1983.

Barnes, C. W. "Landscapes of Northeastern Arizona." In *Landscapes of Arizona: The Geological Story,* edited by Terah L. Smiley et al., 303–25. Lanham, Maryland.: University Press of America, 1984.

Barnes, Will C. *Arizona Place Names.* Tucson: University of Arizona Press, 1935.

Breed, William J. "Molten Rock and Trembling Earth: The Story of a Landscape Evolving." *Plateau* 49, no. 2(1976): 2–13.

————. "Slicing Through the Layer Cake: A Geologist Looks at the Colorado Plateau." *Plateau* 49, no. 1(1976): 6–15.

Brew, J. O. "Hopi Prehistory and History to 1805." In *Southwest.* Handbook of American Indians, edited by Alfonso Ortiz, vol. 9. Washington, D.C.: Smithsonian Institution, 1979.

Colton, Harold S. *The Basaltic Cinder Cones and Lava Flows of the San Francisco Mountain Volcanic Field.* rev. 2d ed. Flagstaff: Museum of Northern Arizona, 1967.

————. *Black Sand: Prehistory in Northern Arizona.* Albuquerque: University of New Mexico Press, 1960.

————. "A Possible Hopi Tradition of the Eruption of Sunset Crater." *Museum Notes, Museum of Northern Arizona* 5, no. 4(1932): 23.

————. "Principal Hopi Trails." *Plateau* 36, no. 3(1964): 91–94.

————. "The Rise and Fall of the Prehistoric Population of Northern Arizona." *Science* 84(1936): 337–43.

————. "Sunset Crater." *Plateau* 18, no. 1(1945): 7–14.

————. "Sunset Crater: The Effects of a Volcanic Eruption on an Ancient Pueblo

People." *The Geographical Review* 22, no. 4(1932): 582–90.

Colton, Harold S., and Frank C. Baxter. *Days in the Painted Desert and the San Francisco Mountains; A Guide*. Bulletin 2. Flagstaff: Museum of Northern Arizona, 1932.

Colton, Mary-Russell F. "Hopi Legends of the Sunset Crater Region." *Museum Notes, Museum of Northern Arizona* 5, no. 4(1932): 17–18.

Cooley, Maurice E. *Regional Hydrogeology of the Navajo and Hopi Indian Reservations, Arizona, New Mexico, and Utah*. Washington, D.C.: U.S. Government Printing Office, 1969.

————. "Physiography of the Black Mesa Basin Area, Arizona." In *Guidebook of the Black Mesa Basin Northeastern Arizona*, edited by Roger Y. Anderson and John W. Harshbarger, 146–49. Socorro: New Mexico Geological Society, 1958.

Damon, Paul E., M. Shafiquallah, and Joel S. Leventhal. "K-Ar Chronology for the San Francisco Volcanic Field and Rate of Erosion of the Little Colorado River." In *Geology of Northern Arizona: With Notes on Archaeology and Paleoclimate, Part I — Regional Studies*, edited by Thor N. V. Karlstrom, Gordon A. Swann, and Raymond I. Eastwood, 221–35. Flagstaff: Geological Society of America, 1974.

Fish, Paul R., Peter J. Pilles, Jr., and Suzanne K. Fish. "Colonies, Traders, and Traits: The Hohokam in the North." In *Current Issues in Hohokam Prehistory: Proceedings of a Symposium*, edited by David Doyel and Fred Plog, 151–75. Tempe: Arizona State University, 1980.

Forney, Gerald Glenn. "Lava Tubes of the San Francisco Volcanic Field, Arizona." *Plateau* 44, no. 1(1971): 1–13.

Hargrave, Lyndon L. "Shungopovi." *Museum Notes, Museum of Northern Arizona* 2, no. 10(1930): 1–4.

Hartman, Dana. "A Chronicle in Wood and Stone: An Archaeologist Views the Wupatki–Sunset Crater Region." *Plateau* 49, no. 2(1976): 2–13.

Holm, Richard. "Holocene Scoria Cone and Lava Flows at Sunset Crater, Northern

Arizona." Flagstaff, 1984. Manuscript.

Krutch, Joseph Wood. "The Paradox of a Lava Flow." *Arizona Highways* 35, no. 6(1959): 6–13.

Lamar, D. L. "Geology of the Wupatki Blowhole System." *Plateau* 37, no. 1(1964): 35–40.

Lucchitta, I. "Development of Landscape in Northwestern Arizona: The Country of Plateaus and Canyons." In *Landscapes of Arizona: The Geological Study*, edited by Terah L. Smiley et al., 269–301. New York: University Press of America, 1984.

Moore, Richard B., Edward W. Wolfe, and George E. Ulrich. "Geology of the Eastern and Northern Parts of the San Francisco Volcanic Field, Arizona." In *Geology of Northern Arizona: With Notes on Archaeology and Paleoclimate, Part II—Area Studies and Field Guides*, edited by Thor N. V. Karlstrom, Gordon A. Swann, and Raymond I. Eastwood, 465–94. Flagstaff: Geological Society of America, 1974.

Nequatewa, Edmund. "The Kana-a Kachinas of Sunset Crater." *Museum Notes, Museum of Northern Arizona* 5, no. 4(1932): 19–23.

————. "Yaponcha, the Wind God." *Museum Notes, Museum of Northern Arizona* 5, no. 4(1932): 18–19.

Pilles, Peter J., Jr. "The Field House and Sinagua Demography." In *Limited Activity and Occupation Sites: A Collection of Conference Papers*, edited by Albert E. Ward. Albuquerque: Center for Anthropological Studies Contributions to Anthropological Studies, 1978.

————. "Sunset Crater and the Sinagua: A New Interpretation." In *Volcanic Activity and Human Ecology*, edited by Payson D. Sheets and Donald K. Grayson. New York: Academic Press, 1979.

Repenning, Charles A., and James H. Irwin. "Bidahochi Formation of Arizona and New Mexico." *American Association of Petroleum Geologists Bulletin* 38(1954): 1821–26.

Repenning, Charles A., and Harry G. Page. "Late Cretaceous Stratigraphy of Black Mesa, Navajo and Hopi Indian Reservations, Arizona." *American Association of Petroleum Geologists Bulletin* 40(1956): 255–94.

Rigby, J. Keith. *Southern Colorado Plateau: Field Guide.* Dubuque, Iowa: Kendall/Hunt Publishing Co., 1977.

Robinson, H. H. *The San Francisco Volcanic Field, Arizona.* Washington, D.C.: U.S. Government Printing Office, 1913.

Schroeder, Albert H. *Of Men and Volcanoes: The Sinagua of Northern Arizona,* edited by Earl Jackson. Globe, Arizona: Southwest Parks and Monuments Association, 1977.

Shoemaker, Eugene M., and Duane E. Champion. "Eruption History of Sunset Crater. Investigator's Report." Wupatki–Sunset Crater National Monuments, 1977. Manuscript.

Smiley, Terah L. "The Geology and Dating of Sunset Crater, Flagstaff, Arizona." In *Guidebook of the Black Mesa Basin Northeastern Arizona,* edited by Roger Y. Anderson and John W. Harshbarger, 186–90. Flagstaff: Geological Society of America, 1974.

Sutton, Robert L. "The Geology of Hopi Buttes, Arizona." In *Geology of Northern Arizona: With Notes on Archaeology and Paleoclimate, Part II—Area Studies and Field Guides,* edited by Thor N. V. Karlstrom, Gordon A. Swann, and Raymond I. Eastwood, 647–71. Flagstaff: Geological Society of America, 1974.

Voth, Henry R. *The Traditions of the Hopi.* Chicago: Field Columbian Publication 96, 1905.

Wolfe, Edward W. "The Volcanic Landscape of the San Francisco Volcanic Field." In *Landscapes of Arizona: The Geologic Story,* edited by Terah L. Smiley et al., 111–36. Lanham, Maryland.: University Press of America, 1984.

# LIST OF PHOTOGRAPHS